FAIRYLAND

FAIRYLAND

A Memoir of My Father

ALYSIA ABBOTT

W. W. NORTON & COMPANY
NEW YORK : LONDON

For information about permission
to reproduce selections from this book,
write to Permissions, W. W. Norton & Company, Inc.,
500 Fifth Avenue, New York, NY 10110

For information about special discounts for bulk purchases,
please contact W. W. Norton Special Sales
at specialsales@wwnorton.com or 800-233-4830

Manufacturing by Courier Westford
Book design by Brooke Koven
Production manager: Louise Mattarelliano

ISBN: 978-0-393-08252-4

W. W. Norton & Company, Inc.
500 Fifth Avenue, New York, N.Y. 10110
www.wwnorton.com

W. W. Norton & Company Ltd.
Castle House, 75/76 Wells Street, London W1T 3QT

1 2 3 4 5 6 7 8 9 0

for my mother and my father,
and
for Annabel, so she may some time
know where her mother "was at."

CONTENTS

I wanted to show children these fishes shining
In the blue wave, the golden fish that sing

—ARTHUR RIMBAUD, "The Drunken Boat"

AUTHOR'S NOTE

To write this book, I've relied on personal memory, interviews with family and friends, articles and history books, and, especially, the papers my father left. These include his journals, poetry, prose, and letters, from which I draw quotes. Informed by my father's work, my own memories, and other research, I've sometimes re-created scenes and dialogue. These are mostly expanded from those described in my father's papers; however, I've also invented dialogue and changed the names of a few individuals in the book, but only when doing so had no impact on the veracity and substance of the story.

PROLOGUE

I

T'S A LATE summer afternoon. I'm watching my father's hands manipulate the rubber-net-wrapped steering wheel of our 1972 Volkswagen bug as we move onto the Golden Gate Bridge. In between his first two fingers is a lit cigarette, its ash long and in need of flicking. He straightens the wheel, and the ash falls, as he tells me again the name of this place where we are going, a place I've never been before: Sausalito. When I hear the word I picture flying saucers taking off and landing and I imagine this party will be held in a flying saucer. I am five years old.

We arrive at a large pink adobe house. Someone with curly hair answers the door wearing sunglasses and a flimsy pink and purple robe. He gives my father a big hug and ushers us into the house. As he leads us through the rooms, the tall man points out to me the items that I can break and the items that I can't break because they are antique. Then he leads us out onto a large pool deck where a punch bowl, chips, and small sandwiches are laid out on wicker and glass tables. Music plays from speakers as tall as I am. There are no other kids.

I don't yet know how to swim, but I want to be in the water. Through the smooth surface I can see the shiny aqua-green tiles at the pool's bottom sparkle as they reflect the sun. I beg my dad, so he takes off my clothes and sets me up on the second of the steps leading into the water and instructs me to keep still.

From my concrete perch, I watch as my father's friends cavort in various states of nakedness. Young men close-dance with other young men around the pool. As I stand there, taking in the scene around me, I feel surreptitiously with my right foot the step under the water next to where I am standing. I step down to it, then, reaching with my foot, find another step below. I float down to this new step where I can stand, my head and shoulders still safely clear of the water. My father, deeply engaged in conversation with the host, isn't watching, so I find with my outstretched toes another step where I can float and stand. The warm water rises to meet my dry skin and I feel as if I've uncovered a secret pathway to a magic place, a mermaid sea.

Lulled by the jets now pulsing in the pool, the thumping loud music, and the golden late afternoon light, I move myself deeper into the water, always finding a step to catch me. Then I reach out for another next step and find there is none, and, just like that, the pool's warm water engulfs me, filling my mouth, my nose, my ears. Splashing frantically to keep myself afloat, I try to yell for help but, because I can't keep my head above water long enough to formulate a cry, I can only call out, "Hell! Hell!"

Peering at me from one of the deck chairs, a young woman calls out to my father, then points to me, "Steve, isn't that your daughter bobbing up and down in the water?" My father yells, "Give me your arm!" then pulls me out onto the pool's rough edge where I cough up water and the bitter taste of chlorine stings my nose and throat. It will be years before I learn to swim, and—like not learning to ride a bike until college and my father's sexuality—this will be a source of secret shame.

My father notes this day in his journal with the headline "Alysia's Swimming Accident," and beneath it a small scribbled drawing showing my thin arm flailing above wavy water. When I later find the journal entry, I smile with delight.

*   *   *

I FOUND my father's journals in our dining room closet four months after he died of AIDS-related complications. I'd always known Dad kept journals. Peering through the French doors separating my bedroom from the living room where he slept at night, I could see him perched on the edge of his sagging fold-up futon, legs crossed, foot dangling as he scribbled away on the spiral notebook balanced on his lap. When I was a girl, I used to wait until he left the apartment to sneak into his milk-crate bookshelves and pull out the two hardback black journals in which he'd recorded our life in the mid-1970s. Crouched on the floor, I sifted pages and pages of these books in search of the capital A, for Alysia, or my childhood nickname A-R, short for Alysia-Rebeccah. I delighted in the descriptions of myself as a toddler—how I inexplicably used to call Dad "my poor little Da-da," or the time I peed in his bed. I took comfort in knowing that as young as I was I already had my own history, and that I had changed from the person I'd once been.

I hadn't read his journals in many years and I didn't expect to find anything new when I decided to clear out our dining room closet that spring afternoon of 1993. At twenty-two years old, fresh off a year of nursing my father and then watching him take his last breath at the Maitri Hospice in the Castro, I thought nothing could hurt me anymore. What I most dreaded all my life, the death of my father and only parent, had already happened.

I also believed there were no surprises left. After my mother's car accident when I was two, my father had raised me on his own and with few boundaries. After our nearly twenty years together as only parent and only child I felt I knew him—his warm cigarette-tinged scent, the twitch of his foot whenever he was deep in thought, his taste for hard candies and chocolate Kisses every time he tried to quit smoking—as well as I knew myself. In the shape of his hands and the length of his fingers I saw my own. Sitting quietly beside him in the solitude of his hospice bedroom in those final months felt as natural and comfortable as breathing.

So I boldly dug into the journals, pulling out a dozen notebooks from beneath a box of dusty Billie Holiday and David Bowie records covered in yellowed newspapers. These journals spanned from 1971, when my father was still in graduate school, to 1991, when AIDS-related CMV retinitis began to strip him of his sight and his ability to write. I honed in on three notebooks dating from 1971 to 1973, which I'd never seen before. These journals recorded the brief time when my mother, father, and I formed a family, and they enthralled me. It was the first time I experienced my mother in that most exciting of verb tenses: the present.

Paging through these entries, it struck me that I shouldn't be reading my father's journals, that I was invading his privacy. But after our last year together and without any family to help sort the fourteen-year accumulation of stuff in our apartment, I also felt it was my due. Besides, as I read on I learned that my dad had anticipated the possibility of my finding them:

> September 9, 1973: Want to start writing again, More than ever! But who will I write for? For John – that deposed dream? For myself I guess. Maybe for Alysia that she might sometime know where her parents were at.

My father's journals indeed revealed where my parents were at. The problem was, his version of our family story was different from the one I'd been carrying around my whole life. Here's what I knew:

My parents met as graduate students at Emory University in Atlanta, Georgia. Stephen Eugene Abbott had resisted the Vietnam War as a conscientious objector and came to Emory to pursue a master's in English literature. Barbara Louise Binder, a self-declared Marxist, was pursuing a master's in psychology. They came together through a common passion for the antiwar movement and SDS (Students for a Democratic Society). The following year they were married by a justice of the peace and nine months later, in December 1970, I was born. We lived happily until, one night late in the summer of 1973, my mother was out driving when her car was rear-ended. She flew into the street, was hit by a car, and was killed instantly.

My version of this story highlighted the tragic. My photogenic mother, who graduated valedictorian from her high school in Kewanee, Illinois, who graduated with honors from Smith College, who loved dogs and lost causes and made a great chicken cacciatore, was only twenty-seven when she died. My father had been desperately in love with her and was so distraught over her sudden death that he turned gay and moved us to San Francisco. From then on he exclusively dated men, making the possibility of remarriage and siblings impossible. All of my hardships as a girl and teenager, from my difficulty fitting in, to my enduring loneliness, to my propensity for keeping secrets, could be traced back to that night in the car. It was an accident. No one was to blame.

Then I read the journals. And another story emerged.

> Atlanta Trip. I go see lawyer. While waiting, lawyer
> talks about his writing. I'm nervous and smoke a heck
> of a lot. Get idea for a novel called "The Gypsy Man's
> Daughter" about Alysia. Begins on my death bed – she
> remembers back how it was growing up with me, about

my boyfriends – diaries, etc. come in. flash forwards &
backwards.

My father wrote this entry in his daily journal in 1975, two years
after my mother died leaving him the single father of a needy toddler. Seventeen years later, I would sit by his bedside as he died.
Thirty-five years later, I am finally telling this story, a story he
envisioned, but in my own way.

PART I
Fairytales

*I sensed our excesses would lead to death, only I assumed
I'd be the one to die.*

—STEVE ABBOTT

1.

WHENEVER MY FATHER described the two-room apartment he shared with my mother on Peachtree Street, he told me about the fish. When they first moved in together, they had little money to decorate. Curiously stained oriental rugs and once proud antique dressers and end tables were picked up at estate sales and hauled home in the back of a borrowed pickup truck. What money they did have, a gift from my mom's parents, they put toward the tropical fish which they bought in a single day of romantic enthusiasm. In the entry-way of their apartment stood a large, thick-glassed tank in which they kept angelfish. Past a curtain of clinking beads, in the den, were two more tanks. In one, kissing gouramis swam alongside tiny blue and green guppies, past plastic trees and a tiny figure of Neptune covered in algae. In the fish tank on the opposite wall swam South American piranhas, which my parents fed raw ham-burger meat each night before bed.

When my parents first met at an SDS party and my father told my mother he was bisexual, she answered, "That means you can love all of humanity instead of just half of it." It was 1968 and everyone was talking about revolution. My father had just returned from a summer in Paris; the city was still roiling from the May riots when students had shouted, "Be reasonable! Demand the impossible!" Now, in the halls of American academia, anti-war students were shutting down campuses from UC Berkeley to Columbia.

My mother was intrigued by my father's open approach to sexuality. She never got hung up on his boy crushes, like his other girlfriends had. She was only jealous of his relationships with women and, according to Dad, even liked the guys he was attracted to. On weekends they went to the Cove and to the other gay and mixed bars that dotted the outskirts of downtown Atlanta. There, my mother picked out the young men my father could never attract on his own—men who'd never consider a gay encounter but who'd be up for a drunken three-way. In those early years of the sexual revolution, it was hip for young people to try new combinations. Sometimes my mom would dress in men's clothing when they went out. Dad said she made a cute boy.

Other weekends, my parents hosted dinner parties, entertaining their antiwar and grad student friends with spaghetti, cheap red wine, and charades. Dad wrote about feeling satisfied at the close of these evenings, seeing himself and my mom as leaders of a salon of intellectually engaged students. As they cleaned up after one such party, my mom suggested they marry. "Landlords won't hassle us so much," she reasoned. "We'll be able to stock the kitchen and house with wedding presents. My parents will give us more money. Other than that, our life won't really change." My father wrote about her furiously sweeping the worn linoleum, "as if all of the loose ends of our life could be gathered in a dustpan and tossed into the trash."

My parents married on February 20, 1969, at the office of a justice of the peace in downtown Atlanta. They invited no family to witness the occasion. They took no wedding pictures. At first they enjoyed the novelty of matrimony. "It was like a game, or a sitcom," my father wrote. My parents used to joke that he was like a flannel-clad frontiersman, coming home from his long day at school to a gracious wife who cooked dinner and washed dishes while he turned to his serious work as a graduate student and aspiring writer. But only a few months after their wedding, their life did change. Grad student friends distanced themselves, deciding perhaps that because my parents were married they wanted to be alone. And my mom seemed to grow restless and bored with the gay scene, just as my dad was growing bored with the domestic scene at home.

Four months into their marriage, my father learned about a disturbance in New York's Greenwich Village. In the early hours of June 28, 1969, a crowd of gay men and transvestites fought off a routine police raid at the Stonewall Inn, a Mafia-run gay bar on Christopher Street. The following nights of violent face-offs and demonstrations would mark what many consider the start of the modern gay rights movement.

Inspired by this event and his discovery of the cultural journal *Gay Sunshine*, my father, then Emory's student government president, wrote a column for the student paper publicly coming out, an experience he later wrote about:

Because I had a wife no one could question my manhood. I obviously wasn't gay just because I couldn't relate to women sexually. No doubt this allowed me to "come out" much more publicly and aggressively than I would have otherwise. Even so I paid a price. I lost friends. What was hardest for Barb, so she said, was her straight friends' "sympathy." "How can you stand it?" they'd ask. They refused to accept that it didn't bother her all that much.

Over the next two years, he helped organize Atlanta's Gay Liberation Front, one of hundreds being organized on American campuses in the wake of Stonewall. He was also named the gay lib editor at Atlanta's alternative weekly, *The Great Speckled Bird*, all the while sharing a life and bed with his wife.

The Great Speckled Bird, cover by Steve Abbott, June 28, 1971. Courtesy of Special Collections and Archives, Georgia State University Library.

Then, on a warm spring night in 1970, a year into their marriage, my mother entered the den where my father was sitting and sternly and needlessly rearranged chairs and straightened the piles of papers that cluttered his desk. I imagine her in a flouncy purple blouse and a brown corduroy miniskirt, which would ride up her bare legs every time she bent over to pick up a stray paper. My dad admired her compact frame, feminine and efficient in its movements. Finally, after straightening a calendar hanging on the wall, she faced him.

In his journal my father would recall how, lit by the gurgling blue-green light of the fish tanks that surrounded them, my mom appeared like a sea creature. With her black eyeliner and mascara accentuating her large eyes, he imagined her as a villainess in an underwater sea lair.

"I'm pregnant," she announced.

"I thought you had an IUD."

"I took it out. Don't you remember?"

He didn't remember. After a moment he asked, "Do you think we should keep the baby? I can't really see us with a baby in this place." He gestured to the apartment, which seemed to shrink as he sat there.

"I want this baby."

"I don't know if we're *ready* . . . And then there's the money. Even with your salary and my fellowship money, we're barely able to support ourselves now. I mean . . . if you want to have an abortion, you know I'd be there for you."

"I want this baby."

My dad felt like Flash Gordon strapped to his chair in this underwater universe. The air felt suddenly heavy and suffocating. He scanned the room for a means of escape. But the serpentine siren flicked her tongue and repeated her demand:

I want this baby.

Five years earlier, in the winter of her freshman year, my mother had taken a leave of absence from Smith College and moved into Chandler House, a maternity home for pregnant girls in Evanston, Illinois, three hours' drive northeast of her parents' house. It was a difficult period. My grandparents worked hard to keep my mother's pregnancy a secret as it would bring shame on the family in their small Midwestern town. My mother signed into the home using a fake name and didn't return to her parents until after she gave birth to her baby. Records from the home indicate that my mother kept to herself, often reading or taking walks along the North Shore, no matter the weather. After the birth of her daughter in May 1965, she signed papers giving her away to people she'd never meet.

During that five-month stay at the home, my mother called my grandmother almost every night. My uncle David, then ten years old, remembers picking up the phone and hearing my mother crying. The rooms were poorly heated, she complained to my grandmother. The housemother was brusque. Every winter afterward, my mother slept with a plug-in electric blanket. It was Kermit green with a soft, nubby texture. She hated to feel cold, my father told me.

So on this spring night in 1970, my mom told my dad she wanted to keep me. Perhaps she thought having a baby would change him, might make him a more attentive husband or make him forget about his young lover, a lean blond undergraduate named John Dale. In his journals Dad recalled her saying that if he wanted to leave, he could.

I imagine their conversation, with Dad crossing and uncrossing his legs. He flicked ash from his cigarette into an abalone ashtray perched on an end table but said nothing. She read hesitation and fear on his face, then came up with a compromise.

"If I have this baby and it's too much for you, you can split. I won't chase you. You won't even have to pay child support. I'll take full responsibility."

My mother took a deep breath and exhaled. Her brown eyes widened and then narrowed in a fixed gaze on my father. He felt, sitting next to her standing figure, like a small boy. He had no argument to offer. "We are married," he wrote in his journal. "She's free to be herself. How can I hold her back?"

JOHN DALE told me that the rain fell softly down the oak-lined streets in front of the Emory University hospital on the night of my birth. He sat with my father in a hospital hallway. My dad smoked a cigarette and talked nervously waiting for his child to be born.

"Sometimes I find myself wanting it to be a boy and then I think, why do I want that?" My dad crossed his right leg over his left, and his one dangling foot twitched nervously from side to side. "Is it because . . . I've been *taught* to want a boy? Or do I need to see a version of myself reflected in this baby?" John shrugged, offering a weak smile. They continued talking when a nurse appeared from a side door. "Mr. Abbott? Your wife has delivered a healthy little girl. She's resting now but you can see the baby in the window of the south ward, just down the hall."

My dad stood behind the window of the baby ward, so close that he fogged the glass with his breathing. He scanned the many baby faces searching for mine. In a letter he later wrote me, he described all the babies as looking "like fruit in a fruit display." When he found the baby with the index card reading "Abbott," he studied my face and wondered if I would be like Angela Davis, the Black Panther activist famous for her Afro, her fist held high in court. "My hope was that you'd grab the world by the ears," he wrote, "and carry on the revolution for 'The Good.'"

But I wasn't named Angela. My parents wanted a hyphen-ated name "like a real Southern belle," Dad would later explain, "like Peggy-Sue or Betty-Joe." After searching through books of names at the hospital, my parents decided on Alysia-Rebeccah, which translates as "captivating peacemaker." They'd call me A-R for short.

Later, in the hospital room, my mother lay holding me against her chest. Her whole body ached. When she saw my dad, she smiled and placed me in his arms. I was smaller than he'd expected. He didn't know how to hold me, and my mom laughed, showing him. My dad said I squirmed like a small reptile in his hand and then peed on his arm. He was elated.

SUNDAY

Alysia – 1 egg, 1 jar cereal. 2 pieces of bread. 1 jar fruit.
Barbara – 1 piece of toast + butter – juice.
Steve – 2 pieces of toast + jelly.

Steve – 3 pieces of bacon – 2 eggs. 4 pieces of bread. 1 glass
     of juice.
Barbara – 1 piece of bread – cheese. Marshmallow. Juice.
     Handful of nuts and raisins.
Alysia – 6 tbls yogurt. 1/4 jar prunes. 1 marshmallow.

This note is a surprise in the middle of my dad's 1971 notebook. It's the only time I've seen my mother's handwriting. Unlike my father's scrunched and tight letters, her script is neat and con-trolled, slanted to the right, leaning toward the future. She writes with a thin, blue, felt-tip pen. Perhaps money is tight. Perhaps she's worried about our nutritional intake. It's a concerned hand, a lov-ing maternal hand that writes out the meals for the day.

The week before, my father had lost his job at the Atlanta Mental Health and Retardation Center, a job my mother had helped him get. So during these months, while my mother was pursuing her master's in psychology and working every day at the clinic, my father worked on selling his comic strips to underground newspapers. He also stayed at home with his eighteen-month-old daughter, playing the revolutionary role of househusband.

Every day, after making calls and mailing off query letters, Dad would put me in the stroller and walk me into Lullwater Park. From a small paper sack, he ripped pieces of stale bread and handed them to me to toss in the water for the ducks. I loved watching the ducks quack and splash as they struggled to get every crumb.

Because of money concerns, my mom and dad moved their fish tanks into a larger apartment, which they shared with a roommate, an antiwar student named Bill. After work one afternoon, my mom came home to find my dad sitting with Bill and his friends Jeff and Phoenix on the sofa while I played on the oriental rug with a pink wind-up musical giraffe. My mom announced that she felt "intense feelings of love for everyone." My father told me how she liked to imagine everyone as part of one big family.

My mom lifted me up and sat me on the sofa while my dad proceeded with his discussion of David Cooper's *The Death of the Family*, which had been interrupted by her entrance. "Cooper shows how the family institution is rife with subtle violence, meant to bring down the individual." Their conversation stopped when the telephone rang. My dad picked up. "It's John!" He took the phone into the other room, but through the French doors my mother could hear his muffled excitement. John was visiting his family in St. Louis for the summer.

"How's Alysia?" John asked.

"Incredible. We have a telepathic connection. It's like I know what she's tuned in to even when she's quiet. Barbara thinks

I 'neglect' her. But I think A-R feels the security of a deep love with me."

John told my dad he'd be up this weekend from St. Louis and my dad could barely contain his excitement. "Really? Friday?" My mom picked me up off the couch and stomped into the side room. Dad felt embarrassed, protectively cradling the phone. "She's making some scene in Alysia's room. I have to go."

Jeff and Phoenix had been tripping on mescaline all afternoon. My mom drove them home as my dad watched me and picked at the lasagna in the kitchen. She returned twenty minutes later and began to cry, black mascara streaming down her face.

"Why do you have to go on about the evils of the family like that, and in front of other people? If you're having a problem with us, just tell me."

"Your response only proves my point! The family structure is corrosive. It feeds paranoia and hostility."

"Shut up with that already!" she snapped. "Don't you ever think about growing up?"

"Have I ever made you happy? Have you ever felt fulfilled with me?" Hearing himself start to yell, my dad tried to calm down. "Or . . . supposing I was everything you wanted me to be? You'd probably still be unhappy. Maybe you're the sort of person who always wants more."

My mom started crying again and walked to the other side of the house with me in her arms. My dad followed her.

"Things have heated up too much here," he said. "I think it'd be best for both of us if I leave for a while. I spoke with Larry the other day. He's got a place set up in Frisco and he's invited me out. I think I'll take him up on it."

*　　*　　*

IN JANUARY 1973 my dad sent me an illustrated letter:

What Daddy Is Doing
Daddy's feet are big feet. Alysia's feet are little feet.
Today Daddy took his feet for a walk in the park.
On the way Daddy talked to the flowers.
"Hi, Flowers."
Daddy saw a doggie. The doggie barked and wagged his tail.
"Bark! Bark!"
But Daddy is thinking about Alysia and Mommy.
When Alysia is asleep Daddy will give Alysia a big kiss.
Soon Daddy will get in his car and drive home.
Then Daddy can play with Alysia again.
"Hi Baby." "Whee!"
Then we can go see the ducks again. Alysia can feed the
    ducks.
"Quack! Quack!"

Detail from letter, 1973

My dad had driven to San Francisco from Atlanta and stayed for six months, exploring the city and peddling his comics at various places including Last Gasp, publishers of the underground Zap Comix. S. Clay Wilson, the cartoonist behind Zap's *Checkered Demon*, had been a friend of my dad's in Nebraska and made a few introductions, but Zap had little interest in Dad's gay-themed strips. When not working, he visited the city's many bookstores, bars, and cafés, where he'd write letters to my mom back in Atlanta.

One evening, he telephoned. "I've felt peacefulness out here alone," he told her. "I've sometimes felt this with John. But with you, there's usually some shadow of anxiety, some worry about the past, or the future. It's hard to imagine just being—*be*-ing with you. Sometimes I think you can't let things just be."

"I just want things to go well with us."

"I think things will go better for us if you can find more fulfillment on your own—not build your life around me so much. Maybe an extended vacation would help. Why don't I take A-R with me to my folks in Nebraska and you can mellow out in Atlanta for a while?"

"No," my mom answered. "I don't want you traveling together without me. What if something were to happen? I'd be left alone."

SHORTLY AFTER his return from San Francisco, it was clear that my father's concerns about his marriage were unchanged:

> June 6, 1973: Going to Frisco it was easy to be born again. How to continue doing so when living in the midst of hassles so familiar is the challenge. Going to Stone Mountain [in Atlanta] with Barb & Alysia was fun at first, then a tired duty which wilted into an unbearable feeling of being trapped, oppressed and sucked dry.

Why is this? Is the insanity in my own head that I cannot be satisfied with Barbara? So at night I go out to the bar, where the dim lit haze of smoke is a backdrop for smiles, drinking, sweaty dancing & seeking sex with some attractive man stranger who may perhaps lift me out of this routinized world I sink around in.

One afternoon that July, after my father had picked me up from the day care center while my mother was at work, he returned home to find my mom's new boyfriend, Wolf, in the living room preparing to shoot up a tab of what looked to my father like psilocybin, which he had mashed with a spoon. Wolf pushed the needle through his arm. Nothing. Then his whole body turned red and he stumbled around the room. His face contorted with what looked like savage pain, his eyes bulging.

"Was there strychnine in this?" he rasped.

My dad felt helpless before Wolf's cramped contortions and shudders.

"If I OD on this," Wolf yelled through clenched teeth, "just take me to the road and dump me."

"What will I do?" My father's mind was racing. He felt his heart beating faster. "Call John – ask him to help me."

Then Wolf fell on the sofa, lifted his leg, let out a fart, and smiled. At that moment, my mom returned from work and Wolf tried to pass the whole thing off as a joke. "But it's a very macabre joke," my dad wrote, "as we both know."

A suicidal patient she treated at the Georgia Regional Hospital where she was working, Wolf and my mom got involved while my dad was in San Francisco. His mother had killed his two brothers before killing herself. She described Wolf to my dad as "incredibly real." When my dad first met him, he was also charmed. With his lank, long hair and sunglasses pushed up onto his head, Wolf looked like Peter Fonda in *Easy Rider*, my dad wrote. And he was open, vulnerable, and appeared to love my mom. He certainly needed her in ways that my dad didn't.

Maybe it was good for her, my dad thought at first. She seemed to finally develop her own emotional life and concerns. So when my mom suggested Wolf move into their house, my dad thought, why not? There were always roommates moving in and out of Adair Street. What's another person?

But Wolf was different. His neediness was strong and intense. He pumped drugs into his veins, and Barbara was starting to do the same. They were spending days together in bed. She began to miss work and was losing weight. The house, formerly kept tidy and swept, was a mess. Garbage and papers covered the floor. Bugs crawled beneath unwashed dishes in the sink. The fish tanks were murky with billowing clouds of algae. Years later, my grandmother would recall the state of their house with tears in her eyes.

TWO WEEKS LATER, my dad received a phone call from my mom. She asked him to pick me up from the day care center because she was doing MDA with Wolf. At about 1 a.m. that night she returned home crying. My father suspected she was drained because of the tension still between them and "too much dope."

Early the next morning, my mother woke my father because she'd had a terrible nightmare and wanted to tell him about it. Their fish tank had broken and all of the fish had flopped into the street. No one would help her save them. After listening and calming her down, my dad fell back asleep, but an hour later he was again woken up. My mother had collapsed while walking through the kitchen, breaking a glass.

Ten days later, my father was sitting at his typewriter when Wolf approached, inviting him to "do up some MDA." Dad had

once done IV drugs with Wolf and my mom, but he didn't like it
and asked that they not do it around him. Taken aback by what he
regarded as Wolf's "gall," my dad demanded that Wolf either lay
off drugs or move out. To make his case, dad read aloud excerpts
from William Burroughs's *Naked Lunch*, hoping to convince Wolf
to make the decision to quit drugs on his own. After hours of listening silent and blank-faced, Wolf finally promised to give up all
drugs "save grass" for three months.

Later that same night, John Dale called and my dad recounted
his troubles with Wolf. John suggested that he move out.

"I can't," my dad said, "for A-R's sake, if not for Barbara's."

Eight days later, Wolf was arrested in northern Michigan for
running drugs and guns across the Canadian border. My mom
announced that she was going to drive up to Michigan the next
day so she could post bail. "How long can this go on?" my dad
lamented in his journal.

The next night, he received a phone call from my mom in Michigan. "Wolf's charges have been dropped. I'm driving with him to
Atlanta. We should arrive by Sunday."

AUGUST 28, 1973. It was raining in Atlanta when an early morning telephone call woke my father. Knoxville Hospital was looking for Wolf's father, reporting that "he has multiple injuries."

"What about Barbara Abbott?"

My dad was directed to call a hospital in Sweetwater, Tennessee.

"What about Barbara Abbott?" he asked again.

After much hemming and hawing, the hospital administrator
said that my mom had "expired." My dad started to shake. "What
to do? What to do?" He called her parents in Kewanee, Illinois.
Her mother picked up. He asked for her father but before he
arrived my dad said, "I have bad news. There's been an accident."

"What accident?"

"Barbara has expired."

"What are you saying?" Barbara's mother shrieked into the phone.

"Barbara's dead."

"Oh God, no." The phone clicked.

2.

RECEIVE THE ARTICLE in a plain brown paper envelope. For nearly a week it sits in the entryway of my home. I don't want to open it until I have time to read and take it in. Even when I find that free time, I want to leave it alone, afraid of diluting its power, or being disappointed by its contents. It is my history, my own secret. Finally I open the envelope, pull out and unfold a scratchy photocopy of the *Sweetwater Valley News* dated August 30, 1973. Thank you, Wanda, at the Sweetwater public library.

Looking at the article, I'm first struck by the picture that accompanies it: a demolished VW bug in the foggy morning of August 29, just as it's about to be towed away. The front of the car is smashed so completely that it doesn't look like a car but like a sloppy metal wound. How anyone survived I can't understand.

Some details in the article confirm what I know: my mom flew out of the car and was hit by another car. Others are new: the car hit a massive pulpwood truck. And there was someone else in the car too, someone who was pronounced DOA at Knoxville Hospital: a nineteen-year-old kid from Michigan named Thomas Hungerford. Was he a hitchhiker? Could he have been involved with the accident? Did he know Wolf? I also get Wolf's full name: Jonathan Dennings Wolfe. He was the one survivor, sent to Knoxville Hospital. A quick Internet search reveals nothing more about him. Still, there's now this proof, resting in my hands. This really happened. These were actual people. They didn't just exist in my dad's journals and in my imagination.

The accident occurred at 6:30 a.m., Tuesday in heavy fog
on a straight stretch of highway in front of the entrance to
the Lil' Daytona Speedway near the East Tennessee Live-
stock Barn.

Reading on, I'm startled by the article's mistakes. "Barbara Bender
Abbott" instead of "Binder." "Her body was shipped to Chicago
by Kyker Funeral Home," instead of Piser Funeral Home. Is this
unconscious anti-Semitism on the part of *Sweetwater Valley News*?

When the morning fog burned off, when all the smashed pieces
of the car and bits of lumber had been picked up and hauled away
("It took more than an hour," according to the *Sweetwater Valley
News*), when the blood on the ground was finally washed away
by the September rains, there would be no more Barbara Binder
Abbott. Only the promise of her. The high school valedictorian
and Smith graduate never to receive her master's. The future suc-
cess predicted by her Latin teacher, Mr. Carlotta, never to be realized. The lover of children and dogs never to get a dog, never to
nurse more than one child. And that child, now motherless.

MY DAD'S SISTER, Elaine, arrived in Atlanta soon after the
accident. She took the first plane she could catch from Lincoln,
Nebraska. When she entered the house, I thought she was my
mother.

"Is that Mommy?"

"No, Alysia," my dad said. "Mommy's not home."

Elaine remembers my mother's fuzzy white bathrobe, which
was still hanging on the back of the bathroom door, and the closet
still full of her clothes. "He couldn't put them away."

One night my dad planned an outing to the better Atlanta
bars, even a drag show to shock his younger sister, who until this

visit hadn't known he was gay. "So that's like two whammies that sent me into shock," she told me. But Elaine hadn't packed any "dress-up clothes," so Dad went into my mother's closet. "Take this," he said, holding out a paisley pantsuit. It fit, so Elaine wore it, though she recalls feeling very strange. And then that night, when she came in and Dad paid the babysitter, she remembers me, a few months shy of three, waking up and asking again, "Is that Mommy? Is Mommy home?"

"No, honey. Mommy's not here."

Eventually, Dad tried to explain that Mommy wasn't coming back. With toy cars, he acted out the accident. Reading the lines from my Babar book, he tried to explain the loss. "Babar's mother was killed by a mean hunter. Babar cried."

But I still couldn't get it. I spent every day thinking Mommy would walk through the door or that I'd wake up and she'd be there in bed next to Daddy. And then one day, as Dad was dressing me for day care, I broke down. Wringing my hands, I cried over and over, "I want Mommy! I want Mommy!"

Dad calmed me, he held me, and again he explained to me, patiently pulling out the Babar book: "Babar's mother was killed by a mean hunter. Babar cried." Then he finished getting me dressed and drove me to the day care center, just like he did every morning. He wrote that I was okay after that day.

She flew out the car window. At some point my father must have shared this detail of my mother's accident with me because it's always been an integral part of my family story. She *flew* out of the car. As a child I imagined her flying, already a ghost in a long white dress.

MY MOTHER'S SISTER, Janet, was asleep in my grandparents' spare room in Kewanee, Illinois, when they received my dad's phone call. She was visiting from Evanston with her kids, Judson, five, and Jeremy, a day shy of three.

"Should I take the kids home, Munca?" she asked my grandmother later that morning.

"No, I like to look at them," she said.

Word of Barbara's death spread quickly in her hometown, population 15,000. The next day, the local *Star Courier* ran an article about her accident and a small obituary. By nightfall, the asphalt driveway of my grandparents' ranch-style home was full of cars. My uncle David, who was only eighteen and about to start his freshman year of college, recalls a constant traffic of people moving in and out of the house. They'd leave flowers and platters of homemade food on the table in the front room. They'd wash dishes and talk in hushed tones with Munca, who never took off her sunglasses.

David remembers Munca's close friend Daisy Gerwig arriving through the front door and making a beeline for Munca, who was sitting in a chair off the kitchen. With her arms outstretched, Daisy said only these words before embracing her: "Hostages! Hostages!"

Only later did David learn that Daisy was referencing a quote from Sir Francis Bacon that would often come up in conversations about their kids: "He that hath wife and children hath given hostages to fortune."

For two days, visitors and friends came to support and feed and mourn with the Binder household, but my grandfather, a distinguished radiologist who was never socially inclined, avoided the scene. Instead of greeting people in the front room or sitting with friends in the living room, he retreated to his bedroom in the back of the house. Behind a closed door, he sat on the end of the stiff sofa under the window, and read a book. He kept the shades closed.

He remained there for hours, undisturbed by the many visitors, until on the afternoon of the second day Munca came in. David remembers seeing her kneeling on the floor in front of Grumpa and pounding the carpeted floor of the bedroom with her fists, crying, "Why didn't they take me? Take me! Take me! Give me my daughter. I'll go!" Barbara was the second daughter Munca had lost; her first child, a tall, dark-eyed girl named Rozanne, died of leukemia at age three.

Munca's friend Millie Jensen heard her crying from the hallway and rushed in to comfort her. She bent down to the floor to hold her close. But Grumpa stopped her by lifting the palm of his hand. Millie moved back to the front room, leaving Munca to her keening grief.

Barbara had died early on Tuesday. On Thursday her funeral was held outside Chicago. It took my grandparents, aunt, and uncle three hours to reach the Piser Funeral Home from Kewanee. They planned to bury my mother in a family plot at Westlawn, Chicago's Jewish cemetery. By the time they arrived, my father was there. He brought me along, though I was not yet three years old. His journal:

I cry when AR sings, "All the little children," and "Happy Birthday to you Mommy."

Barbara's sister Janet waters flowers. Barbara's mother complains about her dry throat. Barbara's brother asks how I like his shoes. The Rabbi asks if I'd like anything in particular said about Barbara. Later, I think I would have liked it if he said she gave her life helping others.

The service is simple, dignified. The rabbi talks about psalms and about poetry. Sounds good but I can't remember a word of it. Barbara's mother says "impersonal" and thinks that's good. They kept the sermon to ten minutes. Only the grandmothers cry, and Barbara's mother when I meet her. We hug. During the service, while I cry my choked, silent cry, Barbara's brother talks with his mother about waterhole golf. Riding to the cemetery Barbara's father jokes about the funeral car being unwashed, how that's rude, how he doesn't think he'll come back here again.

Trying to fit in is such a strain. Some relatives want to joke and small talk. Then a new group comes in with the mask of grief. Uncle somebody squints as if sand had just been blown in his face.

At home at last alone (A-R at daycare center) I read. I feel as if Barbara might walk in at any moment and fill the house with her buoyant presence, her smile, her energy. Does anyone at all know I wonder how I loved Barbara. How I needed & counted on her. I am now free, free of protection. But I loved her.

A-R & I seem to relate as we never have before. A new awareness, a new discovery, a new companionship. We have only each other now.

I'm told that within a few weeks of my mother's death, my maternal great-grandmother asked my aunt Janet if she was going to adopt me. She said she could, if Steve was okay with it. If he had accepted my aunt's offer, I would have grown up in the suburbs with a mother and father, two brothers, and a dog named Pokey. But my dad told my grandmother very clearly that he wanted to raise me, even if he had to do it on his own.

*　　*　　*

BACK IN ATLANTA, Dad floundered. Wallowing in his grief, he sought the company and support of John Dale. But John was no longer interested in Dad's intensity and was too young to sympathize with his anguish. John had also moved in with his girlfriend, Susan, and taken a job at Southern Bell. He met with Dad a couple of times, but answered only some of his letters and phone calls. With nothing left in Atlanta, my dad decided to move to the city that had been so hospitable to him only a year before, San Francisco.

In August 1974, within a year of my mother's death, my father drove us over the Golden Gate Bridge into the city that was to become our new home. His hands tightly gripped the wheel of our beige VW bug as a cigarette dangled from his mouth. In the backseat he'd stacked boxes and suitcases, our oriental rug, my favorite little blue chair, and the smallest of our fish tanks. On the rear bumper of the car, a sassy Minnie Mouse sashayed in a polka-dot dress. From the front seat I looked out the window at the wide expanse of water below us. It was my first time seeing the ocean.

3.

WHEN I REMEMBER Dad now, I mostly remember his innocence. His sweetness. His gentle manner. He wasn't tough. None of the tragedy he'd known—losing his wife in a car accident, feeling rejected by family and lovers—had hardened him in any way that I could tell. His hands were soft. He had pale skin and freckles. He burned easily in the sun, so he generally avoided it.

As a little girl, home from first grade and resigned to cozying up to the television for company as Dad worked on his poems and cartoons, I developed a crush on Mr. Rogers. He was so like my dad, with his slender shoulders, brown hair, and light eyes, the careful way he removed his loafers and laced his sneakers, his gentle manner of speaking and of inviting you into his life. Every day he sang me a song and every day I answered him: "Yes, I will. I will be your neighbor."

You could hear Nebraska whenever my father opened his mouth. His conversations were peppered with folksy sayings and examples of the dry wit he'd admired in his grandma Focht. Widowed young and never remarried, she cared for her two children on a schoolteacher's salary and helped raise my father until my grandfather returned from the Second World War. "If ya burn yourself," she used to tell him, "ya gotta sit on the blister."

I used to tease him—the way he pronounced café "cuh-FAY," the way he called the remote control "the clicker," or the way he called every pasta dish we ate "spaghetti" instead of differentiating between linguine, fettucine, and angel hair as I'd learned to do, a San Francisco sophisticate. When he said "Okey dokey!" and smiled his toothy grin, it sounded old-fashioned and silly. Sometimes his more literary friends made fun of him. They laughed when at a fancy dinner Dad told them a story about his childhood dog, Sparky. But the quirkiness of his speech, as much as I teased him for it, just made him more of the dad I loved.

Dad's sweetness and easy manner charmed people and animals. Whenever we were at a party or at someone's house for dinner, whatever cat was around would inevitably end up on Dad's lap, purring away while he stroked its fur absentmindedly. At many of these parties I was the cat, always drawn to his lap, always calmed by his breathing, his vibrating chest and soft voice. And on his lap he would also pet me with those gentle loving hands.

I have pictures of him at age eight. His parents used to drive him and his younger sister from Lincoln to Denver, Colorado, every summer. In Estes Park you could feed chipmunks with peanuts sold by the bag at the park entrance. In one picture he's crouched perfectly still, his hand balanced on a boulder, his fingers outstretched, clasping a peanut. At the end of that peanut, a tiny chipmunk nibbles away while my father looks content and serene. In the background, his younger sister, Elaine, is in bangs and pigtails, her mouth open in mid-complaint. No matter how much she tried to tempt the chipmunks with her swaying peanut, they were always drawn to Dad.

As a child, I loved looking at pictures of my father's boyhood in Lincoln. There he is riding a tricycle. There he is playing pony express and circus with the neighborhood kids. The scenes of my father captured so diligently by Grandpa Abbott looked to me right out of the shows that aired every afternoon on television: *Leave It to Beaver* and *Father Knows Best*. Grandpa Abbott scribbled titles on the photo backs: "Dancing Steve." "First Communion." "Taking time out for refreshments." These titles unwittingly masked a quiet unhappiness I only understood after reading Dad's journals.

When some people age, you can see a history of disappointment in their face and posture. A smile is creased in the corner, as though it painfully swallowed an unpleasant truth. Sad eyes slant and sag. Cheeks grow pale. Shoulders slump as if weary from carrying the burden of grief, guilt, or unresolved hurt. But look at a photo of this same person as a child and you may see someone else entirely: someone full of lightness and joy and that peculiar, almost stupid hope that can only come from inexperience.

Munca talked about that stupid hope. It was maybe for this reason she avoided looking at pictures of herself when she was young. I once asked about her wedding portrait, which we didn't find until after she died. "I don't know where it is," she said. "I think I saw it once and thought, 'That stupid girl. She doesn't know what she's in for.'"

My father also didn't know what he was in for as a grown-up, but that stupid hope came later. In pictures of him as an adult in San Francisco, with his arms slung around the neck of a young boyfriend or pulling me onto his lap in a cluttered apartment kitchen, he looks relaxed, almost giddy. Posed among a group of illustrious writers in the basement of City Lights bookstore, he appears content and proud. Standing on Haight Street in his beard, fedora, and 1940s topcoat, he looks in his element, like a king surveying his lands, unaware of the invaders at the gate.

You find a different Steve in the Nebraska pictures. As a three-year-old he already looks uncertain. As a child of seven he's often looking away from the camera, while his sister will be smiling and looking straight on. In another photograph, a close-up of him in an Indian headdress leaning against a tree, he sneers. In his eyes, there's an aggressive snarl that seems deeper than the pretend play typical of children. In pictures with his parents, I rarely see affection. His body is stiff next to his mother in a parking lot somewhere in Colorado. Both of them are looking away, as though trying to find their real families. In the family album, I see, in fact, that no one in my father's family hugs. They rarely touch. Hands are in laps or at sides, clenched into loose fists.

Lincoln, year unknown

My father never officially came out to his parents. Helen and Gene Abbott learned their son was gay by reading a letter Dad had written to his brother David, which had been left out on the table. But they had long been suspicious.

Dad wasn't able to be himself, his true self, his naked and profane self, until he left Lincoln for Atlanta and then San Francisco. Once he came out, he was fully out. He could never go back in.

PART II
Motherless

I knew if I wanted to keep Alysia I'd have to stop being crazy. I didn't know if I could but I had to try. Alysia was all I had left in the world and I was all she had too.

—STEVE ABBOTT, 1976

4.

I CALLED HIM EDDIE BODY. At four years old, language was my playground. "Eddie Body's not anybody! Eddie Body's not anybody!" I'd repeat, relishing the near symmetry of the sounds. Eddie Body was Dad's new boyfriend, his first serious relationship after our move to San Francisco in 1974. There'd been different men—good-looking men, funny-looking men, almost always tall and skinny and young—that I found in Dad's bed in the mornings. But it was different with Ed. He was the only one with whom I became close. He is the only one I can remember. We spent six months living with Eddie Body. I loved him.

A twenty-two-year-old kid from upstate New York, Eddie Body had moved to San Francisco to get away from his pregnant wife, Mary Ann. He'd made a pass at my dad one afternoon over a game of chess in the Panhandle Park. Soon after, Ed moved into our apartment, a four-bedroom Victorian located a few blocks from Haight Street.

Haight-Ashbury's "Summer of Love" had ended in 1968 with the arrival of heroin and petty crime. For years the neighborhood was dominated by bars, liquor stores, and boarded-up storefronts. But rent was cheap and soon my father, along with scores of other like-minded searchers, moved in, setting up haphazard households in the dilapidated Victorian flats that lined Oak and Page streets. Many of these new residents, if not hippies themselves, shared an ethos of experimentation and free expression. Many also happened to be gay.

By 1974, the Castro was emerging as the political and commercial center of gay San Francisco, with future supervisor Harvey Milk already running campaigns out of his camera shop at 18th and Castro. The post-hippie Haight was a gay-friendly alternative. Unlike the Castro, where gay men put their sexual identities front and center, the Haight's gay residents fit into a larger bohemian mosaic. They got checkups at the Haight Ashbury Free Clinic, shopped for crafts at Far Out Fabrics, joined the Food Conspiracy co-op, and patronized Mommy Fortuna's, a restaurant which hosted cross-dressing musicals featuring members of the psychedelic, nationally renowned theater troupe the Cockettes and their offshoot, the Angels of Light. This diverse community, which favored aesthetics over activism, gave my father a sense of belonging he hadn't experienced in Nebraska, or even in post-Stonewall Atlanta. It was in this world that Dad and Eddie Body met and fell in love.

In his journal Dad described Ed as "a joy, a help, a comfort and often-times frustrating as hell." When Eddie Body first moved in, he had ambitions of musical stardom. He played guitar beautifully and wrote songs, including a tender ballad for my father. Ed had a job downtown selling high-end pots and pans. But after a few months in our apartment, he'd quit the job and dedicated his waking hours to getting stoned, strumming on his guitar, and halfheartedly watering ferns around the apartment. By early 1975, Eddie Body mostly lived off Dad and the Social Security checks we received after my mother's death.

Dad, Eddie Body, and I lived with two roommates, Johnny and Paulette, on Oak Street. Johnny had spent two years in a Buddhist monastery before moving to San Francisco. After smoking several joints, Dad and Johnny would listen to Tibetan bell music and engage in lengthy conversations about the afterlife. But while spiritually enlightened, Johnny showed little interest in the material aspects of the house. Dad alone scoured neighborhood stoop sales and thrift shops for the mirrors, rugs, plants, and Indian fabrics that decorated the apartment. Dad also picked out colors— Indian earth brown and imperial jade green—and painted all the rooms himself.

Johnny was known in the Haight as Joan Blondell, a drag character named after the old Hollywood star famous for her sarcastic wisecracks. Joan would get all dolled up and yell things like, "Don't you feel hot?" then kick over a chair for everyone's amusement. Dad fondly described Joan as "the bitch of death."

Paulette was our roommate who replaced Suzan, who replaced Wade. Like Johnny, she enjoyed dressing in drag; unlike him, she did it full-time. Originally from Alabama, Paulette embraced a Southern Gothic aesthetic mixed with 1940s film fantasy. She decorated her room like the inside of a casket, stapling drapes to the ceiling and outfitting the corners with mahogany antiques and funereal plants.

Paulette also expected everyone to be her servant, an honor Johnny—and Joan—resolutely declined, precipitating many quarrels. Perhaps Paulette was jealous of Joan's local fame. In a letter, Dad recalled New Year's Eve 1974–75, when Paulette couldn't get into the bathroom and had to wait forever before Joan was ready to come out. "You should have seen the feathers fly," he wrote.

"You actually don't look forties at all, *Johnny*. You look like a— well, a *whore!*"

"I know," Joan replied. "Isn't it *divine?*"

AS WE SETTLED into 1975, our household calmed down, with each of us living in our own world: Eddie strumming his guitar, Paulette grooming herself in the mirror, Johnny meditating in the sunroom. Dad was happy to be left alone to read and write while I drew mermaids by the window.

My mornings were spent at the Haight-Ashbury Daycare Center. Through the center Dad became acquainted with some of the neighborhood's more colorful single moms. Lola's mother, an actress with the Angels of Light, had performed in a Warhol film. Moonbeam's mother sold grass out of her apartment on Oak Street. She had a knack for dating young guys, getting them on General Assistance, and then pocketing their checks.

When I wasn't playing with Moonbeam or Lola, I was often left to myself. "Faggots find her cute but are afraid of her," my father wrote in a letter. "Child = responsibility, the ultimate freak-out for the selfish and the escapists."

But not Eddie Body. Each afternoon he'd pick me up from child care, a big smile on his face. On one occasion, he arrived wearing a dress. The attendants wouldn't allow him into my classroom until I heard his voice and then ran into his arms. After day care, Ed and my dad would take me on long walks in Golden Gate Park.

When I was a little girl, the sun was always shining in Golden Gate Park. Entering the park seemed otherworldly. I knew well the papery, banana-shaped eucalyptus leaves and tiny acorns that littered our path. We walked down a hill to a murky pond framed with fern trees and pointy bushes. I imagined it was inhabited by a lady of the lake, who'd only reveal herself after the sun went down and we'd left the park. After the pond we'd descend into a tunnel designed to resemble a cave: brown painted walls toothed with sculpted stalactites. The home of a wayward dragon. Past the cave, the path spilled into an emerald field where towering eucalyptus and pine trees cast long shadows.

To the right of the field was Hippie Hill. Music was always playing; there was a drum circle, maracas, and someone dancing, limbs flailing loose and free. Dad, Eddie, and I would lie on the grass among the clusters of wanderers. In the 1970s, to be aimless, even homeless, was still considered more a philosophical choice than a product of economic destitution. Eddie would patiently thread daisy chains for me while sitting cross-legged in the grass. Sometimes he teased me.

"Eddie Body, I'm hungry," I said one afternoon.

"Hi, Hungry."

"Nooooo, I'm *hungry*."

"How are you, Hungry? My name is Ed and this here is Steve."

"Noooo. *Nooooo*. That's *not* good."

Dad chastised him. Then Eddie Body gathered me into his arms and squeezed me to his bare chest, his whiskers tickling my neck. He smelled of Egyptian musk and BO.

The three of us stayed in Golden Gate Park as long as the day would have us. When the light faded and the air cooled, we began the long walk home together. The leaves of the eucalyptus trees shimmered in the early evening light, looking like rust-colored sequins.

At home, Daddy made din-din while Eddie Body took a bath. I watched him lounging in our rust-stained claw-foot tub. He washed himself with a thick white bar of soap, the same soap Dad used to wash me each night. Eddie was leaner and browner than my dad. He barely had any hair on his chest and a small migration of whiskers sat precariously above his mouth. When he bent forward, his shoulder-length hair hid his face. Eddie watched me watching him and laughed.

"What's that?" I asked.

"What is what?"

"That." I repeated. "There!" I pointed to two egglike spheres I could make out in the dark mass of hair between Eddie's legs.

Eddie coughed and adjusted himself in the bathtub. A small streak of water spilled over the tub's porcelain edge.

"Those are testicles," he said.

I tried the word on for size. "Tess. Tess."

"They're also called balls."

"What do they do?" I asked.

"Um . . . they help make babies," he answered. "Didn't your dad tell you about this yet?"

"No."

"They help make babies. Men have them."

"I won't have them?"

"No, you won't have them."

After dinner, Eddie and Dad took turns reading me stories before tucking me in to sleep. The next morning I woke up, opened the door to my dad's room, then crawled into his bed. Eddie Body was always there, always happy to see me. "It's wake-up time!" I announced. I cuddled between them and lay there, awake but with my eyes closed, while the two of them fell back asleep. Feeling warm and safe, I didn't want to disturb this special time. Often when I crawled into Dad's bed I'd slow my breathing so that it moved in time with his. Together we'd breathe like one. But on this morning Eddie Body's sleep was less steady. Behind me I could feel his breath move from slow to fast. So I tried to adjust my breath to match his. I then moved between the two of them, always trying to reconcile the difference, but always failing.

In the mornings at school I liked to draw. My drawings at four and five were generally the same: an ocean scene. On the surface of the water two boats bob attached by a rope. The girl boat is full of girls, rendered as triangles with stick legs and arms, each topped with a smiley face circle and long hair that curls at the end. The boy boat is populated with rectangles with stick arms and legs and smiley circle heads. Under the water, vast mermaid families swim together: grandma and grandpa mermaids, dogfish and catfish, and birdfish with wings. This mermaid world was fluid, endless, and real to me.

Living in a boy boat, I wanted to do everything the boys did. Every few weeks, Dad would put Lou Reed's *Transformer* on the turntable. Then, together with Johnny and Paulette, he'd dig into the big closet and pick through baskets of jewelry while Lou Reed seductively serenaded them, calling them "slick little girl[s]."

While Dad dressed up with Johnny and Paulette, wrapping a white scarf around his neck and pulling a plantation-style picture hat over his head—"Very *Juliet of the Spirits*, don't you think?" he asked—I draped myself in sparkly scarves and a heavy faux-Egyptian necklace Dad had found at the local junk shop. The fairies may have outnumbered me, but I was still the reigning princess, able to primp in the mirror along with the best of them.

But it wasn't enough to dress up with the boys. I wanted to *be* a boy and told Dad I wanted to be called a boy.

"You have a vagina," he patiently explained. "Boys have penises."

"Can't I get a penis at the store?" I asked.

"No, you can't."

I also noticed that Eddie Body and Daddy peed as easily among the thicket of conifers in Golden Gate Park as in our toilet at home. When I had to pee in the park Dad had to take me through the tunnel, past the pond, and up the hill to the McDonald's, just beyond the entrance, my bladder barely containing itself. After watching Eddie retreat to the bushes one afternoon, I told Dad that I wanted to pee like him. So that night, in our chilly bathroom, he taught me to pee standing up. With gentle hands he helped thrust my pelvis forward while keeping my legs straight and steady so I could better aim into the toilet. I was small in relation to the seat, so it wasn't hard to pee into the bowl, or at least onto the bowl. After several days of practice, I managed to make it in, not getting any on the floor or down my legs.

"Far *out!*" my dad said. Then he ran into the bedroom to share the news with Ed.

"It's a bad kind of life you're giving Alysia, growing up around queers."

"What do you mean? She's happy," said my father.

"She needs a mother. You should get married to a woman."

"Like you and Mary Ann?" my dad asked.

ROOMMATES (queer or otherwise) weren't simply a way for my dad to save money on housing; they were a source of free child care. On any given night Dad would ask Johnny or Paulette to watch me so he and Ed could go out dancing in one of the many bars that were swelling with excitement in post-Stonewall San Francisco: Sissy's Saloon, the Mineshaft, the Stud. On one occasion Paulette reported that I'd turned on all of the kitchen burners, which she'd discovered only after the smell of gas had permeated the apartment. Another time I drank half a bottle of medicine and suffered a minor tummy-ache.

Reading about these events in my dad's journals, it's hard not to feel angry. My father expressed resentment because I asked him to fix me breakfast when, at age four, I was "perfectly capable of doing it alone." Maybe Dad couldn't understand my needs because our life was populated by so many needy wanderers like himself, young people escaping bad homes and bad marriages, all searching for their true selves and open to anything that might further that quest: Hollywood, bisexuality, cross-dressing, meditation, Quaaludes, biorhythm charts, bathhouses, Sufi dancing. Renegades all, but few truly suitable for raising kids, let alone watching them for a night or two.

Eddie Body said I needed a mother. In truth, everyone in that apartment needed a mother, someone to cook and clean, someone to settle the quarrels and to dispense the love and acceptance that was so elusive to these men when they were growing up. I liked to play the role when I could, a Wendy to Dad's lost boys. I'd call him "my poor little Da-da" and serve us bowls of Jell-O, saving the biggest serving for myself. When Eddie Body and Dad were tripping on drugs and dressed in drag I came up and said, "You can be a boy or you can be a girl, you can be whatever you want to be."

But, of course this was just pretend. Ours was a defiantly motherless world. Sometimes we were like Huck and Jim, beyond law, beyond rules, eating with our hands. We were unkempt but happy, with Dad affectionately calling me his "Wild Child." Other times we were like Tatum and Ryan O'Neal in *Paper Moon*, a traveling father-daughter act pulling schemes, subsisting on our charm, and always sticking together.

We hoped that Eddie Body could share this life with us, but their fights became more frequent. More and more he went out without my dad. And, according to my father's journals, Ed became less interested in sex. Lonely and dejected, Dad remembered my mom:

> Sometimes I think of Barb and how callous I was to her
> for so long, so maybe it serves me right that Ed's like
> that to me sometimes. I had a dream about her the other
> night. I was going around to all the bars alone, feeling
> lonely, and she brings me the car in the parking lot. We
> feel so good being together. "But this really isn't happen-
> ing you know, you're dead." She looks hurt. "It's not that
> I don't love you," I say.

One afternoon, at the Haight-Ashbury Daycare Center, I didn't see Ed at the classroom door. Dad met me and we walked to the park. Back in the trees beside Hippie Hill, we started playing our game of hide-and-seek, a favorite from the time I was a toddler back in Atlanta. I called, "Where you are, Daddy?" He answered,

"Here I am," and I followed the sound. When I found the tree where he'd been hiding, I circled around it while he circled in the same direction so that he was always just out of reach.

"Where you are, Daddy?"

"Here I am!"

Until, finally, I ran and caught him. When I became hungry and tired, we walked home together hand in hand. As we entered the tunnel leading to the opening of the park, Dad told me about Ed.

"Eddie Body and I are having problems," he said.

"What kind of problems?" I asked.

"Well, Ed doesn't seem to like me anymore. He doesn't want to sleep with me."

"I'll sleep with you," I said. And I pulled his hand and started skipping, so that he would be forced to join me, which he did happily.

As we skipped through the tunnel, I began to sing a song I'd learned at day care: "This little light of mine, I'm gonna let it shine." Dad tried to sing along but I yelled at him. I wanted to do it alone. "Let it shine! Let it shine! Let it *shine*!"

The next morning, I went to the airport to spend a week with my maternal grandparents in Kewanee. After my mom died I spent almost every school break at my grandparents. The week I was away, Dad wrote in his journal that Ed had received a letter from the wife he'd left behind in New York. He'd learned that she'd given birth to a baby girl and now wanted a divorce. My dad held Eddie while he cried.

At the end of the week, my father picked me up from the airport. Driving home on Highway 101 at night, San Francisco looked like a glittering diamond necklace strung across the sky. Dad turned to me and asked, "You didn't tell Munca and Grumpa about Eddie Body and I, did you?"

I looked out the window. "I didn't say *nothing*."

Back at home, we climbed the stairs to our apartment. Dad put down my suitcase and I pulled off my coat then searched the house for Johnny, Paulette, and Ed, but no one was home:

"Where's Eddie Body?" I asked.

"He's with Mary Ann."

"Why?"

"He loves Mary Ann."

"He loves Alysia," I said.

"He does love Alysia. But he also loves Mary Ann. And she has a baby."

"Why can't Mary Ann and Eddie live with us?" I asked.

"It doesn't really work that way," Dad answered.

"But I want Eddie Body."

"So does Daddy."

"Daddy is sad?" I asked.

"Yes. Now Daddy doesn't have a boyfriend."

"I make you feel better." I crawled into his lap. "I'll be your boyfriend."

When I left Dad's lap to go to the bathroom, he noticed through the open door that I didn't pee standing up. When he asked me about it I answered, "Munca and Grumpa said little girls should sit down."

"Okay. You can do it that way if it's more comfortable for you. But if you want to pee standing up, you know how!"

"Little girls sit down," I repeated. "I don't know how to pee standing up."

"That's fine, too."

Later that night, after putting me to bed, Dad went out to the Stud, leaving me in the care of Paulette. In the back of the club, he got stoned, took two carbitols, and met a rangy eighteen-year-old named Jimmy, whom he took home.

The next morning, I climbed into Dad's bed, squeezing myself inside the small space between him and the man beside him. My dad was asleep but I didn't recognize the other man with his shaggy blond hair. I fell back asleep and started having nightmares. I called out to him in my sleep, "Daddy, let me *in*!" He reported on the night's aftermath:

> February 15: Alysia's been in upset and cranky mood this afternoon. Maybe upset about Ed leaving. She was more clingy than usual. Her eye hurt. She wanted to be held and cried a lot. I thought it was just because she was tired, not having had a nap. Put her to bed around 4–5. Don't want to go to bar but may go to a party. I think I'll stay home because Alysia may wake, and maybe no one will be here with her unless I stay.

That night after putting me to bed, instead of going out, Dad drew me a Valentine's Day card. In his journals he wrote about making the card as a way to help me cope with the loss of Eddie, which was still so confusing and painful after my mom's death. But looking at it now, I think he really made the card for himself, as a way to articulate his philosophy on love. I see him especially in the angry dog.

Two of my father's lovers—his most passionate love affairs after my mother—were with men who ended up leaving him to return to women. Each of these men explored physical love with my dad, either because of his charisma or because of a moment that encouraged sexual experimentation. But these men, with girlfriends and wives, were still anchored to society in a way that Dad no longer was and never would be again. My father wrote about this coincidence in a letter to John Dale that February:

> You know, it's so weird I chose Ed as my lover, a man like you (I say man because he's refused to become another

February 1975

bitchy queen like so many gay men do – refused to shut himself off from the rest of society). And now, like you, he's going back to his wife. In his case it's somewhat different. He has a kid too now, a little girl who he loves terribly much even though he's never seen her. I love Ed & need him but he wasn't able to find a job here & hated feeling dependent on me. Also maybe his wife & baby need him more, & he them. So I've encouraged him to go . . . I hope [his wife] forgives him & helps him to his feet.

Given how much the breakup hurt Dad, I was surprised to learn that he had actually encouraged Ed to return to his wife. In the back of his journal I even found a seven-page unsent letter Dad wrote to Ed's wife pleading with her to take him back. I can't help but think this letter came from some unresolved guilt Dad still felt about the way he'd treated my mom in the end.

After Ed split, Dad tried to orchestrate a room switch in the apartment, arguing that if he was still paying the most rent he should have his pick of rooms. Johnny didn't want to trade rooms, accusing Dad of "economic imperialism." Dad then moved us to a flat on Page Street, a few blocks away and without room-mates. He regretted losing the Oak Street place he'd put so much time and energy into, but, as he wrote in a letter: "Just living in a houseful of screaming faggots was driving me up the wall . . . I wish I could find some really together people for Alysia to grow up around, instead of all the neurotic, selfish shit-faces that so abound."

Eddie Body moved to New York but returned to San Francisco only a few weeks later. He'd lived with his wife and daughter but left them after deciding it was "too much." He started dating women again, and even moved in with Moonbeam's mom. Since my father had introduced them, their coupling was especially painful for him. He visited us a few times but he never stayed very long, and it always confused me. I missed him and couldn't understand why he wasn't with us anymore.

In the years that followed, Dad had other boyfriends but none lived with us. And after Eddie Body, I stopped paying close attention.

5.

I N 1976 EVERYTHING was new. Dad dubbed it his "bisextennial year." We lived on a new block, in a new apartment, and the walls of this apartment were painted with a fresh coat of white paint. The smell of these walls invigorated me. Even today, freshly painted walls smell to me like new beginnings.

When we moved into 1666 Page Street, with its smell of fresh paint, I decided it was magic. I was five years old, but would soon be six and there were six letters in my name. The Page Street apartment was ours alone, a haven of unconditional love, a place I remember as safe. We kept a cage full of doves. Even when the newspapers in the cage smelled dirty, there was always the loud rhythmic cooing of the birds, a sound full of deep satisfaction.

Sunshine poured through our front windows every afternoon. As the light passed through the crystals that hung in the windowpanes, rainbows shimmered around the room. On weekends and after school we walked to the Panhandle to play. On the way, we passed run-down Victorian houses with chiseled faces, jutting chins, and large glass eyes. Many of these buildings were crumbling at the edges, with cracked and peeling paint, but with their occasional pillars and names like "Queen Anne" they were romantic to me, like the ruins of a lost kingdom.

Every weekend, beneath the Panhandle's grand acacia and cypress trees, Dad learned tai chi from a local teacher, who was later immortalized on the mural outside the Park Branch Library.

For a while Dad had me learning too. The movements were strangely slow. A strong arm reaches forward, then around. A leg stretches out, then down. We looked like people caught in a time warp, stuck on the edge of 1976, trying to swim in midair, trying to escape the trappings of our life on earth.

Months after the breakup with Ed, Dad was still trying to heal himself. In his writings he describes a persistent sense of isolation and disconnectedness. "I fit in neither with the gay nor straight community because of Alysia and because of my attitudes, which are not click-ish nor faddish." In addition to practicing tai chi, Dad quit smoking, drinking, and doing drugs. While I was at my grandparents', he attended a six-week alternative medicine seminar where he learned to meditate and cleanse auras.

In the move from Oak Street, Dad also sold and gave away all of his dresses and most of his jewelry. "I'm just not that into drag anymore," he wrote to John Dale, "not even on Halloween." But he saved the best—the heavy Egyptian necklace and the scarves of Spanish lace—for me. In its place he adopted a butch look: handlebar moustache, plaid shirts rolled at the sleeve revealing furry forearms, worn blue jeans, and a heavy black leather jacket. Though Dad claimed not to be faddish, this look was so popular it came to be known as the Castro Clone. The uniform reflected a changing aesthetic among the city's gay men, referencing working-class machismo instead of the more feminine style of generations past.

The prevalence of the Clone look coincided with a growing number of openly gay men moving to the city. Four thousand people marched in the first Gay Pride parade in 1972. In 1976, 120,000 took part, including Dad with me riding atop his shoulders. The face of San Francisco was being transformed by these new residents, who spent weekends in the Castro, enjoying lunch at the Patio Café, standing in clusters outside the Twin Peaks bar. I was especially fascinated by the well-built men with moustaches and tight jeans, hands in their neighbors' back pockets, knocking back beers, staring and smiling, but rarely at me.

As a girl, I always longed to stay among them, to find my way into what I perceived as their tight sense of family. Dad wanted to as well and whenever he could, he did, leaving me with friends or neighbors while he tried to find love in the many gay bars. "I'm a poet," he used to tell the strange young men. And in San Francisco, in 1976, this still meant something.

My dad was also struggling to find work, any work, to supplement the Social Security paid to us after my mom's death so he could make the monthly rent. He sold blood, did substitute teaching at the Haight-Ashbury Daycare Center where I went each day, and painted their mural: "A jungle scene, the lions, monkey and giraffe looking very spiritual and mystical and happy. Quite colorful."

He was also struggling to find his voice as a writer, and visited different bookstores around the city in search of community. He wrote in notebooks in cafés or at home when I wasn't jumping all over his lap, craving some kind of attention, some kind of something that he didn't quite know how to satisfy.

I still wanted simple things: sunny days, cartoons, and French toast, a dog or a cat, not the birds or fish which we had. In the living room, we kept a tank with guppies and kissing gouramis. Frustrated by a pet that could only be watched behind glass, whenever I was alone I grabbed the small net and scooped guppies into my hand. I watched their tiny blue and silver bodies, wet and squirming, tickling my bare palms. Sometimes a guppy would slip out of my hand onto the rug and I'd quickly retrieve it and throw it back in the tank. Sadly, a number of fish died after these games, but I still played them.

But more than any animal, I wanted my father. I wanted Him.

I wanted him all to myself. Dad tried to oblige me. We still played our games of hide-and-seek in Golden Gate Park. Sometimes we skipped together. At home, he made me spaghetti. We'd "wrestle around the room" until I was red-faced and out of breath. Then we'd watch TV or he'd read me stories: *Jack and the Beanstalk* or *Ten Apples Up on Top*.

Other nights I accompanied him to neighborhood potlucks or to readings where adults crowded the room, a forest of legs for me to push through to find Dad against the wall deep in conversation. I'd crawl onto his lap or lie on the floor beside him, waiting for time to pass. On the drive home, I usually fell asleep. Even if I woke up I pretended to be asleep so that Dad would carry me from the parked car up the stairs of our building to my bed.

But I tired of going out so many nights. One evening when my dad wanted to take me out with him, I told him "No, I want to stay home," and despite the fact that there was no one to watch me, he let me stay home alone.

"Don't answer the door," he said. "Just stay here and play with your Little People." I put on a brave face. I was a big girl of five almost six. After he left, I decided to do what he might have done, like a big girl does. I would wash my hair. In the bathroom by the bathtub I found a clear bottle filled with yellow shampoo. I overturned the bottle and sticky globs poured into my hand. I then massaged the globs into my hair, like Dad did each week, sitting on the edge of our porcelain tub.

I can't remember if I wet my hair but I do remember it lathering into a mass of bubbles and sticky heft. I remember my head being too heavy for my body as I tried to get it under the open faucet. Here the hair seemed to drip, a mass of mess served up on my shoulders, unraveling and falling all over me. The soap dripped down onto my face and made my eyes sting and tear. I was scared because I didn't know what to do. I cried, but no one heard me. The water kept running, the hair kept dripping, my eyes kept stinging, but no one answered. So I shut off the water and walked my heavy mess of head into the living room where I could play with my Little People and try to make the wet hair go away.

Sometime later the door unlocked with a pop and there was Dad. I was thrilled to see him, to know that he'd returned and that I was no longer alone. But a shadow passed over his face when he saw me with my wet hair and the trail of suds and pools of water that had followed me from the bathroom into the living room.

"Why'd you do this?" he wanted to know.

In the bathroom he lifted the bottle—once full, now almost empty. He wasn't happy. He rolled his sleeves up past his elbows. He put me in the tub while he sat on the tub's edge. He rinsed my head under the faucet and it hurt to have my hair washed out. The heavy tangles and knots pulled at my head. I started to cry because I couldn't tell him what he wanted to hear. The smell of the new paint had gone. And there we both were, with eyes stinging, hopes dashed.

ALYSIA'S HAIR ON BEING WASHED

Not flower sweet nor tough as seaweed
Quiet it hangs—
Soft, Damp Spanish Moss
Spun fine as glass, as dreams
And so it grows
Unthought, uncut, unexpurged.

No Legion of Decency hair this
But wild unhairlike hair
Wrapped round impossible boats
Clinging there, growing there, aching there
Like poems in America
Like love
Like life, threatened in your mermaid sea.

O hair of my daughter
Uncombed, unused to water
Medusa head—
For all that,
Still you endure.

6.

I N THE FALL of 1976 my father enrolled me in the French
American Bilingual School, then located at the corner of
Steiner and Grove. Dad had high hopes for me at French
American. It was an expensive private school filled with children
of diplomats and businessmen and a far cry from the grotty world
of the Haight-Ashbury Daycare Center, with its hippie teachers
and single moms into astrology and macramé. "I feel like she's gotten into Harvard!" Dad wrote in his journal after I was accepted.
He enlisted my grandparents to help cover the tuition. "Barbara
would have liked it," he argued. As Munca and Grumpa were both
deeply committed to education, they agreed.

French American required their students to wear a uniform of
white blouse paired with a navy skirt or slacks. Since I had nothing
like this in my wardrobe Dad drove us out to the Stonestown Galleria, the only mall we'd visit together. We wandered the circular
racks of clothing in the children's department as if in a maze. I
click-clacked the hangers, observing the colors and textures with
my fingers, while Dad occasionally examined the price tags with
round eyes. We continued aimlessly until we were rescued by a
saleslady with red hair and shiny teeth, who quickly sized us up
as the clueless pair we were. Chatting up Dad, she learned everything about French American and their uniform. And of course,
she made friends with me. "Entering first grade? That *is* exciting!"

She led us to the rear of the floor and into a dressing room with large mirrors and a heavy green drape you could pull back and forth across the ceiling. "I'll be right back," she said. Elevator music played as I jumped around looking at my reflection and Dad fidgeted with a pack of Carlton Regulars.

Our saleslady soon reappeared, arms stacked high with white and navy clothing. She pulled the drape closed, and with Dad's help, I tried on everything. He zipped me in and out of polyester pants. He buttoned and tied ballooning blouses. He pulled vests and dresses over my head, and then yanked them off, my tangled hair getting caught in the buttons. Every few minutes the lady would return, always bringing more, then cheerfully removing what didn't fit.

Then our saleslady returned, announcing she had something "*very* special." A manicured hand jutted through the dressing room curtain holding a sleeveless quilted blue jumper with a matching white blouse. "We just got this in last week!"

I stepped into the dress and my father fastened me up, struggling with each button in the back.

"How're we doing there?" she asked.

"Almost," my father answered. "There's a lot of buttons."

Dad stood behind me as I considered my reflection, then he pulled open the drapes so I could walk out. But my shoes were rooted to the dressing room floor. My eyes were focused on the girl in the mirror. On the front of my dress I could see a Holly Hobby look-alike wearing a wide-brimmed bonnet and a long dress similar in shape and style to my own. Except that this other girl was standing in profile and she was standing upside down.

Outside the dressing room I faced the red-haired lady uncertainly. A wide smile gripped her face. She turned to Dad for a reaction and then she turned to me. My apprehension must have been evident because without my saying anything, she said: "The girl's upside down to everyone else, but when you look down"— she motioned me to look down—"she looks just right!"

I was still too young to doubt the lady openly, but I could tell that there was something off. The girl on the dress is upside down. This is the truth. There is no way to right her.

Looking at the saleslady's shiny teeth and gums, I got a tight feeling in my stomach and turned to Dad. Surely he'll point out the absurdity of the upside-down girl. He'll take me out of here and return us to the Haight and maybe we'll go to the Panhandle or to Mommy Fortuna's for dinner. But Dad just smiled and nodded at me in that stupid dress. I felt sick. I realized I was alone and yet, even alone, I knew that I was right.

"What do you think?" the saleslady asked again.

"Well, I think it's very pretty," said Dad. "You look like a *real big girl.*"

"I don't like it," I mumbled.

"Is it too tight in the back?" the saleslady asked. "Because we can get a bigger size."

"I . . . don't . . . *like it!*"

Dad woke up from his haze. He looked confused and embarrassed. The saleslady's smile was replaced by a tight-lipped smirk. Dad avoided her eyes and walked me behind the curtain with a firm hand. He pulled off the dress, grabbed a handful of blouses, stockings, and skirts, and paid for them. We drove home in silence.

UNLIKE THE OTHER students in my new class, I didn't know any French. So Dad set me up with a summer tutor. I enjoyed my books, especially *Babar* in French: *"Babar est sorti de la grande forêt et arrive près d'une ville. Il est étonné parce que ç'est la première fois qu'il voit tant de maisons."* "Babar has left the big forest and arrived at the edge of a city. He's shocked because it's the first time he's seen so many homes."

At first-day orientation Dad introduced me to my French teacher, Hortense, but I couldn't understand anything she said.

Mornings were conducted exclusively in French. Like Babar, I felt like a true foreigner, walking on all fours, unused to the ways of civilization. What made matters worse was the fact that Dad and I arrived late nearly every day. No matter how much he tried to get me to school on time—setting the alarm, locating my one pair of shoes—we always seemed to sleep in, to run out of milk or clean stockings. We'd inevitably rush out the door and fall into the dingy VW bug out of breath. After racing down Oak Street, Dad would pull up in front of the school, move the stick shift into neutral, and take a drag from his cigarette. He'd pull me up the stairs and kiss me quickly on the cheek before pushing me through the doors of the white Victorian townhouse. Outside my classroom, I could hear the muffled voice of my French teacher inside. Pulling open the heavy wooden door, her voice suddenly loud and inescapable, I hurried to my seat at the back of the class.

I watched as Hortense moved up and down the aisle that split the classroom, her arms folded behind her back, her triangle of frizzy hair bouncing with each step. Behind rectangular wire frames, Hortense had deep-set, suspicious eyes. She surveyed the students, then she found me.

"Alysia . . . *quel jour est-il?*"

I stared at Hortense dumbly, then looked away.

"Ah-lee-see-YAH." Her heels tapped on the wooden floor as she approached my desk and stood before me in flesh-colored stockings and a brown wool skirt. Her mouth was tight and thin: "*Quel. Jour. Eh-TEEL?*"

The liaison of *"t'il"* was quick and sharp like a whip. Involuntarily I straightened my back. But the question was still impenetrable, like a tangle that couldn't be combed out.

"I don't know."

"*En fran-ÇAIS, s'il vous plaît.*"

"*Je . . . Je . . .*" A girl kicked my seat and I heard laughing.

"Attention!" Hortense commanded sharply, and the class was again silent.

Hortense pivoted on one foot and turned. *"Quelqu'un?"* And a sea of hands shot up. She called on a girl in the front row.

"Il est lundi, Madame Hortense."

"Très bien, Nicola."

Nicola wore two parallel dark brown braids down her back and a shelf of bangs cut straight across her forehead. Her pleated skirt fanned around small knees. Her argyle socks were pulled over firm calves, which crossed discreetly under her chair, ending in polished loafers, perched as if ready to bolt at a moment's notice.

I looked down. My own blouse was rumpled, tucked unevenly into my navy skirt. My chalky white stockings were too small and crept down my backside.

The next morning I asked my dad to tie my hair up like Nicola's, but braids were beyond him. He managed a lopsided ponytail but fastened it with a sticky rubber band pulled from around our morning *Chronicle*. When he removed it that night, he took several strands of my hair as well.

> September 12, 1976: Alysia's been having quite an adjustment to her new school. Friday she spilled her juice and had to wipe it up. Monday, she skinned her knee and a girl behind her was kicking her chair. She says she can't understand her French teacher. A lot of groaning in the mornings. One night she kept me awake grinding her teeth.

Dad, in the meantime, was finally finding his voice as a writer at Cloud House. The building was located on the corner of 16th and Guerrero and we'd pass it on the way to a food co-op in the Mission where, while Dad shopped for organic produce, I roamed the aisles, stealing carob stars from giant plexiglass bins.

At first glance, Cloud House seemed like a crazy house. In the storefront window, poems, hand-lettered in cutouts and Magic Marker, were Scotch-taped to the windows and walls. Above the door we saw a sign: "Walt Whitman Breathes Here." Dad asked the cashier about Cloud House and was told they held open readings every Thursday at 8:30. Dad went the next week for the first time, with me in tow. There were no other kids.

Through the dimmed light I could see the walls were covered with posters, drawings, and photos as well as handwritten and typed poems. A short, intense man with black hair ran in and out of the back room fetching hot water for everyone's tea. He introduced himself as Kush.

"Why Cloud House?" my dad asked him.

"Clouds are families made of evaporated forms," he said. "It's important to put your head *in* the clouds and feel *like* a cloud because clouds release what they have to the earth. Poetic visions aren't just private but can reach others. We do that at the Cloud through open readings. Everyone's welcome. Come, sit down."

He waved us to the center of the room, where Dad and I found several people sitting in a circle around three or four kerosene lamps. We quietly took a seat on the floor behind them. A cassette tape of somebody reading was more or less ignored as joints and conversation were passed around the circle. The air then filled with the smell of burning sage, to "drive out negative energy."

When the tape finished, the black-haired man shook some wind chimes, which hung on a long rope from the ceiling in the center of the room. He then walked around the circle chanting a Native American prayer. His deep bass voice seemed to penetrate the floorboards where we sat. Finally he pulled out a wooden flute, played a few notes, and announced that the floor was open to whoever wanted to read.

A tall young man with an overgrown beard, sparkly eyes,

and a cowboy hat stood up and began reading from a weathered black notebook. After he finished, everyone clapped. Next, a big woman in a floor-length dress stood up. Shifting from one leg to the other, she read nervously, apologizing for every poem. All the while, Kush sat hugging one knee, listening intently. "Why don't you read that again," he'd say, or, "How'd you come to write that?" When people's comments went too far afield, Kush would interrupt, "Let's hear some more poems!"

Then a tall, thin man with a harried expression stood up and everyone yelled, "Moe!" This was David Moe, nom de plume H. D. Moe. He always seemed addled and out of breath, as though he'd just emerged from a space pod. Or maybe this was an expression of his dyslexic poet persona, which was part Beat, part mad scientist:

> *Duchamp pas de deux*
> *electric Voltaire*
> *wombing Ouija!*

After Moe left the stage amid hoots and howls, a man dressed all in denim with a bowl haircut and mirrored sunglasses stood up. "Hullo. I'm Dennis." As he read he manipulated his voice, which buzzed and droned like a futuristic machine. All the while he raised and lowered his body like a wizard casting a spell. I'd never heard a sound like that coming out of a person before. Dad and I were transfixed.

Dad was too shy to read on the first night. When everyone who wanted to read had finished, Kush concluded the evening with a final chant of his own.

Dad returned home in a state of feverish inspiration. After I was changed into my nightie and tucked into bed, he got to work on a comic poem—lines of verse interspersed between comic book frames. The poem was simple, consisting of permutations on the phrase, "Faster than love, your words burn up my fire." He called it "The Poet as Arsonist."

The following Thursday we returned to Cloud House and Dad shared his poem, which was showered with praise: "It's like William Blake!" Kush insisted Dad let him Scotch-tape the poem to the wall. Emboldened, my father began to do a series of comic poems, which he mimeographed at Cloud House as eight-by-ten broadsides, then taped up in cafés and laundromats all over town, with me running just behind him.

Dad had studied poetry as an undergraduate at the University of Nebraska with John Berryman and Karl Shapiro, but stopped writing in 1967 because poetry then seemed to him "an empty, meaningless parlor game." Finding Cloud House reignited his passion. Soon he stumbled on a used copy of Jack Spicer's *Billy the Kid*. The book changed him utterly. In the 1950s Spicer, along with Robin Glaser and Robert Duncan, helped forge an avant-garde poetry which they named the Berkeley Renaissance. Spicer especially showed Dad that poetry was a way to get in touch with his gay identity. "Spicer's work acted like a magnet drawing out mine," he wrote.

We were soon spending several nights a week at Cloud House. I'd find a sun-faded pillow in the corner, where Dad would set me up with paper and crayons. I drew fluffy cloud houses and cloud high-rises, all populated by eager inhabitants arriving on the backs of birds. Kush hung my pictures in the windows, so that every time I walked into Cloud House, it felt like my house too.

So many evenings of my girlhood were spent sitting in crowded, hushed rooms, waiting for the quiet to be pierced by these strings of strange words. Rarely could I follow what was being read. To me it was just background noise, a soundtrack for my curious wanderings, paging through books on shelves or looking at the

Garfield and Snoopy comic books I'd brought from home. Other times, the steady and repetitive rhythm of the readers, the warmth and tone of their different voices, worked on me like a lullaby. I'd climb onto Dad's lap and drift off to sleep, soothed by the movement of his breathing, his warm skinny chest which I listened to as it vibrated in animated conversation. There was no place I'd rather be.

Cloud House readings were often followed by potluck dinners. The grown-ups often drank too much, filling the rooms with their cigarette and marijuana smoke, reciting poetry, then arguing about it.

Poet 1: "In order to bring poetry to the people it has to relate to them personally, to expand their dreams. Protest poetry puts blinders on people."

Poet 2: "But if there's no revolutionary poetry, there may be no revolution!"

Poet 3: "I see the cassette tape recorder as the lethal weapon. We've gotta go out with the cassette players and instead of playing disco, play some consciousness!"

Dad and I always came home late from these evenings. We'd stumble into our respective beds, still in our clothes, and the next morning we'd wake up and rush out the door, late to school again.

SOON AFTER STARTING at French American I began to wet myself. At five and a half, I was three years out of diapers. I was not a bed wetter at home and I have no recollection, nor does Dad record in his journals, of my having accidents at home or anywhere else. But at French American, at the least convenient moments and least convenient places—high on the jungle gym or on the farthest reaches of the schoolyard—I'd have a sudden and uncontrollable urge to pee.

I was old enough that I could simply have gone to the bathroom in the morning or broken off from the single-file march from our classroom to the playground. But during those first few months I developed a deep and abiding wish to disappear. I didn't want to call attention to myself by asking to go to the bathroom and I didn't know how to ask in French. Besides, I'd grown accustomed to holding inside anything that was too embarrassing or too shameful to share: my dad's boyfriends, my mom's death, my pee.

Over the next few weeks, I got to know the unsmiling school nurse and her wordless riffling through a box of lost and found in an effort to find me dry clothes I could change into in the back office. I remember itchy plaid polyester pants that were too short and the astringent smell of my urine-soaked clothing tied together in a clear plastic bag that I carried along with my lunchbox while I waited for my dad to pick me up after school. Other kids smelled it too; I was sure of it. I believed myself stained with the scent. Seizing on my shame, a pair of second-grade girls decided to punish me further. Who was I to argue?

After our class filed outside for recess I'd be playing alone, crouched in a corner of the yard. I'd look up and there they'd be. I can't remember their names but I do remember one bully had blond hair with dark brown eyes and eyebrows, the dissonance of her coloring emphasizing her menace. The second bully, a mousy brunette, had an overlarge forehead. Standing in navy skirts and kneesocks, they towered over me. I remember them marching me to the water fountain at the entrance to the school. They stood beside me, forcing me to drink until I said, "I have to go to the bathroom."

"Then pee!"

But I couldn't pee on command, so they walked me down the hall to the girls' bathroom and told me to sit on the toilet, but with my clothes on. I tried again.

"Do it." Their words echoed in the empty bathroom. "*Do it.* Pee!"

But my body still wouldn't let go. So we marched back to the fountain where I had to drink more water. Then I returned to the toilet seat. Finally, after pushing down my skirt and peeling off my stockings, a small trickle of pee streamed and then surged through my underwear. I would have pulled off my underwear but the girls insisted that I keep it on.

I learned to long for the rainy days when our classes stayed in for recess. Under the sweet watchful eyes of the English teacher, Mrs. Meadows, I spent my recess drawing. With crayon and paper I created large families: A mother in a blue dress and brown bun pushing a baby carriage surrounded by brothers and sisters, grandparents and cousins. I made drawings inspired by television shows, *The Brady Bunch* and *Eight Is Enough*. In these fantasy worlds there was always a sibling nearby to provide company or protection, as Peter Brady did for Cindy when she was being teased about her lisp.

In math class we learned about shapes and were encouraged to find shapes in our environment. The clock was a circle. The door, a rectangle. At pick-up time, I noticed each family formed a shape of some sort. Three kids and two parents formed a pentagon. Two parents and two kids formed a perfect square. Even an only child with two parents formed a triangle. But Dad and I were just two points. A line. Not even a shape.

I could have told Dad about the bullies at school, but deep down I suspected he was more the source of my problem than its solution. I used to pray that he wouldn't pick me up wearing his leather motorcycle jacket. That all the shiny cars and pretty pigtailed girls would be gone before our dingy beige VW bug finally rumbled up to the curb at Grove and Steiner.

When he arrived, he reached across the passenger seat and opened the door while the engine was still running, a cigarette attached to his lower lip. Inside I noticed the cracked and ripped leather seats, which exposed crumbly yellow foam, and the overflowing ashtray that wouldn't close no matter how much I tried to close it.

THE NEXT WEEK we returned to Cloud House, Dad was the first to stand up and read. He was so mild and soft-spoken in daily life that it was strange to see him before an audience, strange to see him magnify his voice to fill the big room. I sat on the dusty floor at his feet. All was silent except his words soaring above my head:

THE DEPARTURE

I suppose it's all over now.
  Brief as a cloudless sky
  Empty as my daughter's mouth
You are flying home for Christmas.

  Back home
  I read this note:
  "Dear Tooth Fairy,
  Tonight's the night!"
  Tooth under her pillow.

Your plane drones on.
I don't know where it's taking you.

I replace Alysia's tooth
With a shiny tin quarter.

(She, so anxious. For days
It just barely hung in there
A dead white star.)

Under my own pillow
I dream fitfully.
A sad, savage bird
Drops you
Into an album of fading wings.

Come morning
I'll be the only good fairy
Left in town.

H. D. Moe was the first to publish Dad's poetry. At a time when many experimental West Coast poets had a hard time getting published, Moe started his own journal, called *Love Lights*. But after finding that a poetry magazine wouldn't pay the rent, or even a few days' bills, he started putting erotic photos of women on the cover and selling *Love Lights* from newspaper vending machines. Unsuspecting leches fed quarters into Moe's machines thinking they were getting porn but found instead pages and pages of absurdist poetry.

Through Moe and Kush, Dad met poets all over town. Dad was frequently asked to produce and put up comic strip flyers for various readings. He embraced the tasks with zeal, not caring whether or not the posters featured his own name. "Poetry was my new religion and I, its eager acolyte," he wrote.

North Beach was the heart of the city's poetry scene since the founding of City Lights bookstore. Its future was argued over in almost every café and bar. In Caffè Trieste, "proletarian poet" Jack Hirschman would read from his recent translation of Jean Cocteau or Alexander Kohav with the conviction of the reborn, his stringy blond hair hanging around his face "like a halo around the death mask of Samuel Johnson," my Dad wrote. Hirschman and Moe argued vehemently about politics and aesthetics. Whenever he was pressed on particular points, Hirschman would laugh and retreat into metaphor. "The Red is the Black," he'd say, waving his arms, then read another one of his translations. Moe, for his part, argued for "Correctionism," by which he meant that everything in life was in constant and interdependent flux. Most poets of the time were coining their own catchwords, one writing "Budada" manifestos, another proclaiming "Actualism." Night after night, Dad listened to these disputes, which were sometimes, he noted, "observed by a shy and aloof Lawrence Ferlinghetti, or mocked by the obnoxious clowning of Gregory Corso."

But poetry didn't clean up our apartment or wash out the crumbs and banana stench from my Scooby-Doo lunchbox. Poetry didn't help me practice reading French at night, or get me to school on time, or bake Rice Krispie treats for the many school picnics and parties. In fact, because of poetry, Dad was even more remote, more irritable when I disturbed him in his room, notebook balanced on his lap, cigarette burning in the ashtray beside him.

> March 13, 1977: Problems with Alysia lately. She's alone a lot, bored with TV. And I want to write, type, read, work at my craft instead of play with her. I try to give her some time each day or night and we talk about the problem. But it's an aggravation to me and a hurt to her. I've been cranky with her. She brought me the Oscar the Grouch book to read two nights recently to clue me in, I think.

At French American, the bully girls were thinking up new ways to harass me. The previous week, they'd forced me to eat orange rinds. Another afternoon, they tried to get me to hurl obscenities at Marc Lovejoy, the meanest-looking boy in the second grade. Weak and weird as I truly thought myself to be, I wasn't stupid. Marc's relative size had already impressed me in games of Nerf football in the courtyard.

"No. I don't want to," I said.

The blond bully pulled a small Swiss Army knife from her pocket and opened it. "You better tell him." I found refuge when the bell rang and we were called to line up with our classes. Later that day I told my English teacher about the incident. Soon after, the bullying ended, and the blond girl was expelled.

My days of torment were over, but the damage was done. I conflated the bullies and my bathroom accidents with an inchoate sense that something was wrong with me. I broadcast my sense of complete otherness through my slumped posture, downcast expression, and extreme timidity. Kids at school called me weird so often that after a while I believed them. I hid myself behind a curtain of tangled hair.

Even though I wasn't gay, I knew "gay" applied to me because of Dad. And during my first couple of years at French American, in between French dictations, math lessons, visits to Kewanee, and hours spent in front of the TV, I learned that gayness was a) "gross" and b) beyond my control. Grossness wasn't something you did; it was something that could just happen to you, or something that you were born into.

So when, early that spring, I found a nest of spiders in my Weeble tree house in the backyard after months of neglect, I didn't think, "Hmm, Daddy should have put this tree house away last fall. I should ask him to wash it out." I thought, "This tree house is gross because it is mine and I am gross." And when I put my stuffed animals to bed under a felt blanket with a plug-in bulb so that they wouldn't be scared of the dark, as I was, and then, after running off to play, forgot the animals under the blanket so that the bare bulb burned a tiny hole in the blanket, emitting a terrible black smell, I didn't think, "How silly! I forgot to put away the animals! I should show Daddy what happened." Instead, I hid the blanket and waved away the offending odor, thinking that the smell was because of me, further proof of my essential badness which needed to be kept hidden.

The experience with the bullies merely confirmed the harshness of the world I'd been thrown into, the difference between the world of Dad, which though far from perfect was still ruled by love, and that of school, which for me continued to be ruled by fear.

Many mornings, I'd be weeping as Dad pulled me up the stairs to French American. I dreaded facing Hortense, who on being told that I was late because the bus we had to take that day was late answered, "Buses aren't late, people are late." Then one day, I abruptly stopped, sucked in my breath, and wiped my face dry with my sleeve.

"What happened," Dad asked. Why'd you stop crying?"

"I changed the channels of my emotion," I announced.

He squeezed my hand and smiled.

"I changed the channels of my emotion," he repeated. "I like that."

I took note of Dad's reaction and at that moment I felt something like the power of language. Whether or not my declaration actually turned around my day, I can't recall. But I liked the way Dad looked at me when I said it, I liked the feeling it gave me, and I wanted to feel it again.

*   *   *

OVER THE NEXT two years Dad integrated me into his writing life. When I memorized a Baudelaire poem for school, he pushed me in front of the open mic at a North Beach coffeehouse to recite it. Few of the assembled poets and poetry fans understood me, especially as I was reciting the poem in French and at light speed, but most thought it "far out" nonetheless, and Dad grinned widely.

He illustrated his first book of poetry, *Transmuting Gold*, with my mermaid and Cloud House pictures. Together we drew the book's cover, just as he sometimes enlisted my help drawing his cartoon broadsides. Later we posed together for his book *Wrecked Hearts*. Dad pulled a medieval robe over his blue jeans. Then, in my best dress, hair combed, I acted out scenes with him in the bushes of Golden Gate Park while a photographer friend snapped photos of us. I loved it.

Then in the fall of 1977, vandals broke into our Volkswagen bug late one night, smashing the back window and stealing our radio. "It doesn't even work!" Dad exclaimed, as though we were the victors instead of the victims. Dad duct-taped the back window with a plastic bag, but weeks of storms ripped the bag to shreds, rain drenching the backseat. Out of the garbage and muck, a mushroom grew. Dad found my reaction worthy of another poem:

IT'S A STRANGE DAY, ALYSIA SAYS

*"It's a strange day," Alysia says, "A green
bug in my room & now this mushroom growing in the car."*

*She's right. Under damp newspapers & cigarette
butts, from the floor, protrudes a slimy brown thing.*

*Maybe I should get a new car or at least
clean it up, fix the windows like the kids say.
But how can I do this & still talk to angels?*

Poets get absorbed in strange quests,
question not the creative regimen of poverty.

I wanted to meditate on this but before I could
  a hitchhiker we pick up crushes the mushroom getting in.

Now the rain wants me I can tell by how
it licks & scratches at the window.

I get so tired of poems that look like this
but say absolutely nothing. Don't you?

In Dad's circle, poverty was not only acceptable but poetic and honorable, a way to "talk to angels." Dad was trying to unlearn civilization at Cloud House, to shake off the order-loving conformity of his upbringing where no child spoke unless spoken to and no glass went without a coaster. In this space he was trying to create, mushrooms were magical, fantastic, the stuff of lyric.

But they weren't for me. At French American, especially through elementary and middle school, our ratty apartment and car, and my shabby, ill-fitting clothing, became a liability, another way I stood apart. Right side up with Dad, I couldn't help but be upside down in school. I learned to move between both worlds, to turn myself over as the situation required.

It would be years—at least until ninth grade, when I discovered rock music and drama class—before I saw my difference in the desirable glow of bohemianism. Even then, I never talked openly with any of my friends and extended family about Dad's orientation. His sexuality was a secret I held on to long after it was useful to do so, a secret I held on to until the physical manifestation of his illness forced me to come out.

7.

EVERY YEAR summer rolled around, Dad would pack me up for another visit to Kewanee, Illinois, the rural town two and a half hours southwest of Chicago where my maternal grandparents lived. Beginning when I was three years old, I was flown from San Francisco to Kewanee for two months every summer. According to Munca, she and Grumpa designed the arrangement to give Dad a break and to spend time with me. Because minors weren't allowed to fly alone before the age of four, Dad coached me to lie about my age, much as he'd coached me to not tell my grandparents about his boyfriends. I never understood why Dad didn't accompany me on these trips, but it didn't matter. I loved flying alone.

Around my neck I'd wear a badge indicating my status, "unaccompanied minor," which opened up a world of privileges. Holding the hand of the uniformed stewardess, I'd board the plane first, visit the cockpit, and meet the pilot. At my seat, I'd be given a bag of toys: a lapel pin I could wear mimicking the shape and metallic hue of the real pins worn by the crew, airline-themed coloring books and word scrambles, and a tiny plastic maze with a ball bearing that you'd tilt from side to side until the ball rolled into a tiny hole. I drank chocolate milk through a straw and made friends with my seatmate. When the flight was over, the beautiful stewardess would return, taking me by the hand so that we would be the first to get off the plane.

I'd see my grandparents at the door of the gate, Munca dressed in her collared tennis shirt, no-iron khakis, and bleached tennies. Beside her, Grumpa would be sitting, looking off distractedly. She'd see me and wave her hand up and down: "Yoo-hoo!" Then she'd nudge my grandfather and he'd see me, stand, smile, and wave. After the stewardess delivered me to them, Munca would wrap her long arms around me and I'd be enveloped by the smell of her house: fine wool and cedar, Jean Naté bath splash, and just the faintest hint of mildew.

Once I was in Kewanee, the world of Dad would recede. No more rumbling Volkswagen with the ashtray that didn't close. The ride in Munca's Lincoln Town Car was as grand and as smooth as a cruise ship. Instead of magic mushrooms, there were magic windows that went up and down with the satisfying flick of a switch. The radio was always tuned to the local public radio station; orchestral music would fill the car, with Munca occasionally exclaiming when she recognized a composer, "Rachmaninov!"

In this clean, comfortable, climate-controlled vessel, I'd travel from Chicago's O'Hare Airport, past the tall fields of corn and the stench-making hog farms that made Kewanee the Hog Capital of the World, to the tan and white ranch house on the corner of Ridge Road. My heart would thrum with excitement at the first glimpse of the house and the rolling clap of the garage door opening to receive us as we pulled into the drive. My mind raced imagining all the house promised: bowls of steaming SpaghettiOs, small glasses of cold orange juice, long white carpeted hallways, color TV sets outfitted with cable in every room, and at bedtime, crisp linen sheets.

Munca and Grumpa, both first-generation Jewish immigrants from eastern Europe, had moved with their small children from Chicago to Kewanee when Grumpa found work as head radiologist at Kewanee Hospital. Munca was a stay-at-home mother but had a vibrant life of her own. She founded the local chapter of the League of Women Voters, played competitive golf and tennis at the Midland Country Club, and did part-time public relations work for the Kewanee Public Library. I asked Munca once, "Are you and Grumpa rich?"

"No," she answered. "We're comfortable."

It was that comfort that I most looked forward to, fantasized about, in the months and weeks leading up to my summers in Kewanee. And for the most part, comfort is what I got. For the first few weeks I was the guest of honor. Munca would arrange day camps and play dates with the children and grandchildren of her tennis partners. She'd take me out for French fries at Hardee's and Dilly Bars at Dairy Queen. I had my pick of twin beds in the back bedroom, Uncle David's childhood room, and would move from one to the other at my whim.

Before bed, Munca would bathe and talc me. After I was dressed in my nightie, hair brushed and smelling sweet, she'd walk me to Grumpa, who would be reading in the den. When he saw me he'd put his book down on the couch. I'd bat my eyes and throw my arms around his big frame and plant a kiss on his cheek.

"Goodnight, Grumpa."

"Goodnight, Bee," he'd answer in his deep baritone.

Then Aunt Janet would arrive with her husband, Jim, and their two kids, Judson and Jeremy, for a two-week stay. I was put to bed on Grumpa's office couch so my cousins could occupy the back bedroom together. Where each day had been planned around my alternating desires to swim at Midland or get books at the library, we now had this family of four to negotiate with as well.

Here, I thought, was a real family— the kind I saw at school and on TV, but one I could watch up close. I was fascinated. But though I was three months younger than Janet's younger son and two years younger than the elder, I have no memory of Aunt Janet scooping me into her arms or helping me with my coat and shoes or tending to me in any way—unless, for some reason, Munca couldn't do it herself.

I always sensed a discreet border. This is the Smith family: the two kids, a mom and dad, like a perfect square. And then there was me.

It was in these moments that I most missed my father. Dad could always make me feel better when the world outside made me feel strange. Dad was the one who loved me best of all.

But my dad was only a whisper on visits to Kewanee, a detail to negotiate among many details—arranging evening phone calls and then, when I was older, receiving his letters and cards, and locating stamps for the letters I eventually wrote to him. He never visited, not during the summers, not during Christmas. And I never heard him discussed or asked after. I don't know if he wasn't wanted in Kewanee, if he never wanted to go, or if both were true. But I do remember this invisible line that I crossed at the airport gate. San Francisco was our world, our fairyland, and beyond it, Dad was gone.

I loved summers in Kewanee. I was driven to the swimming pool each day, fed delicious meals and sweets at my leisure, bought new clothes at J. C. Penney's downtown. I could watch TV whenever I wanted. Yet something always felt off. I didn't know what was missing, but I couldn't escape that feeling of missingness.

The pictures that hung on my grandparents' walls and lined their desks and dressers told me what was wrong:

Here are Aunt Janet and Uncle Jim, posing with their young sons at the annual Hog Days festival.

Here is a nine-year-old Uncle David in a plaid shirt and a sweet smile.

Here is Alysia in first grade wearing a blue dress with a big white sailor collar and white plastic barrettes, which Munca always pronounced accenting the first syllable, BAR-ettes.

Here is a studio portrait of the cousins Judson and Jeremy looking like beautiful little dolls, in turtlenecks and plaid pants.

Here is Janet skiing down a slope in Lake Tahoe and another of Janet with short bangs in darkened silhouette, taken sometime in the 1950s.

Here is Munca smiling at a goose she's encountered on the golf course and, a few pictures over, posing with a five-foot sturgeon she's caught in Alaska.

These were funny pictures, loving pictures, pictures that celebrated adventures and milestones: graduations, travels, weddings, anniversaries. Here is what you did not see:

The picture of my mother at fifteen, shy-eyed, with unflattering bangs and braces. Her picture as a giggling two-year-old in a crinoline dress squeezed into an armchair next to big sister Janet. Her three-quarter profile, looking luminous in white on the occasion of her high school graduation in 1964. The sepia portrait of my parents in full hippie regalia—Mom in paisley, Dad with long hair, beard, and beads—as they look down on their newborn girl. Snapshots of Barbara with me. Snapshots of Dad with me.

I found these pictures only by plundering the depths of my grandparents' closets and dressers. Sometimes I asked to stay home when everyone but Grumpa went to the Midland Country Club. With him reading in the den, I'd busy myself in the back of the house. Digging beneath plastic-sealed winter wools, I'd find old shoeboxes stacked with Polaroids and snapshots, tied with crusty rubber bands. Another box in the back bedroom closet was heavy with framed eight-by-ten portraits, which loudly click-clacked as I searched through them. Only in these dark and musty spaces (how I loved the smell of these spaces!) did I find the set of pictures taken when Barbara first brought Steve home, and those of the solo visit in 1972 when she posed with me on the porch of the old Roosevelt house.

What the pictures on display and those hidden made plain was a certain truth: my parents never occupied the same space as the rest of the family. For a brief time, they, with me, formed a family, but they weren't a part of *this* family. The black-and-white portraits, in faux bamboo wooden frames, depicting my mother growing up were removed from the walls of my grandparents' home after her death. Any framed pictures of me—hanging on the wall in Grumpa's office, or set on Munca's desk or on the dresser beside her bed—were of me alone.

Just as my parents didn't appear in the physical space of my grandparents' home, they never came up in conversation. There was no acknowledgment of September 7 as my mother's birthday or August 28 as the anniversary of her death. No one hid this information, but no one marked these dates in any way. Neither did anyone describe how my mother took her stuffed animals and comic books to Smith College, or recall the time she flushed a half-eaten Christmas fruitcake down the toilet on the Amtrak ride back to Northampton because she couldn't stop herself from snacking on it. I learned these stories from Uncle David when, as a young adult, I joined him on quiet walks or drives past the old house.

It confused me. If the family didn't want Dad around, what did this say about him? And if I loved him and missed him and painfully longed to be back with him, what did this say about me? About us? Was there something unsavory in our world, our San Francisco? Or was there something unpalatable in the story of my parents?

It seemed that my relationship to my mother's family was clouded by the tragedy of her death, especially as I got older and the resemblance between us became more pronounced. At thirteen I cut my hair boy short, as my mom had once worn hers. This prompted my aunt Janet to warn my grandmother before she saw me. She thought the haircut would upset Munca. This reaction thrilled me; if I couldn't remember my mother, I could at least look like her—this lost twin, my other half, my doppelganger. But perhaps I was a walking reminder not of someone Munca loved, but of something that went wrong, of lingering questions. If Steve hadn't been gay, would Barbara still be alive? If he hadn't been gay and had also held a steady job, a *real* job, could we have been as comfortable, as whole, and as picturesque as the Smith family?

It all seemed like a big mistake: something that shouldn't have happened.

Years later, Munca visited me in Paris during my junior year abroad, what she'd call "a successful trip." After an afternoon wandering the Luxembourg Gardens we settled in for tea at a nearby café. Sitting at a narrow table in the window facing the street, I told Munca how important my father was to me. She nodded. "It's not that I don't like Steve," she said. "I just wish he'd never married Barbara."

I understood. Barbara deserved the life of comfort enjoyed by her older sister. She deserved to be living in a fine home in Kansas City, or Lake Forest, or Saratoga, with two kids, two cars, and a dog named Pokey. "Just divorce him," Uncle David remembers Munca yelling into the receiver. "Divorce him, Barb!"

But the truth is, my mother wouldn't have been happy in the suburbs. She loved my dad and wasn't shocked by his interest in men. My parents believed, as did many members of their generation, in revolution—that the rules of family needed to be shattered and rewritten, that there should be room in society and marriage for sexual curiosity, even transgression. But what business did she have leaving her two-year-old to fetch a boyfriend out of jail, a boyfriend who was also her patient?

Sometimes I imagine a world where my mom never met my dad. Or had met him and quickly left him, finding a brilliant Emory grad student with whom she could build her life. She might still be living today. She might be enjoying a distinguished career as a psychologist with the big family and the house full of animals she always wanted.

But then, where would I be?

PART III
Borrowed Mothers

Lincoln, 1978

I don't get it. Alysia and I are really cool.
Why can't we find someone cool to help us on our trip?

—STEVE ABBOTT

8.

S HE WANTED to save the children. In the spring of
1977, a Florida orange juice promoter named Anita Bryant rose to national prominence rallying opposition to
a civil rights ordinance that would have banned discrimination
against gay men and women in Miami–Dade County. Similar
rights bills had been passing across the country, but Miami was
the first Southern city to pass such a bill, and Anita Bryant, an
evangelical Christian and mother of four, would have none of it.
In her TV ads, which compared the wholesomeness of the Rose
Parade with the semi-naked dancing at San Francisco's Gay Pride
parade, Bryant argued that advances in the gay community were
eroding American values and threatening children. In her press
materials she explained her position: "What these people really
want, hidden behind obscure legal phrases, is the legal right to
propose to our children that there is an acceptable alternate way
of life . . . I will lead such a crusade to stop it as this country has
not seen before."

She called her campaign Save the Children, and it was, at first,
very successful. On June 7, 1977, Miami–Dade County residents
voted overwhelmingly to repeal the gay rights ordinance. The victory, which came to be known in the press as Orange Tuesday,
would inspire Bryant to mobilize the first national anti-gay movement, leading to rollbacks of rights legislation in Minnesota,
Kansas, and Oregon. She was the telegenic face of the campaign,

showing up at rallies in her hair-sprayed auburn coif, singing teary renditions of "The Battle Hymn of the Republic."

But as successful as she was, Bryant didn't anticipate how much her fight against gay rights would actually help the gay rights movement, both by bringing the topic into living rooms— that June of 1977, *Newsweek* emblazoned its cover with "Anita Bryant vs. The Homosexuals"—and by galvanizing the community. Gay men and gay women, who'd previously divided along gender lines, now had a common threat. After Bryant's win, they marched side by side in five days of angry street demonstrations in San Francisco and across the country that numbered in the thousands.

A generation of gay men and women, many of whom had moved to San Francisco to enjoy the discos or simply to seek sanctuary, were for the first time politicized. By 1977, over thirty gay political organizations had formed in the city, from the Black Gay Caucus to the Tavern Guild (which succeeded in "gaycotting" Florida orange juice in its bars) to the Lesbian Mothers Union (which fought legal battles to protect custody rights for lesbian moms) to the Coalition to Defend Gays in the Military.

With gay residents now accounting for approximately one out of every five votes in San Francisco, they could not be ignored by city government. Mayor George Moscone, elected in 1975, became one of the first American mayors to appoint openly gay men and women to government positions. And on August 2, 1977, after several unsuccessful campaigns, the first openly gay man was elected to public office in California: Supervisor Harvey Milk.

Dad was a vocal Milk supporter and addressed the political urgency of gay rights in the best way he knew: through art. He wrote a poem about Anita Bryant, which he turned into a cartoon broadside and then, that May, read it live on the community radio station, KPOO:

... O Humanity! When will we ever learn the lessons of history?
If our children need to be saved from anything
It's witch hunters with their pink stars and gas ovens.
Never again! This time we will resist.

For the cover of his second book of poems, *Wrecked Hearts* (1978), he drew a picture of Jesus being gunned down in a gay bar by a thug bearing a shoulder tattoo reading "Anita Forever." Jesus utters "Not again!" as the bullet rips through his heart. The inside title page shows Jesus posed with his open chest—sacred heart imagery my father knew intimately from growing up a devout Catholic in Lincoln, Nebraska. Next to this, Jesus issues a call to action: "What we sissies need is a good revolution."

Six going on seven at the time, I was too young to understand exactly why we'd switched from orange juice to apple juice in the mornings, but I did absorb a sense of persecution: They don't want us. They want to do away with us.

In fact, gay bashing sharply increased after Bryant's win. Gays in the city started wearing police whistles and organizing street patrols. On a late June night, a city gardener named Robert Hillsborough, called Mr. Greenjeans by kids at the playground where he worked, was jumped by four teenagers when he and his boyfriend emerged from their car. One of them stabbed Hillsborough in the chest with a fishing knife, repeatedly shouting "Faggot!" until he died.

I didn't notice the flowers that collected for Hillsborough at that year's Gay Pride parade, only days after his murder, and my dad didn't point them out. Holding his hand, I delighted in the crowd's defiantly jubilant energy, the loud and proud marching. The newspapers estimated between 200,000 and 375,000 turned out for that year's parade. Colorful national flags waved in the air as bare-chested men danced with one another. Everyone cheered when a contingent of Straights for Gay Rights passed. I saw bright yellow balloons and the disco diva Sylvester singing from a glittery float. And everywhere we saw handmade signs: "We Are Your Children."

But even as I felt among friends at Gay Pride, I felt strange at school and at my grandparents' house. I knew what families were supposed to look like, and I knew ours was different. Though I deeply loved Dad, I really wanted a mother. I started writing stories that resolved the problem of motherlessness—stories in which orphaned animals reunited with their mothers or found new mothers, or created families with other orphaned animals. These stories earned me praise from my teachers and from Dad. In the summer of 1977, he considered my desires for family and weighed them against his own:

> July 26, 1977: I find, at present, that my only deep, real and satisfying commitment is with Alysia. For a while, I had a fantasy (especially living with Ed) that I could find a man I loved to live with and that this would also be a good life with Alysia. But Alysia – the more as she gets older – protests against this. She is not getting what she wants and this, in turn, affects me. Whether because of TV or school or grandparent role modeling/conditioning OR because she is simply the honest child saying the emperor has no clothes, she does not want two daddies and with two men, one of them can't be the mommy.

> So what are my options?

> 1) Continue as I am – namely with roommates with whom there is no firm commitment. A drifting life.

2) To more actively seek a man (boy) poet who will share my life with Alysia. This would be ideal but I wonder if it is not based on a fantasy, magical thinking, and thus not a real option.

3) To attempt to overcome my homosexuality and to seek a full time heterosexual commitment.

4) To seek a woman who would accept the homosexual part of me but who would have more than a friendship commitment to me (and me with her) and who would also take a mothering role towards Alysia.

Option 4 seems the most realistic to me at present. The question now is: how to go about achieving this?

A few months later, Dad ran an advertisement in the San Francisco *Bay Guardian*: "Looking for someone creative, especially interested in poetry who would also help with my young daughter Alysia." In December a single mother named Lynda Peel answered the ad. The previous year, she and her thirteen-year-old daughter, Krista, had driven out from their small New Hampshire town to build a new life in San Francisco. Lynda's boyfriend came along and helped them settle in, but when he suddenly left she needed someone to share her rented house in Noe Valley. We arranged a meeting.

Dad and Lynda hit it off immediately. Lynda was a feminist photographer, sympathetic toward gay issues, and intrigued by Dad's writing circle. More importantly, as a divorcee, she could relate to the challenge of pursuing a creative life as a single parent. Lynda said she could help with child care and the details of keeping house that Dad struggled with on his own. Dad would help with rent and groceries and projects around the house, as needed.

I was excited by the prospect of moving in with another kid. We'd already lived with roommates, but few took interest in me and I usually played by myself. Krista was different. She was a kid but something of an adult too. She wore skintight blue jeans and lots and lots of eye shadow. She smelled of perfume and hair spray and would later remind me of the sassy teens from movies like *Little Foxes* and rock bands like the Runaways. I hoped she'd teach me how to wear makeup, or at least play dress-up.

In January 1978, we packed our things and moved into Lynda's place. Hers was a real house, with two floors and a backyard. Far from any street life, it was quiet, which made Dad happy. Our first week, I hoped that I could play with Krista after school, but it seemed she was never around. Then one afternoon a police car pulled up and she emerged with eyes down, her face twisted in a scowl. She'd run away from home. There was lots of talking behind closed doors. My dad tried to smile it all away. "Family stuff," he said. "We don't need to get involved."

The next evening, after Lynda left for her Spanish class, Krista asked my dad if she could take me out to see her boyfriend. She promised that she'd have me back for my 8:30 bedtime. Dad was working on a new poem and, delighted by the prospect of extended quiet, agreed. He helped me with my coat and sneakers, then waved goodbye. The boyfriend, a skinny guy in jeans and whiskers, drove us down 25th Street in his rusted-out car.

Some hours later, I found myself sitting in the front seat alone while Krista and her boyfriend smooched in the back. I didn't know what time it was, but it was dark and I knew I was supposed to be in bed. I had school the next day. At first it was exciting to be there without my dad. The street was lit by flashing red neon. The radio played stories of longing and survival, stories told with thrilling and triumphant orchestration: "If I can't have you . . ." But after a while, I was uncomfortable. I tired of opening and closing the glove compartment. A damp draft blew in through a hole in the door.

"I want to go home, Krista."

No answer.

Bored and cold, I started to worry. Who are these people in the backseat talking to each other? What are they saying? Who are the people walking by the car speaking languages I don't understand? Where are we and how long will we be here? Other children must be in bed, I thought to myself. I imagined them under blankets holding their stuffed animals close.

"I want to go home, Krista. I'm cold!"

"Don't be such a baby."

I nuzzled into the cracked upholstery and tried to lose myself in the songs on the radio. The music sounded like the night— exotic and grown-up, dark and endless. I listened until I fell asleep.

> January 19, 1978: Krista was out till midnight w/Alysia.
> Gary (Lynda's ex-roommate, lover) picked her up at
> 22nd & Mission. Lynda was very angry at me too. After
> taking A-R to school I have long talk w/Lynda. I get into
> some deep emotional feelings & weep (about parental
> rejection partly). Very open, deep conversation but very
> draining . . . Lynda reviewed her hassles with Krista.
> (Who tried to burn down their house last summer, gave
> booze to neighbor kids, etc.) I feel somewhat exhausted
> by it all & bad that Alysia doesn't have sister figure here.
> But house is quiet and peaceful.

Determined to make this alternative family work, Dad tried to adapt us to our new home. Many nights, he and Lynda cooked elaborate vegetarian meals, which were followed by long "rap" sessions where they drained bottles of wine. Dad retreated to his room periodically to smoke since Lynda had a rule against smoking in the kitchen. She had lots of rules.

My father enjoyed Lynda and still hoped that she'd be the household partner he'd imagined in his journal the previous July. When he went out dancing, he'd leave me at home with her and the two of them would make dinner together. But Lynda was an intimidating surrogate mother. Broad and muscular in painter pants and a Mexican peasant shirt, she moved brusquely through the rooms of the house setting up her photo sessions, during which she wanted no interruptions. My playing in the kitchen was enough to prompt her to lumber down the stairs, eyes flashing. She was often angry and she and Krista fought constantly. Slamming doors. Yelling in the halls. It scared me.

Dad knew I was upset and, after putting me to bed one night, resolved to talk with Lynda as they were cleaning up from dinner, a conversation he recounted in his journal:

> I expressed a couple of Alysia's feelings (i.e. that we not talk in her room, that Lynda not come in her room all the time, some fear of Lynda). Lynda said she wanted to deal with AR directly on these things, that I was "rescuing" by acting as a go between. She went "there's a psychological term for that, do you know what it is?" & then went on to tell me I was transferring my feelings onto Alysia. I replied that I resented being put in a category & explained situations when I had to stand up for Alysia before (when people had eaten her food, bothered her at school, etc. – that if parents don't do this, the species couldn't survive. It's survival).
>
> I feel Lynda's trying to have it 2 ways . . . When she's expressing a need, it's "being open with her feelings." When I do it's "bitching at her." Despite this, I do like

her, her strength & buoyant spirit, her dealing with the underneath of interactions. I can see living here being a character building experience for me.

Away from home, Dad continued to focus on poetry. Having established himself at the Cloud House, he now became a regular presence at open readings around town: City Lights in North Beach; a folkie café in the inner Sunset called the Owl and Monkey; and the Rose and Thistle, a straight bar on the corner of California and Polk. But though Dad enjoyed these evenings, he sensed within straight and even mixed audiences a discomfort toward his overtly gay poems. He began reaching out to writers he admired in the pages of *Fag Rag* and *Gay Sunshine*. The papers, both started in the 1970s, published poetry, fiction, and interviews with older writers such as Tennessee Williams and Gore Vidal, along with the work of emerging writers, including Dad and the San Francisco poet Aaron Shurin. In a letter to Shurin, Dad wrestled with questions of identity and writing:

Is there such a thing as Gay poetry or a Gay aesthetic? Is any poem by a Gay poet a Gay poem (some certain unique un-straight consciousness informing it) or is it just certain subject matter & viewpoint field which makes poems Gay?

He told Shurin he wanted to create an intellectual "scene" where he could get feedback on ideas and work with like-minded writers. That February of 1978, Dad organized a Men's Valentine's Reading featuring Shurin and other noted gay writers including Dennis Cooper, Paul Mariah, and Harold Norse. He called the event "From Our Heart to Yours." He illustrated two-color posters, which he printed up in the hundreds but because our old VW's engine had died, Dad had to do all of his promotion via bus and

BART, lugging heavy stacks of flyers and posters to bookstores around the Bay Area. The event was covered by both the *San Francisco Sentinel* and the *Chronicle*. Though the reviews were mixed, Dad was delighted by the attention, cutting them out and pasting them in his journal.

Krista left home and moved in with her boyfriend. I later learned that she'd fallen in with a local Latino gang and started smoking angel dust and pot. Lynda couldn't control her anymore. Tired of the constant battles, Lynda asked Krista to simply make up her mind where she wanted to live so that she could get another roommate. Dad tried to explain to me what was going on and I, having imbibed San Francisco's collective spirit, suggested we all have a meeting with Krista to see what we could do to make her happy. The meeting never happened.

ON APRIL 25, 1978, St. Paul, Minnesota, became the second American city to repeal its gay civil rights ordinance. Anita Bryant took her familiar position in front of the TV cameras: "Once again, as in Dade County nine months ago, the morally committed majority has gained a great victory. The message to the politicians is clear: no longer will God-respecting Americans submit to the oppressive yoke of militant, politically organized immorality."

As news of the St. Paul loss spread, protesters took to the streets of San Francisco by the hundreds. A friend of my dad's called to invite him to a massive demonstration under way in the Castro. Most nights Dad was too busy watching me to take part in the many rallies and protests organized by Harvey Milk and his circle, but on this night he left me with Lynda so he could go.

By the time Dad arrived, the protesters, many wearing "Squeeze a Fruit for Anita" t-shirts and "Anita Bryant Sucks Oranges" buttons, had scattered to various bars. He headed over to Toad Hall, which was teeming with young men in tight jeans and work boots. Dad quickly found some friends, downed several drinks, and started dancing with a cute kid named Stu.

On the crowded dance floor everyone pulsed to a loud disco beat. Previously just a "gay thing," disco music was now everywhere. The Bee Gees' "Night Fever" was that week's number one song and its lyrics seemed to capture the spirit of the night:

> *Listen to the ground*
> *There's a movement all around*
> *There is something going down*
> *I can feel it.*

After settling their tab at the bar, Dad and Stu shared a cab back to our place.

> April 26, 1978: This morning Lynda and Krista are yelling at each other. I take Alysia to school late and when I return this kid Stu is gone as is a box of my antique jewelry and my tape-recorder. The little fool forgot the cord even! Lost my Jack Spicer tape too. Maybe he was desperate for money. I don't know. Can anything really be stolen from me if I don't "own" anything? Such a strange event. The phantom of Toad Hall – if he only steals your heart you will be lucky!

At first Dad tried to keep the theft secret, but then he discovered that some of Lynda's camera equipment was also missing. She was, of course, very "pissed off." She couldn't believe that my father would bring a strange man into her house. Dad wanted to replace everything that was taken but Lynda said she'd been thinking about her needs and wanted to put together a women's collective. "[She] feels she has too much male energy in her life," Dad reported in his journals. Dad offered no argument. He was just as glad to find an out.

The search for a home was on again.

READING THROUGH my father's journals, it's hard to not feel disappointed by some of his choices. Sending me out with Krista the runaway, keeping us at Lynda's for months even after it was clear that hers was an unhappy home, leaving me alone. What was he thinking? How could he put his work and community ahead of my safety? Was he too stoned to see that this wasn't a good situation in which to raise a young girl?

But then I see everywhere evidence of love. Dad considered overcoming his homosexuality for me. He moved in with Lynda and Krista for me. When we later found a one-bedroom in the Haight, he gave me the big room with the balcony, leaving for himself the living room, which only became his room at night. If he was sometimes a failure as a parent, he was always a noble failure. He tried to do what he thought was best even if he didn't always know what "best" was or how to achieve it.

What's perhaps more striking to me is that through it all he never gave up his passion for community. He was determined not only to advance the quality of his own work, but to organize and increase the visibility of gay writers and poets everywhere, to publish broadsides and later magazines on his own dime. My father did all of this while struggling to keep me in bilingual school and pursuing life as an openly gay man. He was a pioneer.

It wasn't easy being a single gay father in the 1970s. There were no books on gay parenting, no Listservs, as there would be decades later. There were no models. For better and for worse, my father was making up the rules as he went along. His only guide was a firm conviction that he didn't want to raise me as he had been raised.

Because he hadn't felt free to be his true self growing up in Lincoln, in our fairyland he raised me with fluid boundaries. In that household, kids were not to speak until they were spoken to and physical punishment was standard; in ours, Dad invited my opinion on everything, from his boyfriends to my punishments. After growing up in a house where he'd been spanked for running onto the lawn naked and displays of affection were uncommon, Dad raised me in a home where a naked man might parade down the hall, where I lived on his lap and called him my boyfriend. There was never a sense that "these matters are not appropriate for children." My father took me everywhere, introduced me to everyone, and worked hard to treat me as an equal. And since I was a precocious child and Dad was a childish adult, in some ways we were equals.

Conservatives like Anita Bryant and California senator John Briggs feared that gay teachers would inculcate kids into a "gay lifestyle," but Dad made no such efforts. In 1975, he wrote:

> I'm not trying to get her to grow up gay. I'm not hiding my gayness to get her to grow up straight. But she can see that there are many orientations and many ways to be. Hopefully, by the time she grows up we will have a society where those dichotomies of whether you're gay or straight, a man or a woman aren't so important. Where people can just be as they feel most natural and comfortable in being.

I always and only saw that people spent time with the people they loved.

9.

D AD'S FRIEND and sometimes publisher, Ken Weichel, heard of all the trouble we were having with Lynda and Krista and offered to set us up temporarily in a pair of rooms in the house he shared with his girlfriend, Patti, in Merced Heights. In May 1978, we moved in.

It was a long drive out to the house—past San Francisco State, past the Stonestown Galleria, and then past a restaurant called the Doggie Diner that featured a fifteen-foot-high statue of a dachshund wearing a chef's hat. But Ken's two-story house was pretty, with wooden shingles and a small patch of grass in the back, and it was quiet. You could hear birds outside the window, and from the kitchen you could see a narrow strip of ocean. When Dad told me we were going to move into the "Doggie Diner house," I exclaimed, "Goody goody gumdrops!"

Despite my initial excitement, I was lonely. I had few friends to play with and spent most of my time after school by myself, since Dad was always writing. Determined to make my room feel more mine, Dad asked Ken if we could paint a mural on the walls. With Dad's help I painted a magic island with palm trees and galloping unicorns and a rainbow that stretched across the sky. It was a place I called Ecnarf—France spelled backward—and I wrote the name in small green letters. I decided to add some water to the paint on the tops of the palm trees, to give the impression that the trees were blowing in the wind. It looked good. Hoping to replicate the effect with the herd of white unicorns, I applied water to their legs, but it just turned them into a large gray smudge. Still, I loved my mural, my room, my own safe place.

Meanwhile, Dad worked on his verse, eventually pulling together the writing that would form his third book of poetry, *Stretching the Agape Bra*. Through his readings at Cloud House and the events he organized around the city, including a reading for the 1978 Gay Pride parade, he was starting to make a name for himself. When a friend asked if he'd like to take over editing the calendar of *Poetry Flash*, a well-known West Coast poetry newsletter, Dad jumped in. When they arrived at the staff meeting at the paper's East Bay headquarters a few days later, they discovered that the old staff, overworked and exhausted, had decided to quit en masse.

Richard Hoover of Hoover Printing Co., to whom seventy-five dollars was owed, offered to take over as publisher, but he needed a managing editor. After a lengthy interview, he asked my dad to take the job and organize a new staff. Dad was initially hesitant but agreed after he was promised he could also write a monthly column—more work, but one that would put forth his own voice.

Just after the meeting, my father walked to the nearby house of Joyce Jenkins. She was a local poet who'd directed the 1978 San Francisco Poetry Festival. Dad knew her by reputation as an excellent worker and as someone strong in areas where he was weak—notably, attention to detail. He invited her to join him as an associate editor and she accepted.

Together Dad and Joyce turned the monthly around. When they started, *Poetry Flash* was in debt. It was also criticized for being conservative and elitist. Over the next five years they would quadruple the monthly's circulation (from 1,500 to 8,000) and expand its size and scope. They worked to avoid favoring any single poetry clique, instead seeking coverage of the best writers in all poetry groups. Sometimes Dad would attend seven or more readings a week, including at Cloud House and North Beach, where he'd been a regular, but also women's readings, gay readings, African American readings, and Asian readings.

Dad's involvement in *Poetry Flash* soon became all-consuming. I would often accompany him on his monthly trips to the East Bay for meetings at Hoover Printing. I remember the loud "ja-*junk*, ja-*junk*" of the press as we descended into the basement offices, the heady smell of ink, and the barren industrial landscape of downtown Oakland. There was absolutely nothing for an eight-year-old to do on these visits, and I felt besieged by boredom. I preferred the meetings held at Joyce's big house in Berkeley. She and my dad would stretch layouts across the big driftwood table in her living room, talking details, while I played with Joyce's refrigerator magnets and a fluffy cat named Jessica.

Joyce had wavy brown hair, large-framed glasses, and a generous smile. She was pretty and sweet, and always feeding me snacks. I liked her immediately. If Dad was spending so much time with her, I reasoned, maybe something romantic would develop. I imagined their marrying and our moving into her big house with its grand views of the Berkeley Hills. When my cousins, Judson and Jeremy, grilled me about Dad's romantic life that summer while I was at my grandparents' in Kewanee, Illinois, I even turned her into his girlfriend.

Most often, if anyone (usually teachers or parents of friends) asked why Dad had never remarried, I'd lower my chin and talk about my mother's death, suggesting that Dad was still too grief-stricken to remarry. I hoped to convince my listener, and maybe even myself, that my dad loved my mom too much to replace her. This strategy, I later learned, worked doubly well with curious strangers. Not only did it throw them off the scent of my dad's sexuality, but it refocused the conversation on my mother's death.

"How did she die?"

"A car accident. A car hit her car and she flew into the street."

This story was so unpleasant that it deterred further prying. But with my preteen cousins, I knew this tactic wouldn't work.

We were sitting in my grandparents' wood-paneled den. I could hear the heavy summer rain drumming the back porch, prohibiting our daily swim. The three of us were snacking while watching TV on my grandparents' massive set. As usual, the brothers were teasing each other, as boys did at that age: "You're gay." "No, *you're* gay." Then Judson turned to me, sitting on the recliner across from him: "Your *dad's* gay." They looked at each other and laughed. I was gnawing on a frozen Milky Way, one of scores of candy bars Grumpa kept stocked in the garage freezer for us.

"No, he's not."

"Oh yeah? He doesn't have a girlfriend."

"Yeah, he does. He *does* have a girlfriend."

"What's her name, then?"

"Joyce."

In truth, as much as I liked to fantasize about Joyce and my dad's coupling, I came to accept that no romance existed between them. In fact, when she did walk down the aisle with her actual fiancé, I was her flower girl. But I had a name and a portrait to go with the name. I knew that, armed with details, my lie would be stronger, and I stuck to it vigorously. "Her name is Joyce and she has brown hair and glasses!" My cousins never asked about my dad again.

MY FATHER wrote a monthly column in *Poetry Flash* called "Up into the Aether," a reference to Jack Spicer's "Heads of the Town Up to the Aether." The column, full of historical and contemporary literary gossip, alternately delighted and outraged San Francisco's poetry community. The poet and playwright Ishmael Reed called Dad the "Hedda Hopper of the poetry world" because of items like these:

> Gregory Corso's back from Europe. I know because he came to my reading with Jack Mueller at the Grand Piano & tried his best to disrupt it. Didn't succeed of course. "Well, Jack," I said afterwards, "When the big guns come after us it must show we're starting to get somewhere."

About a Modern Language Association convention, he wrote, "Academic critics continue to get fat spinning webs of Confucian pedantry while the real movers and shakers of poetry live at the edge of poverty."

According to my father, even the most well-intentioned of these remarks could cause umbrage. Soon he was publicly confronted by snarling poets who felt themselves to be unjustly used. On one occasion, a disgruntled poet named Leon Miller decided to stage a sit-in at *Poetry Flash*. Unfortunately, he barged into a real estate office several doors away.

Better-known poets, however, realized that *Poetry Flash* now had one of the widest circulations of any literary journal in the area, and started to treat my dad with the respect that had previously eluded him. Dad was amused to find himself referred to in magazines in faraway cities and countries as "a leading force in San Francisco poetry." He was amused because, since he'd taken over as editor of *Poetry Flash*, he had little time for his own poetry. He was inundated with offers to read and with requests to contribute to special issues of magazines that had previously scorned his unsolicited manuscripts with the curtest of replies. "How ironic," he wrote in his journal, "that fame should pursue me when once again I am doing nothing and plagued with self-doubts about where I want to go from here."

In the pages of *Poetry Flash*, my father was also the first to seriously consider a new poetry movement, which would come to dominate the Bay Area scene over the next several years. Language Poetry, or L=A=N=G=U=A=G=E Poetry as it came to be known from the magazine bearing that name, evolved in response to the "raw" performance-oriented poetry that the Beat poets and their descendants were doing.

At first, my father found the Language poets appealing for their intellectual disputes. "Our concern's for what's on the page, not on the stage," the poet Ron Silliman told him. This was clearly true, for unlike other poets in town, most Language poets read in a flat, rapid-fire monotone. Even on the page, what most interested them was a language so deconstructed as to be almost totally removed from ordinary discourse. Unlike Dad's North Beach and Cloud House friends, these writers criticized each other's work relentlessly and saw themselves as advancing the Modernist project, in the tradition of George Oppen and Gertrude Stein. If nothing else, this was a great foil for Dad's own writing, especially in the years to come.

WHEN OUR OLD VW bug broke down again, Dad thought I could ride the bus from school back to Ken's place on my own. I was almost eight years old and very tall. He sat me down at our dining room table with the Muni map, carefully drawing out my route. Delivering myself from school to home would take nearly one hour on two buses and a streetcar.

I remember a great stretching openness, a nothing of space that yawned between French American and our home at Ken's. The last leg of the ride, on the M Oceanview, was the most tedious. I'd doodle in my notebooks and seek whatever entertainment I could find. The streets in west San Francisco are named alphabetically—Anza, Balboa, Cabrillo—and as the streetcar wound south I loved to hear the conductor call out the stops in his nasal voice, especially "Wa-*wo*-na, Wa-*wo*-na." I perked up each time we passed Larsen Park at the corner of Ulloa and 19th Avenue, where a decommissioned US Navy F-8 fighter jet sat on a wide expanse of green as a play structure. From the window I'd watch kids climb all over and even inside the plane while their parents sat on nearby benches. Each day I'd pass that plane, and each day I wanted to get off the bus and ride it.

Then one afternoon as we approached Larsen Park, the sunlight flashed on the jet's platinum nose. Just as the conductor was about to close the doors, I jumped off. A thrill of transgression passed through me as I made my way toward the plane, which looked so much larger from the vantage point of the ground. I set my pack down on the soft grass, climbed one of the two ladders leading into the plane, and explored its interior tunnel and many knobs. Climbing onto the silver wing, I lay down, imagining what it would be like to fly above the city. When I first arrived crowds of kids had swarmed around me, but after a short while the sky began to darken and mothers and fathers started to call names and grab hands.

I headed to the bus bench to wait for my train home. An L Taravel and two K Inglesides passed without any sign of the M Oceanview. When a second L pulled up, I decided to board. The L wouldn't take me home, but I knew it traveled some of the same stops as the M and figured it'd be worth getting closer to home. When the L turned toward the zoo I quickly got off, knowing that was the wrong way.

I had to find my way back to the M Oceanview, but was daunted by the prospect of walking back to my original stop, especially as it was now getting dark. When the San Francisco dampness sets in, it chills you to the bone. You can button your sweater, zip your jacket, and still not shake the cold. Just then, a car pulled up to the curb. From the window, a man motioned me over.

"Are you lost?"

"Yes."

"Where do you live?"

"Shields and Beverly."

"That's not very far. I can drive you. Get in."

I considered his offer. I didn't know this man, but he had a nice smile. I just wanted to be home. As I was about to open the door to his car, a woman swept in beside me. "Excuse me, little girl, can you come over here with me?"

She led me by the hand back toward the bus stop and called over her shoulder, "I've got her, thanks!" I turned my head and watched the car drive away. "I didn't want you to get in that car with a strange man," she told me. She wore a pantsuit and purse and had curly hair and large urgent eyes. I didn't know her but I felt like I did.

"Are you okay? Are you lost?" she asked me.

"I got on the wrong bus."

"Where do you live? What's your name? Do you know your phone number?"

I told her what I could but I couldn't remember my phone number. I felt odd, a mixture of embarrassment and guilt. I'd made a mistake and was now tied to this strange woman, whom I needed to make everything better.

"I'm sorry," I said.

The lady walked me across the street to a nearby gas station where she managed to find Ken's number in a phone book. He and Patti came to pick me up. I got into the backseat and watched as the lady exchanged some words with Ken and then waved good-bye to me as the car pulled off.

"Alysia's too young to ride the bus alone," Patti told Ken on the drive back. He just shrugged his shoulders, keeping his eyes on the road. Then Patti turned around in her seat so that she could face me and said, "I know it's not my place to say so, but I think it's irresponsible of your dad."

Back at home, I found Dad waiting in the front room. He'd returned while Patti and Ken were picking me up. After Ken calmly explained to him what had happened, Dad crouched down and looked me in the eye.

"I don't understand," he said. "Why did you get off the bus?"

I rushed into Dad's arms. He started to scold and lecture but with my head now buried in the folds of his flannel shirt, I could no longer hear what he was saying. I knew we were going to move again. Pressing my ear against his chest, I breathed in his familiar smell and I didn't care.

THAT NOVEMBER, the San Francisco that Dad and I knew ended. Within the span of two weeks, a pair of violent tragedies pierced the heart of the city. On November 18, the Reverend Jim Jones, founder of the People's Temple and a major political force in local politics, led a mass suicide of his followers in the jungles of Guyana. Over 900 people died, mostly poor black San Franciscans, including 270 children, all poisoned by cyanide-laced grape Kool-Aid. The Jonestown Massacre, as it came to be called, was the largest single-day loss of American life in peacetime until the events of September 11, 2001.

Nine days later, on the morning of November 27, Mayor George Moscone and Supervisor Harvey Milk were gunned down in their offices. At first there was only confusion in City Hall. Reporters suspected that the People's Temple had dispatched assassins to kill the mayor, just as they had killed California representative Leo Ryan when he flew into Guyana. Then Supervisor Dianne Feinstein appeared, well dressed but ashen faced, and broke the news to a crowd of city workers and reporters: "As president of the Board of Supervisors, it's my duty to make this announcement: Both Mayor Moscone . . . and Supervisor Harvey Milk . . . have been shot . . . and killed." The crowd, which included several seasoned war reporters, erupted into gasps and sobs before Feinstein continued, "The suspect is . . . Supervisor Dan White."

A conservative Irish Catholic, White had been elected to the Board of Supervisors in 1977, the year of Anita Bryant's cries to "save the children," by campaigning as a "defender of traditional values." Before the morning of the murders, White was up all night eating cupcakes and drinking Coke, a detail that would be used by his lawyers.

Word of the deaths rippled across San Francisco. City schools announced the news on loudspeakers. At French American, my third-grade class spent the afternoon writing condolence letters to Gina Moscone, the mayor's widow.

At home, Dad learned the news watching television. He immediately burst into tears. "First Jonestown," he wrote in his journal. "Now this."

By early afternoon, crowds had assembled at City Hall. Among the flowers and pictures, someone placed a handmade sign: "Happy, Anita?"

White's lawyers defended his actions by arguing that his diet of Cokes and Twinkies had pushed him over the edge. The jury, scrubbed of gays and other "new" San Franciscans, was moved by the recording of White's teary confession, hearing in it the cry of a broken man. Though he'd crawled through the basement window of City Hall, shot George Moscone four times, reloaded his gun, and then crossed the hall and pumped five bullets into Harvey Milk, the last at point-blank range, Dan White was convicted of voluntary manslaughter, the lightest possible sentence.

When news of the verdict reached the streets of San Francisco, thousands of protestors descended on City Hall, smashing windows and torching a row of police cars. As a man ignited the last police car, he shouted to a nearby reporter, "Make sure you put in the paper that I ate too many Twinkies!" Police retaliated later that night by taking their billy clubs into the Castro.

Dan White served five years, one month, and nine days in prison. Less than a year after his parole ended, he took his own life, using a garden hose to funnel carbon monoxide into his parked white Buick sedan.

10.

FIRST SAW 545 Ashbury at night. The previous tenant was a friend of Dad's who, coming off a painful breakup with his longtime live-in lover, sold us the apartment's contents for an even $200. He was eager to move to South America with as little as possible, he told us, and wanted to be rid of the "bad energy." On the balcony he had kept his dog, a musty Irish wolfhound named Molly who'd chewed the doorknob down to a ragged nub. Molly's gray fur lined the wall-to-wall carpet of the balcony bedroom.

"This will be your room," Dad said. "We can replace the doorknob and vacuum the rug. Won't you like to have a balcony? Like a real princess!" In giving me the only real bedroom in the apartment, Dad was giving me the gift of privacy and space, a gift he himself hungered for but which he knew was important for a growing girl.

We moved into the Victorian apartment in January 1979. In the picture of the Grateful Dead posing with the Haight-Ashbury street sign, ours is the balconied building to the right of the band, the one that looks like it's wearing a witch's hat. Photos like this would later turn our corner into a mecca for soul-searchers the world over, crowding the street with beggars and camera-snapping tourists. But as the 1970s were coming to a close, 545 Ashbury was ours alone, a beautiful new beginning.

Our first year in the apartment, Dad worked to make it ours, painting the walls of my bedroom my favorite color, lavender, and building me a pine loft bed for my ninth birthday. Each night, I climbed the rickety ladder, lay down on my cut-foam mattress, and looked through the eye-level windows onto Ashbury Street at the many street dramas unfolding, as if on a stage.

Adjacent to my room and separated by a pair of French doors was the living room, which doubled as Dad's bedroom and office. He set up a writing desk in the rounded windows facing Ashbury Street, which he separated from the bedroom by hanging a large square of yellowed Irish lace, stretched taut between four sticks of bamboo. He built a makeshift bookshelf against the wall, stacking orange and gray milk crates separated with horizontal plywood boards that gave me splinters whenever I ran my fingers over them. Over the years, he filled these with layers of books: review copies from small poetry presses and rare and dusty paperbacks he picked up poking through his favorite city bookstores.

The double door frame of Dad's room led directly into the dining room, which was dominated by a twelve-foot-wide spool table. The spool was our dinner table, our meeting table, our drawing table, our *everything* table. I've seen similar tables sealed but ours never was, and over the next fifteen years the crumbs from a thousand meals collected in the table's many cracks and grooves.

A swinging door separated the dining room from the kitchen, which had a bright window over the sink but could fit no more than two people at a time, uncomfortably. The kitchen was painted caramel, with an avocado green refrigerator, a chrome sink, and across from it an ancient oven. The oven had no vent and the walls were streaked with grease, especially where they met the ceiling. But the grime was offset by a large, cheery star someone had cut out of cardboard, spray-painted silver, and hung high over the oven. Seen through the open kitchen door, it seemed to watch over us.

We'd spend close to fifteen years living here, the longest we'd live anywhere.

Because there was so much within walking distance of 545 Ashbury, we stopped driving the car. Dad parked it two blocks from
our house on Oak Street and there it remained from the spring of
1979 into the summer of 1980. Because he neglected to update the
tags, parking tickets quickly and thickly collected under the wip-
ers. Walking to the Panhandle, I could see them fluttering in the
wind, a swarm of white moths, until one day we discovered the car
had been towed.

"What a relief," Dad sighed. "That car was nothing but trouble!"

We never paid to retrieve the bug, nor did we bother to get a
new car. Dad would never get around to teaching me how to drive;
I wouldn't learn until after my fortieth birthday. Not that it mat-
tered. More than half a dozen buses and streetcars were within
walking distance. For a nickel, I could get anywhere in the city
with a transfer that lasted the whole day. Now that I was older, I
could navigate public transportation on my own.

Riding the bus to school every day and to my friend Kathy
Moe's on the weekends, I became fluent in the language of Muni.
Though technically faster than the 7 Haight and 6 Parnassus, I
knew it was never worth taking the 71 Limited home as the after-
work crowds inevitably slowed service. I knew that I could board
the N Judah in the middle of the car before the Dubose Tunnel
then exit the streetcar just after, thereby skipping the fare when
in a pinch. I learned how to get to Fisherman's Wharf from Union
Square on the cable car without paying. And if I was waiting for
a bus or a trolley from behind a hill, I learned to listen for the
sound of the electric current, like the snapping of a giant rubber
band, from the cable above or the track below. This sound would
announce the bus's imminent arrival, like an inverse echo. I loved
being able to read the Muni lines this way. It felt like eavesdrop-
ping on the internal workings of the city's body.

One afternoon, after getting off the bus from school, I reached
into my pocket for my key and it was gone. I searched my back-

pack but found nothing. I rang our bell but nobody answered. I moved my finger down to the round white button next to #2, and after briefly hovering, pressed hard.

Robert Pruzan lived in a tiny studio across the hall from us. I didn't know Robert but I knew his garden, which I'd discovered my first afternoon at 545. Exploring the back stairway alone, I followed a dark and narrow basement corridor ending in a latched door. After unlatching the door I entered the most extraordinary oasis filled with rare and exotic blooms: orchids and lilies and jagged bonsai. I loved playing in the garden. Our electric and gas meters became knobs on a time machine. By setting the dials to the prehistoric age I would arrive next to a swamp, where I'd run from screeching pterodactyls and hide beneath the fronds. An avid horticulturalist, Robert tended gardens all over the city and was famous for his landscaping behind the Haight's Shady Grove Café. He worked to prevent the thinning of Buena Vista Park, and later inspired the AIDS Memorial Grove in Golden Gate Park.

"Hello?"

"Hi. Robert?" I yelled into the whistling intercom.

"Yes?"

"It's Alysia. From apartment one. I left my keys at school!"

After buzzing me in, Robert greeted me at his apartment door with a smile. He was small and trim, outfitted in tight jeans, t-shirt, and vest. With his neat beard and mischievous laugh, he possessed an impish quality. I wasn't surprised when I later learned he'd played the fool in a 1969 Roundabout Theater production of *King Lear*.

"Why hello, A-*lyyy*-sia. Come on in!"

After a quick exchange, Robert walked me through his apartment to the back stairs so that I could check if my back door was unlocked. It was bolted shut, so we returned to his apartment, where I waited until Dad came home. Robert had spent much of the 1960s in Paris studying mime with a protégé of Marcel Marceau and had a delicate, precise way of moving through the narrow confines of his studio. Between my repeated calls home, Robert showed me his collection of rocks and shells, theatrically explaining the provenance of each. When I told him I was hungry, Robert fed me vinegar-soaked artichoke hearts from a jar, the only snack food his refrigerator would yield. Together we watched *Entertainment Tonight* on his flickering kitchen TV until Dad's return.

Since I often lost my keys, I got to know Robert pretty well. It seemed like he was always around. I later learned he lived off a family inheritance, never having to bother with an office job, and spent days in the curtained darkroom he'd built inside his closet, developing and printing photographs he'd take roaming the city streets—Gay Pride parades, Harvey Milk rallies, street fairs. Many of these pictures were for the *Bay Area Reporter*, one of the city's gay weeklies, where he worked as a photojournalist, but most were for himself.

The walls of Robert's apartment were covered with framed portraits of notables he encountered and often befriended: the writers James Baldwin and Thom Gunn, the disco diva Sylvester. In the corners I spied his cameras and wide-eyed lenses and long-legged stands, all looking like pieces of a disassembled robot.

One afternoon, a few weeks after meeting Robert, I was playing dress-up. I pulled on a long white sparkly gown and dug through the remains of Dad's collection of scarves and jewelry from the days when he still did drag. Around my neck, I draped the heavy jeweled Egyptian necklace inlaid with amber and teal stones. Around my wrist, I snapped a cuff bracelet overlaid with faux brass leaves. On top of my head I fastened a long strip of lace. I studied my reflection in the bathroom mirror and, satisfied with my transformation, searched for Dad, whom I found loudly typing at his desk, a cigarette burning in the ashtray beside him. He smiled at me appreciatively but, fingers on the keys, soon returned to his typing. I then remembered Robert and crossed the hall.

I knocked on his door, listening to the muffled sound of opera until he answered. He looked me up and down, the opera now blaring behind him in the doorway, and his face broke into a toothy grin.

"Well, look at you! Okay if I take your picture?"

I nodded enthusiastically.

He turned into his apartment to fetch his Nikon. When he reappeared, he led me to the carpeted hallway that con-

San Francisco, year unknown. Photo by Robert Pruzan. Courtesy of the Gay, Lesbian, Bisexual, Transgender Historical Society.

nected our apartments. I posed, chin up, my arms outstretched dramatically, left one up, right one down, both hands clasping the banister stairs. A few days later, he handed my dad an eight-by-ten print of our session, a picture he called "Alysia in Communion Clothes" and which Dad later published in one of his magazines. Looking at the photo now, I notice my Snoopy watch visible under my glittery sleeve and am surprised to see how small I look against the staircase banister, much smaller and more self-conscious than I felt myself to be at the time.

In the late 1980s, a new landlord forced Robert out of his rent-controlled studio. We lost touch and his fabulous garden was overtaken by weeds. Before then, I called on Robert so often, big-eyed and wanting, that I must have been a pest, but he never gave me that impression. With his Nikon and later his Polaroid, he patiently documented my best dress-up sessions and even took a picture of my cat the day we brought her home from the pound. Robert always made me feel welcome in his apartment, as though I were the most fascinating nine-year-old in the world.

IN THE EARLY 1980s, Dad had no shortage of writing work. His position as columnist and editor at *Poetry Flash* brought offers for book reviews and interviews with local gay papers, a magazine based in LA called *The Advocate*, and several poetry periodicals across the country. But while this work steadily improved his reputation, it provided little money. The social exchange between writers and editors, which valued ideas over economic concerns, helped build a culture that thrived on, and appreciated, art and thinking. It was one of the great things about this era of San Francisco. But we still needed to pay our bills.

To supplement his income, Dad started doing market research from a tiny cubicle in San Francisco's financial district, a job he'd keep for years. In especially lean months, he shaved money off our rent by vacuuming the halls of our apartment building. This work led to a few jobs cleaning high-rises across town. I remember climbing Nob Hill to a particularly ornate building. While Dad got to work, I lay down on the wall-to-wall carpeting and propped myself up on my elbows so I could finish my homework. Looking out the window, I admired the views of downtown, which was in the process of being "Manhattanized" by Mayor Feinstein. The buildings of the Embarcadero were lit around the edges and looked like Christmas presents. In my ears, I could hear the roar of the vacuum. I turned to Dad as he awkwardly wrestled with the extension cord of an industrial carpet cleaner, and I felt a mixture of amusement and pity. "Are you okay?" I asked before moving to help him untangle the thick, veiny cords.

I later learned that he took these odd jobs to help pay for new literary ventures. Now that we were living alone and spared roommate drama, Dad brought real focus to his creative work. As editor of *Poetry Flash*, he tapped into the incredible diversity and vitality of the city's poetry scene. He oversaw several special issues including "West Coast Black Writing" (September 1979), "American Indian Poets of California" (October 1980), the "Grand Piano" reading series (February 1981), and "Gay Writing" (March 1981). Then, in January 1980, he launched *SOUP*, laying out its mission in the debut issue:

> To be in the soup! I found myself in it when I started writing editors: "Gee I like yr mag but why don't you stress history, ideas, politics more; tackle deep & scary subjects; publish more of so & so." They'd reply: "Sounds like it's time you start your own mag." So here it is.

Dad conceived of *SOUP* as a way to showcase new directions in writing. He envisioned a literary magazine that would be both inclusive and progressive, incorporating interviews with and work from gay and lesbian writers (Judy Grahn), minority writers (Luisah Teish), transgressive writers (Dennis Cooper and Kathy Acker), as well as older figures who inspired these newer works (Robert Duncan, Diane di Prima, Jack Kerouac). Our neighbor Robert even contributed photos.

As this was years before the Internet, Dad pulled together his own money to typeset, print, and distribute the magazine. He hoped he'd recoup the cost in sales. The first issue ended up $1,800 in the hole, which was a lot of money for us. With his many jobs

Steve Abbott, January 1980

and daily market research work, the stress was considerable, as evident in a cartoon letter he wrote to John Dale.

Despite the stress, Dad found his calling editing *SOUP*. When it came to promoting his own work—his comic strips and books of poetry—Dad could be quite shy. This reticence was left over from his formative hippie days, when self-promotion, even professionalism, were looked down on as bourgeois. But when it came to promoting other writers, my father had no such hesitations. In his interviews and criticism as editor of *Poetry Flash* and now *SOUP*, Dad fiercely pushed other writers' work, especially if he believed the perspective was sharp, new, and underexposed. He was among the first to seriously evaluate the work of Dennis Cooper and Kathy Acker, but when their fame surpassed his, he felt left in the cold.

Some months after *SOUP* came out, Dad and a friend, an older gay writer named Bruce Boone, were walking down the street when my father pointed out how all the writers they knew were white. Dad and Bruce had just completed a two-week seminar with the Marxist literary critic Fred Jameson and were inspired to ignite change, especially in light of the recent inauguration of Ronald Reagan and the self-declared Moral Majority that had helped elect him. "Well, what should we do about it?" Bruce asked. After discussing several ideas, they decided to put together a two-day conference, which they'd call Left/Write—a play on both military lockstep and the lefty orientation of the writers they hoped would take part. The goal was to bring together writers with divergent, and often competing, aesthetic agendas, in the hope that doing so would foster "an activist sense of Leftist unity."

Over two hundred people crowded the Noe Valley Ministry in February 1981. There were workshops for "Criticism as a Political Tool," "The Political Impact of Lesbian and Gay Writing," "Radical Asian-American Writing," and more. Ron Silliman, the only participating Language poet, implored the audience to "leave our aesthetic differences at the door just as cowboys used to leave their guns at the door." But guns were drawn. Many panels ended in screaming arguments, yet all were sold out.

In the decade before the conference, these different coalitions had held rallies and protests for their individual causes. Left/Write was important because it brought the groups together in conversation with one another, some for the first time. The event inspired future identity-oriented conferences, including Out/Write. Though Left/Write gave him no financial reward, Dad was proud to have fathered it.

DAD'S INCREASING literary commitments meant I had even more afternoons and evenings to myself. More often than not I'd return from school to a scribbled note, and either a Swanson's TV dinner in the freezer or five dollars to buy myself something in the neighborhood. If I didn't want to pester Robert, I set up interviews with our gray tabby, Heidi, so named because of her tendency to hide under the furniture whenever I entered the room. I'd ask Heidi a question, then pinch her ear with my fingernails to elicit a response, capturing the exchange on Dad's playback tape recorder. But this activity only increased her elusiveness.

I was about ten or eleven when I became expert at inviting myself to dinner at friends' homes. Taking the bus to and from French American each day, I made friends with several kids who traveled the same route, a few of whom lived only a short walk or bus ride from my home.

I became especially close with Yayne [YAI-nee], the daughter of an Ethiopian dad and an African American mother. Because she was born on the first day of spring, she explained, she was named Yayne Abeba, "flower of my eye" in Ethiopian. She also told me she was descended from African royalty, a detail I unquestioningly accepted, sealing our friendship. Soon we'd greet each other in the halls of French American yelling our entire names.

"Yayne Abebe Mengeshe Wondafarow!"

"Alysia-Rebeccah Barbara Abbott!"

Yayne's parents owned a local sporting goods store and after school, we bopped around until her mom eventually growled,

"You're driving me crazy!" and sent us out onto Haight Street. We hung out at the local library, reading back issues of *Rolling Stone* and *National Lampoon*, but almost always ended up at Kiss My Sweet, a Haight Street café landmarked by a pair of puckered neon lips glowing pink in twin windows. Here we drank peppermint tea sweetened with gobs of honey. Sitting over steaming teacups, we squeezed the café's honey bear so that the honey would "percolate" in time with the Maxwell House jingle: "*Da* na na na na *na* na / Na na na na *na na*."

We returned to Hoy's Sports just as Yayne's mother was locking up. After she went upstairs to count out the register, Yayne and I turned the spotlights, previously illuminating running-shoe displays, toward the floor. Then we blasted the pop station KFRC and took turns emulating the sultry moves of the dancers we studied on *Solid Gold*, a weekly pop countdown TV show hosted by Marilyn McCoo.

In Yayne's upstairs apartment we played Barbies, imagining grown-up lives, going to college and fetching lusty boyfriends in our purple Corvettes. But when I heard the sound of the dishes being laid on the table and smelled the aromas of dinner, I didn't rush home. My strategy, which began unconsciously, was to hang around until the inevitable shift into mealtime. At Yayne's house, as at the houses of my other friends, I learned how to ingratiate myself and work my orphan eyes. I acted surprised when the invitation finally came, but over time I expected it.

"Would you like to stay for dinner, Alysia?"

"I'll have to call my dad," I'd say.

In the other room I'd dial my number and it would ring and ring, as my dad was still out. And then, returning to my friends' parents, I'd say, "He said it's fine."

During these years I perfected a parent-friendly manner that in the short term could make me a happy addition to the dinner spread and in the long term might inspire future invitations. I was polite, always saying please and thank you, asking questions, laughing easily, always helping to clear the table.

My friends' parents generally seemed glad to host me. My presence sometimes provided a needed distraction for fighting siblings. They also knew that I lived alone with my dad, and over time I was treated like an extended member of the family. Mengeshe, Yayne's cologned dad, used to call me "monster" in his thick Ethiopian accent, and I called him "man star."

I was fascinated by these dads but especially by the moms like Yayne's, who worked, or other moms who stayed home, and always kept the refrigerator stocked with snacks, the bathroom with fresh towels and bowls of potpourri. I loved to look for any physical resemblance between my girlfriends and their mothers, and was sensitive to every display of affection and tension.

Kathy Moe, the daughter of Cloud House poet David Moe, lived with her divorced mom out in the Sunset district, only a few blocks from the ocean. A small-boned painter from Kansas, her mom was always dabbing away at massive moonlit portraits of women who looked like herself: big-eyed and pale. But while their hair was drawn thick and flowing, I noticed her own was thin and brittle. I'm sure raising Kathy alone frayed her nerves. She turned to incense and Buddhism. From behind closed doors Kathy and I giggled as we listened to her chiming and chanting, "Nam-myoho-renge-kyo."

I sometimes spent whole weekends at Kathy's, watching TV (*Creature Features* on Friday nights, *Love Boat* and *Fantasy Island* on Saturdays) while we ate Kraft mac and cheese and bowls of sugary cereal that turned our milk blue-gray. But, as much as I wanted to, I could never return Kathy's hospitality. She suffered respiratory asthma and could spend no more than an hour in my house before reaching for her inhaler.

The dust that troubled Kathy so much was invisible to Dad and me. We had no cleaning person and no cleaning schedule between us. Occasionally Dad told me to do the dishes and I made a game out of it. Our big rubber tub in the sink became a pot over a hot flame and me a chef making "dish soup." Dad and I took turns hauling the garbage down to the alley each week but did no other cleaning. Our rooms were both blanketed in books and paper, the surfaces draped with clothes. We'd only straighten up if Dad hosted a dinner party, and even then, the people he entertained always appreciated a certain degree of dirt and clutter.

Then one evening, while brushing my teeth, I noticed the grime on our bathroom sink and out of curiosity took a piece of toilet paper, wet it under the faucet, and wiped the grime away. What a feeling! It was fun to make something dirty clean, like erasing pencil markings from a sheet of paper. So periodically I'd "clean" the bathroom, ripping off some toilet paper and dabbing it under the faucet, always feeling a little proud as Dad never asked me to attend to the sink but always noticed my efforts.

With so many evenings and weekends spent at friends' homes, I have to think I annoyed some parents, who'd maybe not planned to feed an extra mouth. But I was extremely sensitive to this possibility. If I detected the least hesitation when a friend asked if I could stay, if I heard any behind-door whispering or glimpsed the slightest eye roll, I'd quickly absent myself and make my way home. I always had Haight Street.

When we moved to 545 Ashbury, the Haight was still recovering from its threadbare past. Bars and liquor stores dominated the strip and several storefronts were boarded up. But as the 1980s progressed, the neighborhood went upscale. Stores like Coffee Tea & Spice, Bakers of Paris, Auntie Pasta, and Yayne's family store catered to a growing gourmet-eating, health-conscious middle class. At the same time, many of the new shops opening up were gay-owned, and these among others had suggestive names. In addition to the Kiss My Sweet café, there was a craft shop called The Soft Touch, a vintage furniture store called Sugartit, and a large toy store with a gurgling fountain called Play With It. I loved the Haight as a kid.

On weekends, Kathy and I grabbed sandwiches at Viking Sub then roller-skated into Golden Gate Park, our long straight hair flying as we descended the hill into the tunnel. At the Big Playground, skates off, we rode the half-moon swings and then sped down the long cement slides on ripped pieces of cardboard. Eventually we skated over to the Legion of Honor near where the roller boogie dancers set up every weekend. I loved their bright-colored short shorts and their undulating grace, the way they maneuvered around overturned cups and did fancy tricks off ramps while Donna Summer sang from a battery-powered boom box.

After school I often went to Wauzi Records, catty-corner from my apartment. The high ceilings were hung with spinning cardboard displays, the far walls were plastered with posters, and music thumped through the speakers. I spent hours there browsing rows and rows of vinyl, moving from pop to rock to heavy metal to R & B. I always paused at the wildly suggestive covers of the Vanity 6 records, which featured three women in white, black, and red teddies, all heavily made up, posing and pouting under the scrawled title "Nasty Girl." In the heavy metal section I studied records by Judas Priest, the Scorpions, and Black Sabbath, which featured seething demons strapped into straitjackets, vengeful skeletons with mullets wielding axes or crawling out of graves, all stills from a nightmare. Before YouTube, before everyone had their MTV, this is how we surfed culture, how we weighed style choices. Where do I fit in? I used to wonder. Which tribe is my tribe?

Walking down the Haight in the 1980s, the air would be thick with the smells of pot, piss, and patchouli. In your ears, a constant whisper: "Doses, doses." Or "Buds, sweet buds." Candy was my drug of choice then, and with the five dollars Dad left me for dinner I could fill up on a fried chicken leg from Fat Fong's and still have plenty of change left over for penny candy at Coffee Tea & Spice.

The bell hanging from the door would ring as I entered, its chime followed by the powerful and slightly bitter smell of fresh-ground coffee. But my attention focused on the polished wooden counters lined with large glass jars full of candy: chocolate-covered raisins, black and red raspberries with tiny sugar "seeds" that crunched between your teeth. Next to these were the German gummy bears I coveted, which cost 25 cents a pound. I watched eagerly as the clerk's small metal shovel scooped and dropped the bears with a delicate thud into a small white bag on a scale. On good days, I'd get eighteen bears; on not-so-good days, sixteen.

As at all the stores I frequented in the Haight, I got to know the clerks, who were captive behind their registers. At Coffee Tea & Spice I met Sean, a Kentucky native with dazzling blue eyes, a Victorian wax-tipped moustache, and an exotic Southern lilt. He flashed me the brightest smile and was always generous with the scale, often giving me nineteen or twenty bears for my quarter. So when I received my sixth-grade school pictures, I carefully cut out a two-by-four-inch print, walked over to Coffee Tea & Spice, and handed it to Sean across the counter. When I next came in, he invited me behind the register to show me where he'd taped the picture and scribbled horns on either side of my head. The photo would remain on the register for years.

After Coffee Tea & Spice, I went to Etc. Etc., a novelty store whose greatest draw was the rolls of stickers my friends and I collected in three-ring binders: unicorn stickers, scratch-and-sniff stickers, and round stickers that revealed a rainbow sheen when you tipped them in the light. I also fingered Garfield page-a-day calendars, glossy Betty Boop and Popeye plates, fruit-flavored lip smackers sold in narrow slide-top metal tins, and stuffed animals of every type and size. I especially coveted a black-and-white Felix the Cat clock, which hung high on the wall above the register. It had jeweled eyes and a tail, which moved left-right, left-right, with each tick.

Kent Story, the owner of Etc. Etc., was exceedingly nice and let me interview him for a sixth-grade school assignment. He and I sat on the store's back stairs, with Dad's playback tape recorder heavy on my lap and a set of questions I'd scribbled on a sheet of paper in my hand. "What's the most expensive thing in the store? What's the cheapest?"

A few years later, Kent would contract AIDS, and like so many in that first wave quickly became sick. Etc. Etc., like the other stores he owned on the street, would change hands and eventually be replaced by brightly lit chains, just as Gaston Ice Cream on the corner of Haight and Ashbury would become Ben & Jerry's and Wauzi Records across the street would become the Gap, and next to the Gap, Seeds of Life would become Z Gallerie. And on, and on.

At the beginning of the eighties I believed in unicorns and rainbows, the transformative power of sparkly shoelaces and cherry lip smackers. My friends and I sang along with Styx and Olivia Newton-John, believing these were "the best of times." That we were all, indeed, "magic." That, like Newton-John in the movie *Xanadu*, we might be muses in the guise of mortal roller skaters. I believed that this decade might carry us away on the back of a winged horse. But by decade's end, the fabulous creatures had mostly perished. I didn't believe in unicorns anymore. We were not magic. We were not able to transcend our fleshy selves but were, in fact, slaves to these bodies and their tragic fragility.

*   *   *

AS MUCH AS I enjoyed exploring the Haight, I still longed for time with Dad. In the summer of 1980, while I was staying with my grandparents in Kewanee, Illinois, I wrote him a story telling him so:

> Once a father did a poem about his daughter Alysia. When he read it the audience was amazed. It was the best poem they ever heard. It made the rest of the poetry sound like chicken feed. It was so good he read it on radio and television! He did more excellent poems about Heidi as well as Alysia. One time, the president asked him to read them during an election because it was so boring.
>
> What happened to Alysia, you ask? Well, she was at home with Heidi, miserable and lonely because her dad was working. She was the reason for the "sudden success" but she didn't get any credit. So she decided to write a letter telling him what had happened with such success. When he read the letter he decided that no success would stand in the way of his daughter and Heidi.

After my return from Kewanee, Dad decided we should share a special dinner together one night each week. Sometimes he'd fix one of my favorite meals: spaghetti with butter, or baked chicken, which we ate at the round wooden table instead of on our laps in front of the TV. Other weeks he took us out to one of the neighborhood's many restaurants.

At All You Knead, I was just tall enough to look over the counter and watch the pizza chef make our ham-and-pepper pie, which we ate in a wooden booth. At the Grand Victorian near Clayton Street, the blond, moustached waiter led us to our favorite table in the window facing Haight Street. The restaurant's easy elegance, the white tablecloth and vase with a single red rose, always inspired me to sit with a straight back and long neck.

My favorite restaurant was Friends, an Upstairs Café. You reached the restaurant by climbing the narrow staircase of a three-story Victorian. Inside, the apartment was lined with tables for two, the walls adorned with framed black-and-white pictures of stars from Hollywood's golden era: Joan Crawford, Elizabeth Taylor, Bette Davis, Veronica Lake, Marlene Dietrich. Under the glamorous gaze of these women, I ordered linguine with clam sauce. The round plate of pasta was always too big for me, but I liked working at it until it resembled a gleaming crescent moon.

On each of these outings, Dad and I sat across from each other, he sipping a glass of wine, me 7-Up over ice. I told him about school and my new neighborhood friends and he told me about his memories of school, or asked me questions, or just smiled appreciatively. After dinner we walked down Haight Street toward home, hand in hand, taking in the shop windows: the punk mannequin displays at Daljeet's, the delicate stained glass at Acacia Glass. Along the way, both of us watched as the many street characters made their mischief into the wee hours.

PART IV
The Quake

Maybe it's normal for teenagers to be rude & sullen & rebellious but I don't particularly like to be around it. In fact I hardly have the energy to govern or properly love myself, let alone take on added tension.

—STEVE ABBOTT, *letter dated July 30, 1985*

11.

D
ESPITE THE FREEDOM I now enjoyed living at
the corner of Haight and Ashbury, I suffered a peculiar feeling. It came over me many afternoons when I
got home from school, rereading the scribbled note Dad left me
on our dining room table. It came over me as I peeled back the
foil on another Swanson's fried chicken dinner while listening
to the opening song of a TV sitcom I'd long since memorized. It
took shape in my growing awareness that on these nights Dad was
somewhere else, somewhere that had nothing to do with me, with
someone who had nothing to do with me.

Dad tried to shield me from this feeling. He still took me to his
places when he could, adult worlds of writers and words and ideas
that were usually bigger than me and which I rarely understood.
Sitting to one side as my dad interviewed Robert Duncan in his
Berkeley home or sitting beside Dad at his *Poetry Flash* meetings,
I could never follow what was being said and strained to find anything that might engage my imagination.

But inside these worlds of Dad's I was, more often than not, the
only child among adults and the only girl among men. Just as in
the halls of French American, I felt like I was the only kid in the
world with a gay parent and no mother.

There's no one like me. There's no one who knows what this is like,
I used to think.

In fact, there were many children who had gay moms or dads—

sometimes both—in the seventies and eighties. More often than not, these gay parents had had kids with straight partners before coming to terms with their sexuality. They either came out, divorcing their spouse to pursue same-sex affairs, or else remained closeted and married, privately despairing or seeking furtive encounters. In some ways I was lucky. Though often romantically disappointed, Dad at least was free to be himself and was spared the confusion and self-loathing that afflicted so many closeted parents.

I didn't meet any children of gay parents until I was an adult. And among these "queerspawn," as some have chosen to call themselves, I've felt a powerful bond, especially around that peculiar feeling, something like loneliness but more akin to isolation. In those first decades after Stonewall, our families had no way to connect, to make sense of ourselves and where we belonged. We had no Provincetown family week, no openly gay celebrities like Ellen or Dan Savage, no *Modern Family.* We saw no versions of our parents in books or on screens. And so we considered ourselves outside the social fabric, cut off from "the normal." As kids, we often existed in a state of uneasiness, a little too gay for the straight world and a little too straight for the gay world.

To grow up the child of a gay parent in the seventies and eighties was to live with secrets. For me, there was the secret of Dad's boyfriends, whom I kept hidden from friends, teachers, and family, who maybe knew or suspected Dad was gay but didn't want to know details. There were the pastels of naked strangers I found in the backs of Dad's hardcover sketchbooks where I doodled my own landscapes. Who were these men? I wondered. What happened with them? And there was Dad's poetry and prose, which so often depicted the struggles of openly gay men and what those men did together.

My father never asked me to keep quiet about his sexual orientation. He himself was as proud to march in parades as he was to write and publicly read his gay-themed poems. But I couldn't yet share that pride. Waiting for the bus with a cluster of my fourth-grade classmates one afternoon, I pointed to a sun-faded "No On Prop 6" campaign poster stuck in the window of a nearby Victorian. Proposition 6 was an initiative sponsored by Senator John Briggs that would have banned gays, lesbians, and anyone who supported gay rights from working in California's public schools.

"My dad has that poster," I offered, not knowing what it was about.

"Ewww!! You know what that means, don't you?" exclaimed one of my classmates. "That's when boys like boys and girls like girls."

Determined to escape unwanted attention, I said nothing, trying to distance myself from the "gross" association. And in the years that followed, I worked hard to hide the details of our queer domestic life.

When, in the spring of 1983, Dad grew a wispy rattail on the back of his head and bleached it blond, I chased him around the house with scissors trying to cut it off. At first he thought it was funny: the precocious preteen girl shocked by the rebellious antics of her father! But I was truly angry. He was ruining my efforts to fit in. I persisted in chasing him with the scissors until he sharply told me to put the scissors down. *Now.*

If school friends planned to stop by the apartment after class, I'd spend twenty minutes rearranging Dad's clutter in an effort to hide evidence of his transgressive lifestyle—the issues of *Gay Sunshine* and *Fag Rag*, the peacock-feathered roach clips, the plastic baggies full of pot. It was easier to just not have friends over.

But my unusual position, as it turned out, would become both my greatest complaint and my greatest comfort. As I grew into a teenager, I came to see our difference as something powerful, like a secret weapon. Dad and I weren't just odd, we were *set apart.* We may not have enjoyed an expansive lawn in Marin County, as so many of my classmates did, or even a working car. But we were artists.

As ridiculous and pretentious as this might sound, I sincerely believed and needed to believe that our position in bohemia was born of our separation and that the pain of our separation could be redeemed by our brand of bohemia.

Camped out on the sagging fold-out futon in the living room that doubled as Dad's bed, I'd page through his many books and comics, skipping over the weird and dirty bits, focusing instead on the potential for transformation. In a cartoon panel he made when I was five, I was no longer a timid and bullied first-grader but a fierce and proud monster-killer! Studying the cover of Dad's poetry book *Stretching the Agape Bra,* I didn't see a lonely nine-year-old in Nikes but a Victorian ghost-child dressed in white sleeves with a mysteriously somber expression.

In Dad's second issue of *SOUP,* published in 1981, he transformed me from an uncoordinated, so-so French student into Sylvan Wood, the sassy lead singer of an up-and-coming rock band he invented called Toxic Schlock! He posed my friends Kathy as the bassist Sarah Lee Wood and Juliana Finch as the guitarist Twinkie. Yayne was supposed to be our drummer Picture Tube, but because she cancelled on the day of the photo shoot Dad played the part with a blanket over his head.

Across from the attitude-dripping band photo (the photographer told us to look bored), Dad wrote up a fake interview and inserted lyrics to our new hit single, "Burning to Speak." He even had me copy out the lyrics in my own loopy ten-year-old script.

> *Burning to speak, burning to speak*
> *Been waiting on the phone for nearly a week*
> *Burning to speak, burning to speak*
> *I guess you think I'm just some kind of have-to.*

Sometimes I'd sing "Burning to Speak" to myself, making up my own tune, jerking my body from side to side in my bedroom mirror. Dad's lyrics channeled my own yearnings, my desire to have him to myself at least some of the time. Though I was still in love with Dad and assumed he reciprocated my love, I worried that I was for him, "some kind of have-to." So I jumped at any chance to play the role of poet's muse, the occasional Alice to Dad's Lewis Carroll. If I had to contend with some funky mushrooms and a crazy queen or two along the way, it was worth it.

ONE EVENING in the fall of 1983, my father showed me a letter he'd received inviting him to participate in the One World International Poetry Festival in Amsterdam. The annual festival encompassed four days of talks and readings culminating in a lavish cocktail party held at the house of the Lebanese ambassador to the Hague. Dad was invited to read, along with such leading poets and writers of the day as Marguerite Duras, Richard Brautigan, Robert Creeley, and William Burroughs. The invitation legitimized him as a serious writer and editor. It was an opportunity he couldn't miss.

The Dutch club that hosted the event offered to pay for Dad's airfare and hotel. He could have easily sent me to stay with my grandparents or with local friends but he was determined that I should accompany him. He'd long imagined our traveling to Europe. In 1978 he wrote: "I am thinking of Paris . . . & fantasize drawing Notre Dame again with Alysia @ my side, drawing pad also before her. Urchin child of the artist." Dad took on extra writing assignments and temp work, and even borrowed money from his reluctant parents, in order to cover my airfare.

"You know, I didn't get to Europe until after college," Dad told me over breakfast our first morning in our first stop, Paris. "It was

1968 and the streets were full of revolutionaries, not as commercial as it is now. There were no McDonald's." He waved his hands across the street as I took a sleepy bite of my buttery *tartine*.

We were sitting in a dingy café in the 19th arrondissement, weary and jet-lagged. Since it was October, we sat inside the large café window facing the street, our luggage pressed against our knees, scanning the passersby for Michael Koch, the pony-tailed poet friend of Dad's who was to host us in his nearby apartment. Michael had moved to Paris with his painter wife and their three-year-old daughter, Piaf. He supported his family with translation work.

"Piaf's a poet like her father," Dad said by way of introduction when Koch arrived. "The other day, when Michael was helping her on with her socks, she spotted a hole and said, 'A hole in my sock, a balcony for my toes!'" I listened sullenly to Dad's story. I wondered, did he secretly wish that I was more poetic and writerly? Should all poets have poet daughters?

The next day, Michael and his family joined us for breakfast and a tour of the Pompidou Center. We capped the afternoon with a visit to Berthillon, an outdoor ice-cream shop on the Île Saint-Louis that attracted crowds even on chilly fall afternoons. Licking my dainty cone of berry sorbet, I started banging my body against Dad's side as he chatted with Michael about living as an American poet in Paris. After twirling away from him into the crowd of people, I banged back into him again. But in one of my twirls I felt something strange, a hand touching the back of my jeans between my legs. My whole body stiffened and I whipped my head around and caught the stare of a short man with greasy black hair. His eyes boldly looked at me and then darted to a tall blond woman beside him, who I assumed was his girlfriend, then back to me. I quickly returned to my father's side but felt too embarrassed to tell him what had happened.

"I want to go back to Michael's," I said, pulling his arm toward the nearest Métro.

"Wait a second. Let me finish my ice cream."

"I want to go back!"

Later that night, sleeping next to Dad on Michael's living room floor, I dreamed that I was kicking the man with the black hair. I kicked him and kicked him as he lay rolling in the gutter. Again and again I kicked him in the gut.

So when, the next day, our last in Paris, my father and I were walking across the *quai* toward the Eiffel Tower and he asked me, "How'd you like to live in Paris?" I answered, "I don't want to."

"You've been having a good time, haven't you?"

"No."

"But you already speak French! We could probably transfer you to a school here."

I shuddered, then suddenly, and violently, spat on the street.

"I hate Paris. I *hate* it here."

I refused to tell Dad why I was so against the idea, and he didn't push it. I never imagined that I'd return to live in Paris, not once but twice. And I never imagined that ten years later, on an overcast February morning, I would seek out a spot on the bank of the Seine on the Île Saint-Louis, walking distance from the Berthillon ice-cream shop, and that there I would scatter my father's ashes from a gilded cardboard box, finally granting him his wish to live in France.

THE NEXT MORNING, we took the train from Paris's Gare du Nord to Amsterdam. The International Poetry Festival was being hosted by the Melkweg, or Milky Way, a former dairy factory which had become a gallery and performance space catering to aging Dutch hippies and a growing Euro-punk scene.

We arrived on the second day of the conference but quickly found our way around. While readings took place on the main stages, poets speaking French, Danish, German, Hungarian, and Dutch took over the club's dusty back rooms and upstairs. I quietly watched them sipping weak coffee, nibbling on stale pastries, and gossiping amongst themselves.

During our first couple of days in Amsterdam I talked to no one but Dad, who like me was feeling shy. Soon, though, I felt free to wander around the Melkweg alone. That's when I started hanging around with an odd American writer named Richard Brautigan, famous for his 1967 novel *Trout Fishing in America*. Over six feet tall and barrel-chested in a red "Montana" t-shirt, Brautigan was a formidable presence. But with his round wire-framed glasses, poofy hunter's cap, and red, bushy handlebar moustache, he looked almost cartoonish, like a sad-eyed Yosemite Sam.

Brautigan took a special interest in me. He was estranged from his own daughter who, though ten years my senior, had been about my age when he'd last seen her. After a couple of afternoons chatting amiably in a back room of the Melkweg, he decided to offer me advice that he said he wished he could share with his daughter. "Be careful," he warned. "If you see a small blister on the tip of a man's penis, stay away." At twelve, I hadn't yet kissed a boy, so his words hung in the air around us, compelling but never belonging to me. "That's herpes," Brautigan added. "It's not pretty." I sat through his warning and other rambling stories, flattered by his interest and, though not always understanding, curious to hear the next weird thing he might say.

The next afternoon I overheard a conversation between Dad, Brautigan, and Jan Kerouac, daughter of Jack, who was also reading at the festival. They were comparing anecdotes about the peculiar poetry that comes so naturally to children. Kerouac described a moment when, as a girl, she mistook the moon for the sun and woke up her mother. "It's daytime, Momma," she explained as she started to unravel her mother's long braids. My dad recalled the time I asked, "Why is the moon following us?" a quote that he worked into one of his poems. Brautigan described a day at the beach with his young daughter. She was playing with a brand-new pail when a big wave came in and carried it out to sea. Distraught, Brautigan ran into the water, frantically splashing around trying to find it. His daughter, watching from the shore, exclaimed coolly, "Forget it Daddy. It's gone," as though she were the adult and he the anxious child who needed soothing.

In the years since this trip, I've held on to the memory of this conversation like a stone in my pocket, rubbing it between my thumb and forefinger until it's become flat and smooth. I always longed to be part of my father's dialogue, the necessary append-age to his writer's life. This moment, among others, was the fulfill-ment of my bohemian fantasy.

That evening, I sat and watched my dad read in one of the Melkweg's dark, smoky galleries. His final selection was "Elegy," the poem that closed his last book of poetry, *Stretching the Agape Bra* (1980). In it he writes about all the deaths he's known in life, including the death of my mother:

> *When I learned my wife's skull was crushed by a truck,*
> *   my head*
> *swam like an hourglass into a TV set. All the channels*
> *   went crazy.*

My dad had never spoken with me in detail about my mom's car accident, and it felt uncomfortable to hear him sharing something so personal with an audience of foreign-tongued strangers. It was also strange to see the power of my father's words on this other-wise boisterous crowd. His voice unfurled like a heavy bolt of fabric across the room, hushing conversations and quieting clinking glasses. As he continued, his words filled the room and cleared the smoke until all attention focused on the pale and slender man onstage, until I could hear only his words, words he seemed to speak only to me:

> We distance ourselves for protection,
> Wear scarves when it's cold.
> What seems most outlandish in our autobiography
> Is what really happened.

The last night of the festival, the Lebanese ambassador had all the poets in the festival bussed to his tightly guarded mansion for a cocktail party. The ambassador wrote poetry himself, it seemed, and he wanted to play them a rare recording of Apollinaire on his old gramophone. But none of the assembled writers paid much attention, preferring to smoke and drink on his many plush sofas.

As there were no kids to play with, I brought along my camera to occupy myself. I took a photo of my dad in conversation with several poets, his hands hard at work explaining a complicated thought. I took photos of Brautigan in his vest and blue jeans, sitting uncomfortably on the edge of a couch. He kept getting up to fetch a fresh martini at the open bar, each time asking that his martini be "a little more dry" until, finally, the exasperated bartender simply handed him a bottle of gin. Brautigan laughed when he returned to the poets on the couch, showing off the bottle like a trophy. He again brandished the gin on the bus, knocking back swigs for the duration of our trip back to the town center. All the grown-ups were by then pretty drunk, sitting on each other's laps, French kissing, and dancing in the aisles despite the driver's repeated admonishments. I continued taking pictures.

"Hey Alysia!" Brautigan called. "Take a picture of me. I need to sober up." So I snapped my camera inches from his face, setting off a bright flash of light. The photo would later reveal Brautigan's face bathed in white, with only the contours of his round glasses and poofy cap visible. He blinked into the distance. "Thanks, darling."

The highlight of the trip for my dad took place our last morning in Amsterdam, when we shared a private breakfast with William Burroughs at the hotel. I had no idea why Dad was so nervous about meeting this creaky old man in a three-piece suit and hat. Even my dad was a little disappointed, later writing about the meeting, "our talk at breakfast was rather banal (about cats, living in Lawrence, Kansas versus more urban areas, etc.)." But the notorious author of *Naked Lunch* was very interested in hearing about the two years my father had spent studying in a Missouri seminary before grad school, an experience he was in the process of fictionalizing for his novel *Holy Terror*, for which Burroughs would give him a blurb. Dad presented Burroughs with a copy of the third issue of *SOUP*, which he liked.

My favorite moment of the week took place the last night of the festival, when the German punk singer Nina Hagen performed to a packed house at the Melkweg. That week, thousands of Europeans had converged in the capital of West Germany to protest the further deployment of American missiles across western Europe. All this collected anger and energy coalesced on the floor of the Melkweg. From a staff balcony, I watched the scene below: crowds of punks with neon-striped mohawks, wearing metal spikes and ripped clothing and makeup the color of bruises, all pulsing to the rhythm of Nina's spastic singing. The crowd pushed forward and back, dancing. But this dancing looked like fighting, with writhing bodies slamming together and apart and together again. The visiting poets showed only passing interest in the punks below, but I was mesmerized. The energy! The violence! And I could see it all from my own private balcony.

A year after Dad and I returned to San Francisco, I found a picture of Richard Brautigan in our morning paper. He'd killed himself with a .44 Magnum in his home in Bolinas, California. No one knew the exact date of his death. His decomposed body was found on the floor in front of a large window overlooking the Pacific Ocean. Next to him a suicide note read simply, "Messy, isn't it?"

12.

O N A DAMP EVENING in November 1983, a couple
of weeks after our return from Europe, I picked up
the television from the stacked milk crates in Dad's
room and carried it into our bathroom. I carefully set the TV
down on the floor in the corner, plugged it in, and turned the dial
to channel 7.

As I undressed and eased myself into the rising bathwater, I
watched the opening titles of a made-for-TV movie called *The Day
After*. It didn't seem strange to me to watch television in the tub.
Dad was out for the night and I needed a bath, but I didn't want
to miss this "TV event," which had been advertised for weeks.
While running a soapy washcloth over my arms and legs, I followed the life of two Kansas families leading up to, and following,
a Soviet-led nuclear strike on the US. After the bomb hit, channel 7 stopped breaking for commercials, and I was quickly drawn
into the horror of the drama. A young boy stares at the blast at
the moment of impact and is blinded. Homes become scorched
rubble. Hundreds of bystanders become vaporized silhouettes. I
watched as the blistered survivors slowly died of terminal radia-
tion sickness.

I was unable to get out of the bathtub until the movie ended,
long after the water went cold, and I sat shivering in my nakedness. I climbed into my loft bed with pruny fingers, feeling with-
ered and deeply shaken. "What is this world?" I asked myself. I lay
in bed until I heard my father come home.

I had a hard time falling asleep that night. Lying in bed, I listened to the skinheads, new to our neighborhood, who gathered at the corner of Haight and Ashbury. They hurled obscenities in shades of anger and grief, and empty tin cans that echoed in the streets.

As I walked to the grocery store that week with Dad, and later alone, I watched them. Wearing lace-up Doc Martens, they roamed in gangs. I was fascinated by their corner dramas and curious uniforms, especially the skinhead girls who'd shaved their heads but left locks of hair softly curling around their ears and foreheads. The skinheads never bothered me, nor did they ask me for change. Mostly I was ignored, but once or twice a skinhead girl smiled in my direction and said, "Hey." I shyly looked away each time but wondered if she or her friends ever saw me as one of them.

As 1983 moved into 1984, I felt increasingly isolated from the world around me. The *CBS Evening News*, which Dad and I watched most nights over dinner, was filled with diplomatic maneuvering that barely concealed the incomprehensible and too-plain fact that any day the leaders of the world's two superpowers could kill hundreds of thousands of people with the flick of a switch. President Reagan had deployed troops in Grenada, El Salvador, Panama, Nicaragua, and Beirut, where in October, the same night as the Lebanese ambassador's cocktail party, 229 Marines were killed by a roadside bomb. Down our street, posters in the window of the local pharmacy warned of a "gay cancer." In addition to the Cold War there was *The Big Chill*. Baby boomers seemed caught in a navel-gazing spiral of shame, trying to reconcile their sixties ideals with their eighties pocketbooks.

That spring, I was running through the dials on my stereo when I discovered a new radio station: KQAK, the Quake. The station played music that sounded like nothing I'd heard before, certainly not like the Def Leppard and Michael Jackson then dominating the FM dial. The Quake played music that celebrated weirdos and loners, music that addressed the darkness of our atomic age with a peppy, synthesized beat. This music spoke of disillusion and fear, what the band Tears for Fears called a mad world. I couldn't get enough.

Every day after school I'd retreat to my room and switch on the Quake, scribbling down the name of each band the DJ played. The Quake broke local bands (Romeo Void and the Call), but mostly played British bands before their albums were released stateside: Scritti Politti, Depeche Mode, the Cure, Peter Shilling, the Smiths, New Order, Tears for Fears, and Duran Duran. I especially loved these British bands, with their exotic provenance and sexually ambiguous lead singers. The harder I worked to learn about them, the more attached I felt to their music.

At Wauzi and Rough Trade Records, I stared longingly at import albums and twelve-inch singles I couldn't afford to buy on my allowance. So I set up Dad's tape recorder, the one he used for his interviews, and, placing it at the foot of one of our tall stereo speakers, captured hour after hour of the Quake, stopping for each commercial and then hitting "record" once the commercial ended. Most of these tapes were muddy, riddled with clicks and distortions. But for me it was audio gold. I loved the tapes, because I could play them whenever I wanted, on my stereo and, after my thirteenth birthday, on a cheap Walkman.

By myself in my room, headphones on, volume up, I spent hours familiarizing myself with Thatcher's depressed England, made romantic by the Smiths' angst. Bands like Depeche Mode and Tears for Fears conjured an industrial landscape with synthesizers and electric drums, the sounds of pipes being knocked together. This world sounded like the future, and by listening I felt like I was a part of this future. More importantly, this was a world I was choosing instead of one I was simply inheriting from my father.

At the newsstand, I hunted down imports like the *NME, Melody Maker,* and *Smash Hits!,* skimming the pages for any news of my beloveds, delighting in the discovery of their faces, their hair, their habits. I couldn't afford to buy the magazines so I hungrily absorbed every detail I could, furiously flipping pages until the shopkeeper kicked me out.

New Wave, as it was called, was a world where cool boys wore eyeliner and cool girls wore men's clothes. At thirteen, I was still skinny, flat, and late to bleed. Here was an androgynous aesthetic I could embrace with stylish ease.

I cut my hair boy short with a peekaboo curtain hanging over one eye, and I started to borrow liberally from Dad's closet. I donned his old button-down shirts and a pair of his Levi's, the man's waist fastened with a large paper clip, the knees ripped, the thighs decorated with my in-class doodles. I wore a single silver bat earring dangling on a chain from my left ear, a pair of cuffed leather Beatle boots, and a lapel pin I picked up on Haight Street: "Punk Preppy." The centerpiece of my uniform was Dad's 1940s gray fedora, which I kept firmly planted on my head, removing it only to shower or sleep.

BY MY THIRTEENTH YEAR I had outgrown most of my pre-teen friends. I saw less of Yayne, who'd left French American, transferring into a public school. Kathy Moe was getting into a heavy metal scene, favoring thick foundation and spraying her feathered hair into stiff armor. She started hanging out with the WPODs (White Punks on Dope), a Derby-wearing gang that ruled the Sunset district and had a taste for LSD that I didn't share. My other girlfriends, who'd been so good to me at eleven and twelve, hosting me for sleepovers and pancakes, now just seemed too good, with their ribbon-threaded barrettes and Miss Piggy wall calendars.

I gravitated toward a new set of girls at French American who, like me, loved David Bowie, the Cure, and Duran Duran. Each girl was a child of divorce and each possessed an edgy humor and sense of style. Niki routinely gave one of us the DF (Dumb Fuck) award each day for stupid behavior. Andrea wore a permanent scowl, her preppy V-neck sweaters turned backward, her eyes rimmed in black.

At lunch, the five of us would meet in the back stairs of the parking lot behind French American, and after school, we'd ride the Haight Street bus to my place. Where I'd once been ashamed of bringing friends to my apartment, I now knew it was something cool I could share. If the weather was warm enough, we'd situate ourselves on the thick ledge of balcony overlooking Ashbury Street and Anne-Marie and Andrea would smoke Marlboro Lights pilfered from their moms' purses or single Export-A's bought at Pipe Dreams around the corner. Long-legged Anne-Marie, the oldest and most experienced among us, would twist the rings on her fingers and sweetly giggle as she told us about the latest with her boyfriend, while Camille, her blond bob wrapped in a long white scarf, coolly looked on.

Sometimes Dad would be home, scratching away in his spiral notebook, but most often he was out. Either way, I was very protective of his space, not allowing anyone into his room, which I closed off behind a trifold screen. I didn't do this so much out of respect for his privacy as for my own. I still thought I could cordon off all that I couldn't control. I was convinced that his orientation, our "weirdness," would be revealed in his mess— certainly in his bookshelves, where anthologies with titles like *Man Muse* and *Men on Men* could easily be spotted. Even in my circle of enlightened outsiders, I didn't feel comfortable "coming out." Anne-Marie and Niki would later tell me they knew Dad was gay and sometimes talked about it privately. They recognized the Castro papers that littered our table and noted how, when Dad was home with friends, there were only men, never women.

On weekends, the five of us went to eighteen-and-over clubs that advertised themselves in glossy neon four-by-five cards with embossed lettering that we found stacked on the counters in the Haight's growing array of punk boutiques. A couple of us had fake IDs and the rest were let in by lax doormen. At the IBeam on Haight Street, the Noh Club in Japantown, and the Palladium in North Beach, I danced away my anxiety about my too-slow-changing body and the too-fast-changing world, my anxiety about Dad and all that I didn't understand.

One Friday I told Dad that I was going to spend the night at Andrea's house. Andrea told her mom that she was staying at my house, and we both met at the house Camille shared with her sister and divorced mother in Stanyan Heights. At Camille's, the three of us applied lipstick and electric-blue mascara in the bathroom mirror and then split a cab into North Beach. Inside the Palladium, everyone danced looking at the floor. I coiled my hands into fists and pedaled my arms close to my body, as though my shoulders, arms, hips, and knees were a series of small gears shifting and turning toward and then away from each other, in rhythm to the music.

The music I listened to on the Quake now echoed through the Palladium, filling my ears, the bass beat thumping into my molars. From the ceiling, lights cascaded across the floor, flashing blue–red, blue–red, then switched into black light, making everyone's teeth and eyes glow neon, revealing white bras and undershirts. This made us smile. We were all electric now, plugged into the same beat, all dancing alone, but still powerfully together. One of my favorite songs of the night, Billy Idol's "Dancing with Myself," even celebrated this communal isolation.

Just before 1 a.m., the Palladium finished the night, as they did each week, with the Smiths' "How Soon Is Now." The crowd lifted and rolled over the wave of Johnny Marr's perverse reverberating guitar line, which seemed to cut us into two, three, four, chopping us into bits before Morrissey's cool voice and smart lyrics put us back together again.

When the music ended, I found Camille and Andrea at the door, and together we pushed through the crowd and stumbled onto Broadway and into the fresh December air. The streets of North Beach were thick with people and it seemed like everyone knew everyone. The same black eyeliner, the same black clothes, the same pale skin and dyed hair. Without saying anything or doing anything, I felt an electrifying sense of belonging. Keeping close, we hurried through the smellier streets, past the flashing "Live Nude Girls" sign at the Lusty Lady. We passed the Big Al sign, his machine gun at the ready. We passed the tall cartoon Carol Doda sign that advertised the Condor Club, her flashing neon nipples looking like hard cherry candies. We peered into doorways where strippers sucked on cigarettes and men tried to lure us inside with rapid-fire lines and overactive eyebrows.

We averted our eyes as we scurried past, staring at our pointed shoes, counting the blocks to the massive house in Pacific Heights where Andrea's dad lived with his new family. Though Andrea lived with her mom, she figured she could avoid her mom's curfew by crashing at her dad's undetected.

Cars honked at us on our walk home, but we ignored them. Someone yelled, "How much?" and I yelled back, "You couldn't afford me!" And then we all laughed and I flipped them off for good measure.

At Andrea's, we entered through the back door into her step-brother Deke's basement apartment, where we crashed on his couch and floor. When he found us the next morning, sprawled in our smeared makeup and clothes from the night before, he laughed at his little sister's teen antics. In my zip-up black jacket smelling of cigarettes, I waited for the bus home. Twenty minutes later I arrived at my apartment and was surprised to find Dad sitting upright on his folded futon, looking at me sternly.

"Where were you last night?"

"What do you mean? I was at Andrea's."

"I talked to Andrea's mom last night. You *did not* spend the night there. Where were you?"

"We slept at her dad's house."

"Andrea's mother didn't know that. *She* didn't know where you were. And neither did I. Do you know how hard that is for a parent? To not know where your kid is?"

"We were fine, Dad."

"I'm sure you were. But you have to call. I didn't know where you were!"

"Sometimes I don't know where *you* are."

Dad just stared at me. He knew I was right. What authority did he have to punish me? Freedom to come and go as we each saw fit soon became the unspoken rule of our house. If Dad started keeping me on a curfew, then he couldn't feel free to wander in and out at all hours of the night either.

"I just want to know you're okay," he said. "Did you have fun, at least?"

"Yeah. I did have fun."

DAD HAD COOL new friends too. Frustrated by the infighting and lack of professionalism he saw at Cloud House in the late 1970s, Dad started attending writing workshops at Small Press Traffic, a bookstore located in a Victorian townhouse in Noe Val-

ley. There, writer Bob Glück ran several workshops in a tiny parlor next to the kitchen with some money that came from an NEA
grant. Dad attended a few of these but became especially close
with the members of the gay writers group, including the lanky
intellectual Bruce Boone and the Tab-drinking Kevin Killian.
Killian would marry writer Dodie Bellamy; the feline pair evolved
into San Francisco's avant-garde "it" couple. Each week the gay
writers group would bring in a new piece of writing to discuss—
sometimes a work by lesbian poet Judy Grahn, a piece of feminist
theory, or an essay by Roland Barthes or Georges Bataille (whom
Dad introduced to the group). They then vigorously workshopped
one another, always trying to push their writing in new directions.
Meeting for years in this cramped Victorian parlor, the writers
became very close.

San Francisco's literary scene was now dominated by the Language poets. In *Biting the Error: Writers on Narrative*, Bob Glück
wrote, "It would be hard to overestimate the drama they brought
to a Bay Area scene that limped through the 70s . . . Language
Poetry's Puritan rigor, delight in technical vocabularies, and professionalism were new to a generation of Bay Area poets whose
influences included the Beats, Robert Duncan and Jack Spicer,
the New York School (Bolinas was its western outpost), surrealism and psychedelic surrealism. Suddenly, people took sides. . . ."

Dad was among those who took sides. Initially intrigued by the
group, he ultimately found their work too abstract and formal. In
a 1979 issue of *Poetry Flash* ("Language Poets: An Introduction")
he chided the poets to remember that "obscurity is not a virtue in
itself." In his monthly column, he questioned the group's powerful influence on the scene and how they hindered other voices:

I see the moral guardians are at it again: Should Kathy Acker
write this or should Bruce Boone talk that way summed up
questioning at 80 Langton poetry and politics forum. It's the

same old saw that separated [Robert] Duncan & [Denise] Levertov years ago. Theories are fine but one must go where one's poem or novel takes one (a passivist view?) and if you can't say what you want in your own writing, as Kathy pointed out, then where, pray tell, can you? Which isn't to suggest that questioning certain modes of discourse isn't beneficial (here columnist does a dance of Subtle Distinction, trying to avoid stepping on anyone's toes).

These others writers, including Acker but especially those Dad met at Small Press Traffic, approached their work with a deeply personal and often political consciousness that wasn't found among the Language poets. Kevin Killian wrote that the group wanted to "recuperate narrative from the trap of modernism by rearticulating it as a postmodern conceptual art." In my father's second issue of *SOUP*, published in 1981, he named their style "New Narrative."

The community Dad found in New Narrative was not only professional but personal. In an untitled essay on Georges Bataille, Dad wrote, "Real friendship is based on extremity where the boundary lines between people break down. It's like if you're in an elevator with a group of strangers and the elevator breaks down. Suddenly you look into each other's eyes and you're no longer strangers. You can only have real communication when you realize you're facing possible disaster."

The disaster, as Dad and others saw it, was the emerging AIDS crisis and the cultural attacks instigated by conservatives against gay men and women in the early 1980s. It was found in the cruel indifference of President Ronald Reagan, who wouldn't publicly address the epidemic until the end of his second term, after twenty thousand Americans had died, and the hostile rhetoric of conservatives close to Reagan like Jerry Falwell, founder of the Moral Majority, and Pat Buchanan, Reagan's future speechwriter.

In 1983, Buchanan wrote of AIDS, "The poor homosexuals—they have declared war upon nature, and now nature is extracting an awful retribution."

AIDS transformed the landscape for gay men in the 1980s. For writers like Bob, Bruce, Kevin, and my dad, this new landscape couldn't be addressed with Language Poetry, which, focused on pure language, was detached from everyday experience. Since Language Poetry worked to remove the "I," New Narrative formed as a way to reclaim personal space in writing, a way to address this communal crisis.

By 1983 and 1984, Dad regularly entertained versions of the New Narrative group for dinner or drinks in our apartment, often introducing them to visiting writers and artists, our spool table acting as a rotating salon. Over the years, he hosted film-makers (Curt McDowell and George Kuchar), literary lions (Bob Kaufman, Gregory Corso, and Robert Duncan), and various odd characters Dad was profiling at the time, such as the anthropologist Tobias Schneebaum, who was notorious for books in which he confessed he had sex with the Peruvian and Pacific Islander tribes he was studying.

As a teenager, I viewed these frequent visitors as nothing but eccentric intruders in our tiny one-bedroom apartment. When I complained about our chronic semi-poverty, which was especially hard for me attending private school, I openly questioned the legitimacy of Dad's work. "What kind of writer are you if *no* one's heard of you, and you make *no* money?" Furthermore, and more importantly, Dad's appetite for transgressive outsiders threatened my own fragile sense of identity. There was a thin line between cool and weird and I didn't want to be on the weird side anymore. So I was aggressively indifferent to Dad's crowd, all except for a twenty-something writer as handsome as the British rockers whose images wallpapered my room: Sam D'Allesandro.

Dad discovered D'Allesandro in 1984 when he reviewed his

poetry book *Slippery Sins* for *The Advocate*. Born Richard Anderson to a humble ranching family in Modesto, California, he changed his name both to add glamour to his persona and to protect his more conservative parents. Sam convinced me he was the son of Joe Dallesandro (whom I'd not yet heard of at age thirteen), and was later sued by the Warhol actor when Sam read at an LA venue around the corner from his home. Dad's friends weren't as impressed as Dad was by Sam's first book of poetry, but when Sam starting writing prose he developed a pure and poised style. Kevin Killian even considered him a "genius."

I knew nothing of Sam's writing but, like everyone, I was captivated by his beauty. He was tall and lean, with piercing blue eyes and pillowy lips. And he was radiant, as though lit from within; I couldn't help but stare.

I flirted with Sam shamelessly, never seeing his sexuality as an impediment to his affections. (It never was with my father.) And some of my dad's friends noticed my crush. Kevin jokingly called it a waste. But Sam returned my attention. He frequently joined Dad and me on walks into Golden Gate Park or out to the movies or to go shoe shopping. Since I didn't know Andy Warhol, he gave me his back issues of Warhol's *Interview* magazine. Sam even showed up at my birthday party, giving me a Hallmark card written in Spanish, crossing out the text and adding his own in an energetic hand.

Sam seemed especially sympathetic to my teenage boredom, my need for excitement and newness. Sam would take me to the Double Rainbow café on Haight Street, where the boys wore dyed hair and thick-soled creepers and the girls dressed in crinoline skirts, cowboy boots, and red lipstick. Sam also introduced me to Jono, a young painter friend of his who lived across from the Double Rainbow.

I'd sometimes pop over to Jono's after school. He'd buzz me

Photo by Jono Weiss

into his cavernous floor-through, filled with his large canvases, glossy color-block portraits of long-faced, lean-nosed men like himself. The Mutants or Talking Heads would be blasting as he painted. I was content to just watch him, to eavesdrop on his goings-on: receiving phone calls, making plans, and painting. In this way I imagined my own life as a grown-up, filled with friends and music and art.

That spring, I returned to the English Haight Street hairdresser who'd first cut my hair short. I asked her to sheer my bangs so that my hair resembled an overgrown crew cut. When she finished, I immediately went up to Jono's. I can't recall whether I asked him to take my photo or if he offered. I just remember being fourteen, hair dyed black as pitch, posing in front of Jono's big-nosed paintings. Pictures show me in a slate-gray pillbox hat and a vest with snap buttons, a black t-shirt, leggings, and red, red lipstick. (As with my photographer neighbor Robert, I relished the possibility of transformation in these poses.)

When Sam stopped by Jono's that evening, I asked him if he could buy a bottle of bourbon for my friends and me. We were planning a weekend outing to Golden Gate Park. He laughed, saying he had done the same as a kid, and agreed to meet me on Friday night outside Cala Foods on Haight Street. In the parking lot I waited with my friends, all of us dancing and jumping in place to ward off the damp cold, when Sam's sinewy figure emerged from the shadows. He smiled, said hello, and I handed him the ten dollars my friends and I had pooled together. He passed me the paper-sheathed bourbon and I felt flush with warmth, proud that this hip, good-looking guy was my friend.

Sometime later, totally by accident, I discovered Sam was going out with Sean, the smiling Southerner who'd sold me gummy bears at Coffee Tea & Spice only a couple of years earlier. Sam had seen Sean working behind the counter of the shop. Sam wrote his number on a matchbook cover, pushed it into Sean's hand, and said, "Use it." But Sean was intimidated. "He was so good-looking and so intense," Sean later told me. Not until he ran into Sam five years later in a downtown coffee shop did they finally start dating. When Sam became sick with AIDS, Sean nursed him. When Jono became sick several years later, Sean took him out to expensive lobster dinners. But though Sean was diagnosed as HIV-positive, he never got sick himself.

When I meet Sean again nearly twenty-five years later, his moustache is gone, along with much of the dazzle in his eyes. "I'm one of the few people I know from that period who was diagnosed with HIV and is still around," he tells me. "Nobody can relate to it. The whole topic is so . . . It's as if it's something in the past."

HANGING OUT with Sam and Jono, immersing myself in the Haight's New Wave scene, I built up confidence at school. Where before I preferred to lose myself in the lines of my art-period drawings, or hide behind my camera at the middle school dances, I now paraded the halls of French American wearing an anti-Reagan t-shirt Dad got for his fortieth birthday and a bright blue nylon Fiorucci jacket he'd picked up in Europe.

I tried out for Bac A Dos, the school's evening of bilingual one-act plays, which included Tennessee Williams's *This Property Is Condemned*, and nabbed the lead. I played Willie, a girl who lives alone in an abandoned home after "quituating" school. She spends her days walking the railroad track in her dead sister's evening dress, singing to herself, and clutching a grubby baby doll. It was the highlight of my stage career. Ginger, a redheaded senior, told me she cried watching my performance. My English teacher called me "Willie" for weeks after the play ended to see if I'd still answer, and I always did—gladly. The play earned me a public respect that I'd never before known, a sense that I was carving a version of myself that was my own, apart from Dad, and one that was worthwhile. In my yearbook, a senior boy who'd starred in the French-language one-act would write that, like the heroine in Williams's *Glass Menagerie*, I should be careful because "beautiful glass unicorns have a tendency to lose their horns."

Then, one morning in the corridors of French American, a popular transfer student named Sarah said she liked my Fiorucci jacket, but when I smiled back she added with a smirk, "You might want to wash it, though." Only then did I look down to notice

how the cuffs and seams were creased with dirt from my constant
wear. She laughed her rich-girl laugh—deep and chesty—as she
proceeded down the hall, and I got a sick feeling in my stomach,
wishing I could disappear completely.

Another afternoon, my dear friend Niki quietly pulled me aside
after class and asked if I used deodorant. When I gave her a puzzled look, she added, "When you become a teenager you can't just
take showers." When I again looked confused, she sighed, rolled
her eyes, and gave me the talk my father should have given me.
"Your body goes through *changes*. You have to wear deodorant."
She then pulled from her bag a smooth blue block, labeled, appro-
priately enough, Secret, and gently put it in my hands. "I bought
this for you. You need to use this . . . every day."

The following week, I was out with Niki and the girls at Uncle
Gaylord's, a tall-ceilinged ice-cream parlor around the corner
from French American where we'd sometimes nurse caffe lattes
after school. I noticed a couple getting up from a nearby table,
leaving behind half of an ice-cream sundae. Nonchalantly, I wandered over and picked up a spoon and started to finish their ice
cream.

"What are you doing?" Niki cried.

"Finishing their ice cream," I said, swallowing a spoonful of hot
fudge.

"You can't do that!"

"Why not? It's just going to be thrown out."

"Come over here. Come *over* here. You can't eat other people's
leftovers. That's disgusting."

Sheepishly, I put down my spoon. Though I didn't exactly see
what the big deal was, I suspected Niki was right, and I felt overcome with that familiar feeling of confused shame.

Why was it still so difficult to contain my weirdness, to hide
my dirt and mask my scent? These are painful memories to revisit,

even now. "I hope you weren't too embarrassed," Niki would later tell me. "Someone needed to tell you."

Munca, my grandmother in Kewanee, Illinois, wanted to be that someone. But I only saw her in the summers, and though she taught me how to discreetly dispose of "menstrual pads," I cringed whenever she talked with me about my impending "menses." Furthermore, she neglected to tell me about deodorant or even tampons (Niki would later reveal this other womanly secret to me).

And then there was Dede.

When our television broke I moped around the apartment, complaining of boredom. Dad decided to sign me up with the nonprofit Big Brother Big Sisters of America, which paired motherless and fatherless children with childless adults. On the application form I put down that I liked music and animals. I was soon put in touch with Dede Donovan, a law professor in her late thirties from La Jolla, California, who liked Cat Stevens and Irish wolfhounds and had yet to marry. But Dede and I only saw each other once a month. She'd pick me up in her Dodge Colt, the backseat covered in dog hair, and take me out for dinner. She was always kind, but we were never very close, certainly not close enough to talk about puberty.

Why couldn't my father give me that talk? Although he took me out on weekly movie dates—alternating between my Brat Pack picks (*Sixteen Candles, Breakfast Club, St. Elmo's Fire*) and his grim art house fare (*The Killing Fields, 1984*)—and though he was always generous with hugs and encouragement, he had little clue how to raise a teenage girl. He had no idea what I was up against in a private school.

Just as when I was a bullied first-grader, these experiences revealed to me that fundamentally I was on my own, and on my own I was subject to the unpredictable judgment of the social world, where I could be weird without wanting to be, without even being aware that I was being weird. (Fairyland's untidy corners stuck out from beneath the closet door.) As a result of this realization, I increasingly turned inward. What I found there was anger.

ON A BRIGHT afternoon in June 1984, my father was readying himself for that year's Gay Pride parade. I had always loved the energy of Pride but I hadn't gone in years. The sun was pouring into the dining room through the window behind me and I could tell from the light-footed way Dad moved in and out of the bathroom that he was in a good mood.

I could see him looking at himself in the bathroom mirror, tying a red bandanna around his forehead and then finding a red lipstick to paint his mouth. He came over to me, where I sat eating a bowl of cereal, and sweetly asked, "How do I look?"

I was mortified. I'd just come back from hanging out with my gang of girls, where I so wanted to fit in, so wanted to be cool. Dad did not look cool. He looked like the lead singer of the rock band Loverboy, but with red lipstick. Emboldened and sassy, I blurted out the first thing that came into my head.

"You look *so* queer, Dad."

I said it the way I heard classmates say it, meaning lame, stupid, weird, embarrassing. As a teenager, I believed it was my right, my duty even, to be honest about everything. Not only did I point out that the emperor was wearing no clothes, I had to describe what was wrong with the emperor's naked body.

Just as the word "queer" left my lips, Dad's whole face changed. His hopeful smile gone, his eyes hardened with reproach.

"You can't say that."

He now appeared so hurt and serious that all I could do was

look at him. I don't remember him slapping me. But it felt like he did. My face suddenly flushed, and I stared at the floor.

"You can't use that word," he repeated.

I didn't say "sorry." I didn't say anything. I simply stared at the floor until Dad walked out of the apartment, leaving me alone with my confused guilt.

As a small child I had no problem accepting Dad, in all his beautiful queerness. Whether in pants or a dress, he was still my daddy, the one who stirred my oatmeal with milk and honey, the one who pushed me on swings in the park each time I yelled "Again!," the one whose lap quaked whenever he laughed his enormous up-and-down laugh.

But as I got older and became attuned to the world around me, I craved, more than anything, acceptance. His queerness became my weakness, my Achilles' heel. Not only might it open me up to possible ridicule and rejection, it was something I could not contain. Fine, I thought, if Dad was gay, he was gay! But did he have to *look* so gay? And in *public*?

At least I had some degree of control over my own oddity, but here was Dad, out there, doing anything he pleased, saying whatever he wanted, dressing however he wanted, dating whomever he wanted. Including Charlie.

13.

ONE AFTERNOON in 1984, I came home from school, set my backpack down on our large wooden spool table, and called for Dad. Hearing no response, I scanned the cluttered surface of the table and found a note:

Alysia —
  I'll be home at 8pm. Here's $5 for dinner.
  Please take your drawing things out of my room.
      Love,
      Your Pa

With hours to myself, I walked into Dad's room, located his large orange marble ashtray and a folded cardboard matchbook, and placed these together on the hardwood floor. Then, walking around the apartment, I set about claiming items of trash: hair from a hairbrush, magazine, newspaper, rubber eraser, and a straw that had been cut in two.

Sitting with my legs tucked under my knees on Dad's oriental rug, I bent over the large ashtray with my piles of things and matches. Inside the hollow palm of cut marble, I set the lit match to different items to compare how each burned. The hair pulled from the hairbrush burned the fastest. With a sizzle and a pungent burst of smoke, it evaporated as soon as it touched the match flame. A ripped piece of newspaper burned faster than a piece of magazine cover, which I determined must be a result of the heavy stock and shiny color surface. The rubber eraser hardly burned at all but browned at the tip, emitting a fabulously strong scent. But it was the half straws that were the most fun to watch. The sides of the straw melted down and, when cooled, hardened into new plastic shapes. The few times I pulled out the orange marble ashtray I sought out these half straws, which for some reason were scattered about the apartment.

It wasn't until months later that I figured out why there were so many half straws around the house, and later still before I learned the role Charlie played in any of it.

Dad met Charlie at Finella's, a massage parlor and sauna that used to be next door to the Café Flore in the Castro. Charlie worked the desk. Tall and skinny, with a heart-shaped face and scraggly layers of dirty-blond hair, Charlie was typical of the guys Dad attracted. My father had an appetite for lost-sheep types—semi-employed young men who'd as easily steal our hair dryer as say hello, and often did. The previous summer, while I was at my grandparents, a nineteen-year-old Dad met lived in my room. In exchange for room and board, he did dishes and cleaned house. Only after he'd left did Dad discover he'd pinched the $200 we'd been saving for our trip to Europe.

My father often lamented his taste in boyfriends, wishing he could have a relationship with a more appropriate peer, but this rarely happened. "I think it's a character defect," he wrote in his journal. "I've only been attracted to those younger and less powerful than I . . . Is it because inside I feel weak, lost, helpless?"

I can imagine now why Dad might have liked Charlie. He was playful, open-minded, and quick to laugh. And aside from his $1,000-a-month coke habit, he was into healthy living. He rode his bicycle up and down the hills of San Francisco no matter the weather. He took gardening classes, enjoyed knitting, and was a strict vegetarian.

But I couldn't stand Charlie. It wasn't the drug use—which Dad kept hidden from me until he stopped using. It wasn't that Charlie was unkind to me. What I couldn't stand is that he *was* kind to me. Just as he refused to ever cross a picket line, he tended to sympathize with me, the "oppressed" teenager, in any of my arguments with Dad. One evening when the three of us were watching *Dynasty* in Dad's room, which doubled as our living room, Dad wanted me to leave so he could be alone with Charlie. When, after I'd been asked to leave several times, I defiantly refused to budge, and Dad said I was acting like a bitch, it was Charlie who left the apartment in protest.

I didn't want Charlie siding with me. I didn't even like to be in the same room with him if I could avoid it. With his dingy jeans and chenille scarves stinking of patchouli, he looked like the kids who bummed for change on the corner. I quickly and definitively branded him a loser. I certainly didn't think Charlie worthy of my father's attention, especially when it was redirected from more worthy concerns, namely me. And I felt free to share my distaste with Dad, hewing to my policy of total honesty, which prompted many fights.

But as I think it about it now, I suppose I should give Charlie some credit because if it weren't for him, Dad might never have gotten sober.

ANOTHER FALL AFTERNOON home from school, another note on the table:

Alysia –
  Meet me at Charlie's: 1236 Cole, Apartment 4G.
  We'll go to dinner from there.
        Love,
        Dad

It was my first time going to Charlie's place, an apartment in the neighborhood he shared with two other guys. I rang 4G and was buzzed upstairs. As I climbed the four flights of stairs, I noted the red, navy, and gold paisley carpet, which from its psychedelic pattern and dank, musty smell I concluded dated from the high hippie days. As I approached the fourth floor, I considered how to greet Dad. In my mind I kept repeating, "The carpet leaves much to be desired," imagining how amused Dad would be by my witty phrasing. Chin high, I repeated the phrase over and over in my head, accenting different words for effect: "The *carpet* leaves much to be desired. The carpet *leaves* . . ." each time more convinced of my precociousness. Finally, I arrived at 4G, knocked, was let in by Charlie, then dramatically announced to everyone within ear-shot: "The carpet leaves *much* to be desired!"

Charlie's face fell.

"Steve, your daughter's here."

I turned to Dad, who was staring at me, eyes flashing. He quickly apologized to Charlie then led me into the hallway with a firm grip on my arm.

"Charlie just spent the entire afternoon vacuuming the hall-ways," Dad said. "Where do you get off coming in like some prin-cess bitching about the carpet?"

Blindsided by my father's anger, I said nothing. Didn't he cel-ebrate this sort of bitchiness in *Dynasty*? Surely he must at least appreciate my turn of phrase.

"I was just trying to be funny."

"Well, it wasn't funny. You always have to act like such a jerk around Charlie," my father continued, "when you *know* how important he is to me."

But I didn't know how important Charlie was to my dad. How could I? It would be years before I would see my dad as anything more than the source of devoted love, attention, and money that

I felt was my due. I used to think that because my mom had died, Dad was obliged to make up for her absence, to offer me twice as much love, twice as much support as he normally would. This made perfect sense to me. Charlie did not.

But here was Dad asking me to consider him an independent person, an adult seeking the solace of a romantic relationship. It wasn't until well after my father died and I studied his journals that I realized what Charlie meant to my dad. That Charlie made him happy. "I like to be w/ Charlie just because I enjoy it. No reason or analysis. Why does one enjoy flowers, for instance?" But who wants to think of their parent's sexual and romantic needs? At thirteen and fourteen, I still clung to the idea of my dad's unrelenting love for my mother, whose death broke his heart so irrevocably that he *turned* gay. I suspected, even then, that this was a shaky story—but as a very convenient story, it wasn't easily abandoned.

Sometime after the carpet fiasco, Charlie started spending more time with a neighborhood coke dealer. My father was convinced Charlie was seeing him for access to free coke. In the two years of dating my dad, on and off, Charlie was never monogamous, no matter how much Dad wanted them to be. He recalled their disputes in his journals. "I don't know if I can take this lover-ship stuff," Charlie told him one night. Charlie accused Dad of being "too attached," adding that he'd never been with anyone who loved so much "like a woman."

My father tried to date other people, but this opened him up to a different set of risks. "Maybe I've not overcome my emotional dependency at all but merely spread it around more," Dad wrote in his journal. "A lot of sex would be okay except for the dangers of AIDS."

He felt too attached to Charlie to quit their relationship, yet it continued to hurt him. Sometimes Charlie failed to show up for

dates or showed up late, his pupils dilated, clearly high. Though
Dad enjoyed smoking pot and sometimes dropping acid with
Charlie, he tried to curb his coke habit, which he felt was taking
a toll on Charlie's health. "Is there any way I can stop you from
doing coke besides getting you busted by the cops?" he pleaded.
But Charlie argued that cocaine was "no more harmful than eating sugar," adding that he could do more, without a toxic reaction,
because he was a vegetarian.

In love with Charlie but increasingly jealous and helpless to
control Charlie's comings and goings, Dad became obsessed, filling pages of his journals with unsent letters and fantasies about
how he could get back at him. Dad considered puncturing Charlie's bike tires, or putting superglue in his bike lock. Deciding these
were too risky because he might get caught in the act, he settled
on another plan. With a felt-tip pen and a stack of white stickers
my father wrote out, "Hi. I'm cute, blonde and will have sex for a
half-gram of coke. Call Charlie at this number." Dad then posted
the stickers in the bathroom stalls of cafés and bars all over town.

Most of the stickers were torn down the first week, with only a
couple remaining at Café Flore. At first Charlie didn't know who
was behind the stunt and complained to Dad about the "character
assassination." But then one morning, after sex, Dad confessed.
"Charlie's eyes widened," he wrote in his journal. "He pushed
me away, reached for his clothes & started dressing. He was hurt,
angry, but more perplexed by it all. I don't know why I told him."

Needless to say, Charlie wanted nothing more to do with my
father after that. Frustrated and despairing, Dad started fantasiz-
ing about getting a gun and killing Charlie. When he confided
these fantasies to a friend over the phone, the friend recom-
mended Dad admit himself to Narcotics Anonymous, which he
did that very night.

I didn't know then the extent of what went on with Charlie.

Even now, almost thirty years after the fact, it's painful for me to see my dad so out of control, acting quite this crazy. And there's part of me that wants to hide these details, to keep them squirreled away inside the pages of the private journals where they belong. To protect Dad from Dad. But would I feel this way if he weren't my father? If he weren't my father, I'd just focus on the story. This is what happened, and maybe this behavior's not so unusual for drug addicted gay men in 1980s San Francisco. But he's not just anyone. He's my dad. And even if he's not walking around out there, I'm still afraid of how his actions and choices will reflect on him. Does this behavior confirm the worst stereotypes about gay men: promiscuous, morally compromised? And then, I'm afraid of how his behavior might reflect on me. The sins of the father.

I didn't know about the dramas with Charlie while they were going on. I never even noticed Dad's drug use (which included coke, speed, and LSD) until it ended. He was always in and out of the house at odd hours. He was always a little preoccupied, though usually with work. Only now, newly sober, did he start to get into *my* business and play the asshole in earnest. Just as he used to lecture me about the evils of excessive television, he now made me read articles on how "addiction runs in the family." If I showed any impatience for some deferred treat—new clothes, a movie, TV— it was evidence of my need for "immediate gratification," more proof of my "addictive personality." Suddenly he noticed I wasn't doing my household chores, though the house wasn't any messier than it had been before he quit.

"If you're going to act like this," I told him, "I wish you'd get back on drugs."

My father even coerced me into joining him at one of the twelve-step meetings he attended four nights a week at "Our Lady of Safeway," as he called the church on Market Street across from the supermarket.

I sat next to him in the circle of facing chairs, while everyone sipped on Styrofoam cups of coffee. But I could barely suppress my laughter as the addicts went around the room, introducing themselves in turn: "Hi, my name is Dan and I'm an alcoholic and a drug addict," followed by a deafening chorus: "HI DAN!!!"

It all seemed so pathetic and ridiculous. What losers, I thought. Then assorted members of the group would stand up from their rickety metal folding chairs and share a sob story about their addiction, about when they knew they'd "hit bottom." And each of these stories would be punctuated by someone else in the group calling out one of NA's many slogans:

"Let go. And let God!"

"It works if you work it!"

"Take it one day at a time!"

"Turn it over!"

Each platitude seemed more insipid and cringeworthy than the one that came before. But instead of anyone involuntarily rolling their eyes, as I did, the room all enthusiastically nodded or *mm-hmm*'ed in agreement. What kind of cult is this? I thought. The meeting ended with everyone in the group clasping hands and collectively putting their faith in a higher power.

It was almost too much for a teenager to bear.

WHILE DAD was concerning himself with getting sober, I was concerning myself with getting money. At fourteen and fifteen years old, everything I wanted cost money. I knew that cash was cold, hard, and in high demand. *Newsweek* declared 1984 "The Year of the Yuppie." Even the shops on Haight Street sold cheeky t-shirts that asked: "Nuclear war? What about my career?"

Dad talked about money all the time too. From the other room I could hear him yelling. He yelled when he knocked out another filling from his mouth. "That's seven hundred bucks!" He yelled about the phone bill. "Fifty-five dollars!" He yelled when I lost the five dollars he gave me for my Muni Fast Pass. "I was depressed that day," I said, pleading mercy. He yelled when I knocked the TV off the milk crate in a rush to get the phone and he cursed as we watched the broken knob roll across the floor and behind his bookshelf. Dad couldn't afford to fix or replace the TV, so we started changing the channel with a pair of pliers, which always seemed to go missing.

At French American I had money for lunch, but not snacks. A skinny fourteen-year-old with a fast metabolism, I was constantly hungry. I'd often ask for bites of my friends' snacks. I didn't think it such a big deal until a kid named Xavier noticed and started calling me "A-leech-a." Since he was among the popular kids, classmates took notice and I stopped.

I didn't want to ask my father for money because I didn't want to quarrel. So I started borrowing money from my friends and their mothers, which I then had to pay back. In the mornings, while Dad was asleep, I'd sneak into his bedroom. On the floor I'd find his jeans, scrunched like an accordion, then quietly pull out the smooth leather billfold from the back pocket. I'd open the wallet and slide out a ten, sometimes a twenty. He won't notice, I thought. And he never did.

I hated the sneaking and lying, but I wanted money to buy clothes and magazines and records and snacks. I found a job baby-sitting every weekend for a single mother who worked at Daljeet's, the punk shop next to the IBeam. She and a pair of her jewelry-designing sisters had come out from Philadelphia and lived in a three-bedroom apartment off Polk Street. While I loved her three-year-old son, how he called me his "girlfriend," and I loved watching her MTV, where I would slog through countless videos by Rod Stewart (please, not "Infatuation" again!) hoping for the one Duran Duran or Billy Idol, my $15-a-night salary didn't take me far.

So that December, I applied for my first job as a cashier at a local health food store. Sun Country Foods sold fresh-pressed wheatgrass juice for the neighborhood hippies and overpriced gourmet sandwiches for the neighborhood yuppies. The owners of Sun Country required that all their applicants—from manager to cashier—take a lie detector test. I heard the owners had been into EST, a popular 1970s self-assertion cult, as though this might explain their paranoia. But I didn't question the requirement. I just wanted a job, so I made an appointment and headed over that week after school.

Inside, I met the administrator and handed him my application, neatly printed in ballpoint pen. He led me upstairs, where there were two chairs, a table, and large windows that overlooked the store below.

I sat on the far chair with my back to the windows while this stranger wrapped thick white tape around my index and middle finger and then stretched a band around my waist.

After he set everything up, he sat across from me with a notebook on his lap and asked if I was ready.

"I guess so."

Following a series of questions confirming my work experience, my name, and my address, he cleared his throat and asked, "Ever been arrested?"

"No."

"Have you ever stolen anything from a store?"

"No."

"Have you ever stolen anything from an employer?"

"No."

"Have you ever smoked marijuana?"

"Yes."

The administrator jotted something down in his notebook but gave me a gentle look as he did so. Maybe he could detect my nervousness, or maybe he felt strange giving a lie detector test to a teenage girl.

"That's okay. Lots of people have. Ever done LSD?"

"No."

"Meta-amphetamine?"

"What?"

"Speed."

"No."

"Cocaine?"

I paused. I remembered Dad and those half straws around the house, the curious way they burned and melted into amorphous, unpredictable shapes. And I felt myself getting nervous. The wand started to move back and forth. I watched the administrator's pencil moving as he noted something in his pad. I thought I'd better say something. He repeated:

"Have you ever taken cocaine? Snorting or shooting."

"My father does. *Did*. He doesn't anymore. He's in NA."

The administrator looked at me.

"Narcotics Anonymous."

My breathing was still uneven. The wands were moving again. I heard them scratching on the rolling paper and I could feel my face getting hot, my eyes starting to fill. I'd not talked to anyone about Dad's drug use. I didn't know what I felt or even how I was supposed to feel. I was still trying to figure out where Dad's crimes ended and where my own began.

"That's okay," the administrator said reassuringly. "We're almost done."

When it was all over, he removed the tape from my finger, the band from my waist, and then he complimented me.

"Most applicants have done a lot more drugs than you."

And I smiled, feeling pretty good about this.

The next afternoon when I came home from school, Dad was on the phone but handed me a piece of paper. "Sun Country store manager called. Twenty hours a week. $5.25 an hour. Start Saturday?"

TWO DAYS before Christmas 1984, Dad and I were eating dinner at home when he asked me to attend John Norton's Christmas night party with him. I refused. The prospect of joining John Norton or any of Dad's other boring old writer friends for a whole evening filled me with nauseating dread.

"I already have Christmas plans," I told him. "With Yayne."

Even though Yayne and I now attended different schools, she still treated me like family. Every Christmas she invited me to spend the day and night, an invitation I always accepted. Yayne had just the sort of rambunctious family I longed for during the holidays. She only had one brother, but her mother was the oldest of six siblings, all living in San Francisco. Each holiday the aunts and uncles and assorted baby cousins with their pom-pom pigtails and animated braids would gather at Yayne's grandmother's place, the grown-ups and kids assembling in different rooms. Since Yayne was the oldest cousin she was the de facto sitter, and with me as her helper we ruled the roost, determining what TV to watch, who was in trouble for talking back, and who had to sit where to eat. I loved the food especially—sticky yams, buttered corn bread, rich corn casseroles—and the sense that I was welcome, my presence never questioned. I could just watch TV and disappear.

But my father was insistent. "I want you to come, if only for some of the party. You might even enjoy yourself."

"I have a free soul," I shot back. "You can't force me to go and you can't force me to enjoy myself."

We sat in silence at the spool table while I traced the wooden grain of the tabletop with my fingers. Our arguments would often stall like this, the ongoing silence signaling to me that my father had capitulated. He usually didn't have the energy to face off against my will for very long. I was used to winning arguments. But on this evening I took no satisfaction in my victory.

Hoping to pick up the mood, I asked him to draw me. If he could draw me, I decided, everything would be okay. We would return to our special place. We would be us again.

"I can't draw you tonight, mouse," he said. "I'm too tired."

"Can we go on a walk somewhere then? Somewhere in the neighborhood, or we can take a bus to a café or someplace we've never been?"

"I'm too tired."

"Or maybe we can just sit on the roof together? It's really nice up there."

We ended up staying home and talking. Dad told me that he needed me and confessed that because of his "addictive obsessions," his drug and alcohol abuse, he hadn't given me that much time or attention. "I'm sorry," he said.

We made plans for Christmas Eve. We went to Friends for linguine with clam sauce. After dinner we walked home, opened presents, and drank big mugs of hot chocolate with tall peaks of whipped cream.

On Christmas morning, I went to brunch at Dede's house in Bernal Heights, while Dad attended a Narcotics Anonymous marathon, a full day of meetings which he broke up with John Norton's Christmas party. I attended some of the party with him, something we agreed on, and even had fun, watching MTV with a friend's eighth-grade daughter. After the party, we went our separate ways again.

At 3PM Alysia and I left. She to go to Yayne's and me back to NA Marathon. It was intense – two people

spoke about being near suicidal and I got into some
deep feelings of my own, which the two suicidal people
responded to. I felt emotionally drained after all this.

At 10:30 on Christmas night, my father came home from the
marathon to an empty apartment. He called me at Yayne's.

"I want you to come home."

"But Yayne invited me to spend the night."

"I want you home."

"We've already set up sleeping bags in the living room!"

"I said, *come home*. Why do we have to argue about everything?"

When I came home twenty minutes later, I avoided Dad's eyes
and refused to speak to him. After letting myself into the apartment, I marched into his room and turned on the television. Dad
complained that I was invading his privacy, and I blew up. Here he
had forced me to come home and he wouldn't even let me watch
TV!

"That's *so* unfair," I yelled. "You are such a dictator!"

My father's face turned red. He charged at me, and grabbed me
by the shoulders. "Up until now I haven't given you much spiritual
guidance, but it's time I do. Let's start with some self-discipline,"
he said, still trembling. "You. Have to get over. This need. For
immediate. Gratification."

He then started to detail the drug excess he and my mother
were into when I was little, his "drug and booze fuck-ups" since,
and what his recovery and NA meetings were about now. I pressed
my hands against my ears. I couldn't stand hearing him talk this
way. *This is not what I want to be about,* I thought to myself. *This is
not where I want to come from.*

Now crying, I backed out of Dad's room into the dining
room. I was shaking my head as I looked at him, blurred through
my tears. I wanted to erase everything he said from my memory. Leaning against the dining room closet, I sank down to the

hardwood floor. Dad looked scared and confused. He tried to hug me but I wouldn't let him. I closed my eyes and imagined my mother.

Whenever I felt uncertain about myself as a teenage girl, I'd bring a picture of my mom to mind and meditate on that image. Our life might feel like crap, filled with drug-addict losers, weighed down by loneliness, disappointment, and sometimes squalor, but I knew, at least, that I came from this beautiful, brilliant young woman. The first-chair clarinet. The straight-backed valedictorian. The Smith graduate.

"I want you to draw me," I said to Dad.

"Draw you? Right now?"

"Yes. I want you to draw me."

After another moment of silence, he reached into his bookshelf and pulled out his drawing pad and charcoals. He asked me to pose in his room, but I insisted on maintaining my position against the closet door, even though I turned my back to him. I could hear his charcoal pencil scratching lightly against the paper, but I kept on crying, still imagining my mother.

When Dad finished sketching, he called me over so that I could see what he'd drawn. But the version of myself I encountered on his sketch pad wasn't pretty or interesting or even remotely poetic. I was just an ugly amorphous mass, huddled against a door.

"I hate it."

I started crying again and Dad looked puzzled and struggled to find something to say. Then I went into my room and climbed up the stairs to my loft bed and, looking out the window, watched the characters of Haight Street until I fell asleep.

IN THE NEW YEAR Dad refocused his creative work, which had languished during his ordeal with Charlie. He organized a benefit reading, co-sponsored by City Lights and the Art Institute, for poet and Living Theater founder Julian Beck, who was sick with cancer. He did a daylong interview with Allen Ginsberg to be published in *The Advocate* and *Poetry Flash*. Dad had first met Ginsberg at an SDS conference when Ginsberg was traveling cross-country in 1966. Dad, then an undergraduate at the University of Nebraska, invited him to read at the university. Ginsberg wrote "Wichita Vortex Sutra" on the way to Dad's house. For the *Poetry Flash* interview, our neighbor Robert Pruzan took photos of them walking together through the arboretum in Golden Gate Park, both looking distinguished with their beards and glasses.

Dad also redoubled his efforts to stay sober and healthy. He started swimming three days a week at a public pool in inner Richmond. He went to NA meetings four nights a week and he started sitting zazen at a gay-friendly Zen Center on Hartford Street in the Castro. He had learned about the Zendo when profiling its founder, Issan Dorsey, for the *San Francisco Sentinel*.

Over the next few months, Dad started meditating in the Zendo basement several times a week and even picked up a meditation pillow at a stoop sale so he could meditate at home. He initially found it difficult to empty and focus his mind, but with the help of a two-week all-juice diet and the book *Zen Mind, Beginner's Mind*, he found his way. I also noticed how the practice changed him. When he first quit drugs, my father had been irascible and impossible to be around. Zazen seemed to calm and focus him.

But even with his Buddhism and swimming, his regular meetings, and my increasing independence, Dad questioned whether he had the stamina to be a single father. On top of his persistent loneliness ("I don't like cruising," he confided in his journal; "I'm afraid to make eye contact & get scared when I do") and his fragile state as a recovering drug addict, there was me at my most obnoxious and now, inconveniently, smoking pot every weekend with my friends. On top of this, I failed to support Dad in his sobriety.

I refused to attend any other meetings with him and derisively rolled my eyes whenever he discussed them.

In fact, while twelve-step meetings helped Dad clarify what was behind his using—"Tonight's meeting focused on fear," he wrote in his journal; "I probably started drinking & doing drugs because I was shy – afraid of being lonely and unloved, too inhibited (unable to be gay & feel okay about it). I've clung to Charlie because I'm afraid w/out him I'd have no love – that I'd never find another"—I hated thinking about my dad "in recovery." The idea of him sitting in a roomful of strangers and introducing himself, "I'm Steve Abbott and I'm an alcoholic and drug addict," made me sick. Living in our one-bedroom apartment, just the two of us, I felt suffocated by these feelings. His struggles became my struggles, his romantic disappointments my romantic disappointments. I hated it. And Dad wasn't happy either.

> For much of the past 6 months I've wished I didn't have Alysia. I have no privacy at home, feel she interferes (perhaps prevents) me from having a relationship. I greatly resent this. I've raised her by myself for 12 years & I'm exhausted. Don't want the responsibility or the hassle. Then I feel guilty. I love her and enjoy being with her lots of times. Perhaps this is the only as well as the best relationship in my life."

Whenever I felt particularly down about my life, I turned on the television. Dad was never into TV. He had one or two shows he liked—*The CBS News with Dan Rather, Saturday Night Live*, and sometimes *Dynasty*, for its campiness—but otherwise he preferred to read, visit with friends at cafés, or go for walks to the beach. TV was important to me because, especially in the late seventies and early eighties, it was rife with situation comedies revolving around reconfigured families. Some of my favorites:

- *Laverne and Shirley*: Two single women who are best friends live together in a run-down basement apartment in 1950s Milwaukee. Antics ensue.
- *Silver Spoons*: A father and son are filthy rich but, without a mother, must take care of each other. Antics ensue.
- *Family Ties*: A pair of former sixties liberals raise their three kids, including a hard-core Reagan conservative. Antics ensue.
- *Mork and Mindy*: A man from outer space moves in with a woman in Boulder, Colorado. The alien is played by Robin Williams. Antics ensue.

While the backstories of these TV shows differed (with some characters from working-class urban families, others from professional suburban families), the spirit of each, summed up in the catchy theme song that opened the program, hewed to the same hopeful note:

"We're going to make our dreams come true, for me and you."
"Together, we're going to find our way."
"And there ain't no nothing we can't love each other through."

As saccharine as these songs could be, I found reliable solace in them. I believed in their premise, that we could heal our collective pain and broken homes with humor and love as long as we stayed together. And so, for a while, I turned to these shows obsessively. I watched them in prime time. I watched them in reruns during afternoons when I wasn't working or when my friends were busy. And I watched them after the ten o'clock news, before bed. I knew the characters intimately and longed to enter their worlds, where "everybody knows your name" and no problem is so big that it can't be resolved within a twenty-four-minute format.

I always thought Dad and I could get beyond the comedic pain of our situation: "Forty-something gay writer in recovery tries to raise a teenage daughter by himself in a tiny one-bedroom. Antics ensue." But when, in the early summer of 1985, Dad was struggling to build a life without Charlie—whom he continued to see biking around the Castro—and without drink or drugs, and while I was continuing to be a narcissistic jerk—borrowing his clothes and art supplies without asking, failing to deliver his phone messages, and leaving the house a mess—a rehab counselor he was seeing suggested Dad put me in foster care.

> I realize that when Charlie left my life my emotional sexual support system collapsed. And w/o drugs the stress is harder to take still. I keep looking for someone outside to "fix" me. Some of it is simply how I look at my life. I have health, a place to live that's okay, enough money, good friends. To what extent am I being a baby & just refusing my responsibility?
>
> On the other hand, I simply cannot meet Alysia's needs or be good for her if I'm a mess myself. Visitors point out that we're not good for each other. Our needs mix like fire and oil. Or maybe I can do okay, but the addition of her problems, personality, or simply "teenage changes," becomes the straw that breaks the camel's back.
> My options:
>
> a) foster home
> b) grandparents
> c) here, w/ <u>improved</u> relations & therapy.

Dad opted for a variation of c). The missing piece, as he now saw it, was zazen meditation—for me. If I would agree to sit daily zazen with him at the Hartford Street Zen Center, he felt I would

find a semblance of calm and peace. If I refused, he would send
me to live with my grandparents in Kewanee for good. Naturally,
I thought he was nuts. "Absolute power corrupts absolutely," I
told him.

In July of 1985, I flew to Kewanee for my annual visit. Dad and
I talked on the phone every week. He continued to feel strongly
that only meditation would set me on the path to peace at home,
and I continued to think he was off his rocker. Then he talked over
our conflict with our friend Sam D'Allesandro, when he was over
one afternoon. Sam said he thought I was doing fine and that Dad
couldn't make me do zazen. After he left, Dad wrote this letter. It's
the only typed letter he ever sent me.

30 July 85

Dear Alysia,

I was writing you a rather stern, serious letter last Saturday when Sam came over. After talking to him I decided I
was too extreme to expect or insist that you do zazen with
me every day.

What it is, I think, is that I feel really exasperated &
unhappy about certain aspects of our relationship. When
I love someone I tend to give my power away & be dominated. And that's very unhealthy, especially when it inverts
the parent/child relationship.

Authority means authorship. The parent is the author of
the child. The child comes from the parent's seed at birth
& is shaped, authored by the parent who feeds it, clothes
it, teaches it to crawl, to walk, to talk, etc. Authority does
not mean dictatorship. Take a story, or a poem – I write it,
have to decide what changes to make etc. But the story or
poem also has somewhat an energy or life of its own too.
For instance language, the stuff a poem or story is made

out of, comes to the author already charged. Language
by itself wouldn't make a poem or a story, however. Language by itself doesn't even make a dictionary unless some
author puts it into that shape. So a good story or poem
can only result when there is a proper balance or relationship between the independent, charged spirit or energy of
the language and an author who shapes this energy while
respecting its independence.

I raised you from birth showing a lot of encouragement of
your independence. But now I sometimes wonder if I have
not erred too far in that direction because independence
with no respect for any discipline or rules is anarchy and
chaos, a big mess. You have will power, yes, but you mainly
seem to want to put it at the service of momentary, self-
indulgent impulses: I want, I want, I want & I want NOW!

I think one of my own character defects is that I want
to escape from reality, to escape from doing anything
unpleasant. So maybe you've picked up these habits from
me. But even during the worst days of my alcohol and drug
addiction I achieved something! Since 1978 I've published 3
books of poetry, written two novellas, and published about
100 interviews, essays and reviews, published and edited 4
highly respected issues of Soup magazine, for 8 years edited
the monthly Poetry Flash and was a contributing editor
and columnist for other magazines. And I've been invited
to read & participate in conferences & poetry festivals in
other countries. All this didn't happen by accident. I had
to want it, plan for it, work constantly for it regardless of
whether I was happy or unhappy & often in opposition to a
particular mood or impulse.

I guess the reason I wanted you to do zazen with me is
that it brings harmony, clarity, serenity & discipline to a

person. And I think you are very much in need of these virtues.

Maybe it's normal for teenagers to be rude & sullen & rebellious but I don't particularly like to be around it. In fact I hardly have the energy to govern or properly love myself. And I'm not at all sure it's good for you to be around me when I'm so angry & unhappy & depressed. All the ways I used to cope with stress are gone: booze, drugs, cigarettes & most importantly, my relationship with Charlie. I feel as if I didn't have any skin, that my raw nerves are constantly exposed.

So if you don't like any of my ideas on how things could be made better between us, what ideas do you have? I want to emphasize that I don't think you are a "bad" person or that the problems that exist are your fault, or that the one solution is for you to live with your grandparents or elsewhere. I would consider that only as a last resort & have mentioned it far too often, I think, because I get to feeling so exasperated so quickly (perfectionism, lack of patience – other traits of alcohol/drug addict personalities). Getting counseling, trying to work out agreements that we could stick to without fail (like your doing the chores around the house without my having to nag or blow up at you to get it done) would be far, far preferable.

Otherwise everything is fine. Glad to hear you are swimming and getting tan. I do love you sweetie pie—even through my anger, frustrations & various depressions (many of which go back a long way and have nothing to do with you). I realize how I've been these last several months or longer makes it very hard on you too.

Hope to hear from you soon.

Dad

I saved this letter, but not until years later, after my father died and I was sifting through our apartment's copious stacks of papers, did I reread it, and only then was I able to absorb its contents. The truth is: I did want to be my dad's poem. I wanted to be his drawing, his novella, his most refined work of art. I wanted him to shape me with his love and intelligence. I wanted him to edit out my mistakes and many indulgences, with a sharp red pencil or a clean eraser.

Unfortunately, he was often fast and loose in authoring me, many times just improvising on the page. He didn't have the time. He was tired. He was lonely. He was too wrapped up in his own dramas, his own failed romances and career struggles, to manage this "already charged" teenage girl. And too often he made the mistake of sharing these struggles with me, when I was too young to understand them or to bear their weight on my shoulders. Yet we both knew I was a work in progress, so we never really worried. We had each other. And we had the will, and the desire, to keep returning to the page, to keep working on that draft.

But what happens to an unfinished poem if the author dies?

14.

I N THE FALL of 1985, my sophomore year of high school, I
transferred out of French American Bilingual School into
George Washington, a public school in the Richmond district. During my last year at French American I'd been more interested in friends than studies. Though I excelled in music, art, and
drama, my report cards were otherwise mediocre. Disappointed
with my grades, my grandparents announced they'd no longer
foot the bill for my education. Dad couldn't afford to keep me at
French American, and his journals reveal that he started substitute teaching there in order to pay off unresolved bills. That same
year, my friend Andrea transferred to Urban, a local private
school, Niki and Anne-Marie both moved away, and our band of
girls dissolved.

Relocating from a private high school of fifty to a public high
school of three thousand was a big adjustment. During my first
year I was slow to make friends and preferred to spend lunch
breaks doing homework in hidden corners of the school hallways
and stairwells to facing the social dynamics of the football bleach-
ers or "the Wall" behind the school, where students broke into
cliques. Instead, after school, between the hours of 3:30 and dinner, I roamed the Upper Haight, bouncing between bookstores,
boutiques, record stores, and most of all the coffeehouses—
Chattanooga, Double Rainbow, and For Heaven's Cake (formerly
Kiss My Sweet)—and the friends I found there.

There was sixteen-year-old Rudy di Prima, son of famed Beat poet Diane di Prima, Carlos with his red-rimmed eyes (always in trouble), and Father Al Huerta (always trying to keep Carlos out of trouble). There was long-haired Lara, who went to Urban but who lived with her hippie parents only a block from me. There was twenty-one-year-old Eddie Dunn, whose father ran the local recycling center, and his best friend, an Andrew McCarthy look-alike who'd take speed to meet his deadlines programming for Apple computers. And there was towheaded Christopher, a teen-ager who lived in a van at the end of the park, panhandled on the street ("Spare a smile? Spare a smile?"), and sometimes showered at Lara's. Some of my friends were students from the local private schools: Lara and Andrea (Urban), Camille (French American), and Red Head Jed (University). Others were high school dropouts who worked in the local cafés (Jeff). Many dealt drugs, like Steve (pot), Aragorn (mushrooms), and Andrea's boyfriend, Colin (acid). Others were addicted to drugs, like Creature (speed). But everyone was up for the ride, open for conversation, or just hang-ing out over coffee or a joint. There was among us, it seemed, a shared expectation of curiosity and tolerance.

We saw old movies at the Red Vic, holding hands across thread-bare sofas that stood in for theater seats, wooden bowls of but-tered popcorn (yeast optional) balanced on our laps. Sometimes we dated. Lara dated Eddie Dunn for some years. I dated the Andrew McCarthy look-alike for ten days. Sometimes we smoked pot and then frolicked in the playgrounds of Golden Gate Park or groped each other after hours in the Tactile Room of the Explora-torium, San Francisco's science museum, where friends of friends worked as "explainers" and got us in for free.

With the freedom I had, I could have been shooting heroin or turning tricks in the Tenderloin. But I was never that kid and my father knew it. After witnessing all the NA craziness with him, I wanted always to maintain at least a veil of control. Sure, I tried speed—the night of Red Head Jed's high school prom, I stayed up all night, chatting the ear off of anyone within reach. And I took mushrooms a couple of times, once at Double Rainbow with Andrew, Eddie, and Lara, all of us stumbling back to Lara's bedroom afterward to marvel at her soft skin and "baby hands." But I was, for the most part, a good kid. I never did acid. I never touched a needle.

Many of my teachers advised me to take my work more seriously. "Alysia would do better if she just applied herself" was a frequent refrain in parent-teacher conferences at French American. But by the time I graduated from George Washington in 1988, I had several AP classes under my belt and a 3.5 GPA. Besides, if I flaked on my term papers, which I did too often, I was getting an education in the cafés of Haight Street. Dad was frequenting many of these same cafés, with friends (such as Father Al Huerta, who helped Dad get a job teaching expository English at the University of San Francisco) informally keeping an eye on me.

Ultimately, Dad wanted to give me the same freedom he himself enjoyed, the freedom to live a public life, that of a flâneur, where we could trade the boring concerns of home for the intellectual gymnastics of coffeehouse banter, the unpredictability of the street. This was our chosen life.

Though I sometimes met up with Dad at For Heaven's Cake, or Café Picaro or Café Macondo in the Mission, his main stage was, and would always be, Café Flore. The Flore, as it was also known, was a sunny, foliage-infested patio café with a corrugated tin roof located at the corner of 16th and Market. Since opening in 1973, it had become the social and intellectual heart of the Castro district. At the Flore, men and women, young and old, black and white, gay and straight (but often young gay men), would go to meet friends and make friends with interesting-looking strangers.

Deep inside the café, behind the bar, an illustrated circus poster of Kar-Mi, a fortune-teller in turban and moustache, surveyed the colorful scene, acting as a calming presence.

Dad would spend full days at the Flore, filling spiral-bound notebooks on the café's copper tabletops. When he started working as a weekly columnist for the *Sentinel* in 1986, and a sometime essayist for the *B.A.R.*, *SF Weekly*, and *Bay Guardian*, he found many of his ideas there, amidst the conversations he took part in, or overheard, at neighboring tables. The finest of these articles helped get him nominated for the Cable Car Award for Best Gay Columnist and were later assembled in his essay collection, *View Askew* (1989). He was always chatting up younger men at the Flore, trying to find out what creative work they were doing and then recommending books to read and people to meet. He sometimes hoped these friendships would develop into romances. They rarely did. Nevertheless he loved playing an avuncular role in the community. Some believe this was among his greatest contributions.

I'd often find myself at the Flore, meeting Dad or visiting with a cute band of twenty-something gay boys who always sat at the same outside corner table and who counseled me through my ill-begotten crushes and occasional flare-ups with girlfriends. I had the unfortunate habit of pursuing cute guys who were more interested in fooling around than in commitment. I confided my problems to café friends like Aboud, so striking with his olive skin, black hair, and green eyes. He'd tell me that these high school boys were threatened by me. "Female empowerment. *That's* what it's all about, honey." Then he'd laugh—a joyful burst—and I felt I was let in on a secret.

Although I still spent the bulk of my social time in the Haight, I loved these afternoons at Café Flore. I'd been going to the café since I was little, and it always felt safe to me. There was no real threat, no feeling of awkwardness or competition as I sometimes felt among my girlfriends. I was always the kid, singularly young and straight, simply a member of this peculiar San Francisco family.

Soon the young men at the Flore would age before our eyes, shrinking beneath thick layers of scarves and sweaters and wool caps. They walked with canes or were pushed in wheelchairs, their vitality snuffed out, feathers plucked clean. Between the years of 1983 and 1985, the numbers of Americans with AIDS went from 1,300 to over 12,000, but San Francisco was the first city to experience epidemic levels of the disease. By the time the first HIV test was introduced in 1985, close to half the gay men in San Francisco were already infected. My father was one of them, but neither he nor I were talking about it.

FOR MOST of the country, AIDS was still something that happened out there to other people. That changed in the summer of 1985, only a few days after Dad mailed me his letter equating child-rearing with writing a poem, when Rock Hudson ended months of speculation by announcing that he had AIDS. By October he was dead. That same summer, thirteen-year-old Ryan White, an Indiana hemophiliac who'd contracted AIDS while receiving injections of a clotting agent, was barred from his school. These high-profile cases changed the face of the epidemic. AIDS was no longer dismissed as the gay plague, the disease of deviants—drug users and promiscuous gay men. It happened to famous people, to "innocent" people, to people you might know.

That summer and the months following, AIDS made the cover of *Life* ("Now No One Is Safe from AIDS"), *Time* ("How Heterosexuals Are Coping with AIDS") and *Newsweek*, which after running a picture of Rock Hudson on its August cover put AIDS on its September cover with the headline "The Fear of AIDS" and a picture of schoolchildren holding up signs that read "No AIDS Children in District 27."

The problem with all this media attention was that there was so little known about the disease, even among experts. On one episode of the *CBS Morning News* in 1985, a doctor from the University of California said that straight men rarely contracted AIDS from women; moments later, a Harvard doctor said they could. In late 1985, the Reagan White House blocked the use of CDC money for education, leaving the US behind other Western nations in telling its citizens how to avoid contracting the virus. Many Americans still thought you could get AIDS from a toilet seat or a glass of water. According to one poll, the majority of Americans supported quarantining AIDS patients.

This heightened awareness set off waves of anxiety across the country, which was often expressed through jokes (Q: What do you call Rock Hudson in a wheelchair? A: Roll-AIDS!) and violence. Between the years 1985 and 1986, anti-gay violence increased by 42 percent in the US. Even in San Francisco, where Greyhound buses still dropped off gay men and women taking refuge from the prejudice of their hometowns, carloads of teenagers would drive through the Castro looking for targets.

In December 1985, a group of teenagers, shouting "diseased faggot" and "you're killing us all," dragged a man named David Johnson from his car in a San Francisco supermarket parking lot. While his lover looked on in horror, the teenagers kicked and beat Johnson with their skateboards, breaking three of his ribs, bruising his kidneys, and gashing his face and neck with deep fingernail scratches.

As a teenager, I heard about this attack and it haunted me. Returning on a bus home from Café Flore one day, I saw graffiti spray-painted on a billboard that read "Kill Fags!" Riding home from school another day, I saw a message scrawled in black marker on the back of a Muni bus seat: "Gays, get help—not AIDS!"

I knew it was only a matter of time before my father became a target. It turns out he already had been. I just didn't know it.

IN THE 1980S, Black Mountain poet Ed Dorn started a magazine called *Rolling Stock*. In issue number five, published in 1983, there appeared, written in collaboration with the poet Tom Clark, "The AIDS AWARDS FOR POETRY—In recognition of the current EPIDEMIC OF IDIOCY on the poetry scene." The page featured a large illustration of a test tube of reddish liquid, presumably infected blood, which was the "prize." The recipients of this "award" included Dennis Cooper, Robert Creeley, Allen Ginsberg, and my dad.

Dorn's homophobia was no secret. In his 1984 poem "Aid(e) Memoire," he warned those who "screw and are screwed" by everyone all day and all year that they'll get a disease so they might as well go and "drink directly from the sewer."

My father was deeply wounded by the personal attack of the "AIDS award" and a few years later wrote about it in the epilogue to *View Askew*. "They mock us as we die, knowing full well that anti-gay humor leads to anti-gay violence."

His friend Kevin Killian was so pained by the incident that, after Dad died, he wrote an open letter to the editors:

> I write on behalf of one on whom a beaker of poisoned blood was poured by the talented staff artists of "Rolling Stock," one who on his deathbed, still strove to understand the motives behind this attack, one who tried to forgive, one who tried so hard to forgive it broke my heart. He is no lon-

ger alive, but I am, and why shouldn't I say exactly what I feel? . . . A great wrong has been done and memory will never be silent. Memory persists in squawking its fool head off trying to make sense of the evil done to innocent sufferers. I'm hysterical today, let my hysteria explode inside the great white apex of Ed Dorn's heart.

I don't remember ever talking with Dad about the "AIDS award." In fact, I can't recall talking with anyone about AIDS while I was in high school—not with friends, teachers, or family.

The strange thing is—and I find this really curious—I have no recollection of learning that my father was HIV-positive. With everything that I do remember about my life in San Francisco and our life together, all the hundreds and thousands of details I have had to cut when writing about him for the sake of flow and sense, why can I not remember this most important of moments?

My father's journals reveal that he twice tested positive for the AIDS virus while I was still living with him in San Francisco— the first time in the summer of 1986 and then again in the summer of 1987. But I've no memory of finding this out, or even of discussing AIDS with him before I left for college. I can imagine how a conversation might have gone, maybe over one of our dinners in front of the CBS Evening News. Dad could have turned to me at a commercial break, plates of tuna and noodle casserole balanced on our laps: "This is something we should talk about. I know you're scared. I'm scared too. Here's what we're going to do about it." But I can remember no such exchange.

Does that mean it didn't happen? Or does it mean that I've blocked the memory?

What I remember instead is a moment when I still thought he might never get AIDS. In November 1987, the fall of my senior year, I was selected to represent my high school on a ten-day trip to Israel sponsored by the American–Israeli Friendship League. In my application essay, I wrote about my mother, about how she'd been Jewish but how I knew nothing of Judaism since she'd died in a car accident when I was a small girl.

Each of us traveling to Israel was called a "young ambassador," and for ten days we toured the country by bus. We visited Haifa in the north, worked on a kibbutz in the south, sipped tea in Tel Aviv, and floated in the slimy waters of the Dead Sea. At night we stayed with host families. During the day we took guided tours of sites. In Jerusalem at the end of the trip, we made plans to visit the Wailing Wall, the renowned prayer site in the holiest of holy cities.

On the bus ride over, our guide explained how the 187-foot wall, believed to be the sole remnant of the Holy Temple, had been a place for Jewish prayer and pilgrimage since the fourth century. She said, "The sages state that anyone who prays in the Temple in Jerusalem, it's as if he has prayed before the throne of glory because the gate of heaven is located there."

I decided that I would pray when we got to the Wailing Wall. I descended from the bus and walked down to the dusty base of the wall. Standing amongst Hasidic Jews draped with prayer shawls, all bobbing back and forth, I peered up at the Wailing Wall's uneven surface. The midday sun, reflecting off the white stones, forced me to squint, but I could still make out hundreds of tiny papers—other people's prayers—folded and rolled, poking from the cracks in the layers of sediment above.

On the bus, I'd written out my wish in pencil, earnestly hoping that sticking a prayer into the holiest wall in the holiest city on earth really meant something, that there was a reason so many people were swaying and bobbing and kneeling in front of this sacred place.

So, standing amongst scores of murmuring strangers, I felt along the rough stone above, found my spot, and jammed my tightly rolled prayer inside the crack. I pushed it deep, deep inside the wall so that it wouldn't fall out, and as I did so, I repeated my prayer, under my breath:

Please don't let my father get AIDS.
Please don't let my father get AIDS.
Please don't let my father get AIDS.

Since traveling to Israel, I've enjoyed visiting and praying in many of the world's most venerable holy sites. I've prayed in Istanbul's Blue Mosque barefoot and completely prostrate. I've kneeled in the Cathedral of St. John the Divine in New York, lit candles in Notre-Dame in Paris, and climbed the thick stone steps of Buddhist shrines in Kyoto, thighs burning, beads of sweat running down my back. Sitting in a plain wooden pew, I've enjoyed the extended silence of a Quaker service in a Brooklyn Friends Meeting House dating from 1857. I'm always moved by these different expressions of faith, these nuanced forms of prayer, the alternating grandiose beauty and powerful humility of these different houses of worship, all built and sustained by believers. But I've never been able to attach myself to any single faith, nor have I felt moved to believe in a single, all-knowing, all-powerful god. After that blinding day at the Wailing Wall, after all the senseless devastation that's been known in our community, I can't believe in a divine plan.

IN FEBRUARY 1988, three months after my return from Israel, Dad received a call from Kevin Killian. Sam D'Allesandro had died of AIDS. Sam was the first friend we lost: beautiful Sam. He came to my sixteenth birthday party and then disappeared. After a few months of not seeing him, I asked Dad if Sam could join us at the movies and he told me that Sam was sick. I said we should visit him but we never did. And then, some months later, the phone call. In his journals Dad wrote about how shocked he felt: "I thought he was better."

Sam's boyfriend, Sean, later told me that Sam had been diagnosed only six months before he died. But he'd been sick for more than a year. He had CMV retinitis, an AIDS-related condition that causes the retina to detach from the eye, blinding its victims. He had tuberculosis in his adrenal glands. He had HIV pneumonia many, many times. But he refused to go to the doctor. Outside of Sean and Sam's roommate, Fritz, nobody saw him. Nobody. When Sam started to go downhill, he retreated, quitting his job at the travel agency, never leaving his apartment. For a long time he refused to believe that he had "it," even if a diagnosis meant more services and better treatments. "If I have AIDS," he told Sean, "I don't want to know about it." Sam was only thirty-one when he died.

Sam was one of many men in the city who, after becoming sick with AIDS, disappeared from view. The gifted poet Karl Tierney, a colleague of Dad's from the Small Press Traffic gay men's writing group, dropped out of the scene once he was diagnosed. Karl had been twice a finalist for the Walt Whitman Award, a finalist for the National Poetry Series, and a Yaddo fellow. In 1995 he rode his bicycle to the Golden Gate Bridge and jumped off. He was thirty-nine.

Sam's denial about having AIDS didn't absolve Dad and me from our responsibility as friends to visit, to say goodbye, but it felt as if we inadvertently did the right thing. I can only remember Sam as full-lipped and beautiful, with that thatch of soft blond waves, an eighties Adonis. Maybe that's how he wanted to be remembered.

But then, when I recently did an image search for him online,

I found, amongst the beautiful shots, a photo taken by Robert Giard. After seeing *A Normal Heart*, Larry Kramer's play about AIDS, Giard took hundreds of portraits of gay and lesbian writers. In this portrait, Sam looks gaunt, with hollowed-out eyes, like a grinning skull in a wig and sweater. When I found it, tears sprang to my eyes and I turned away. It pained me to look. Why did he pose? Kevin Killian thought Sam might have been thinking of the big picture . . . that he wanted, not his own peers perhaps, but future generations to know something of the horror of AIDS.

The story of how we lost Sam troubled me long after he died and I left San Francisco for college. In that fall's freshman composition class I wrote an essay about him that dealt with homophobia and AIDS, about how the loss of Sam turned me into someone who'd speak out whenever a cousin or a classmate yelled, "Don't be a faggot!" But in this essay about my newfound bravery, I never mention that my own father is gay. I never mention that he could be HIV-positive and might die of AIDS himself. Just as Sam didn't want to admit that he had "it," I didn't want to admit that Dad might get "it." The fear and shame wrapped up in the diagnosis was too powerful to shake. Given my own level of denial about my father's illness, in all likelihood my feelings about Sam were encased in worry about my father.

AFTER MY TRIP to Israel, I set my sights on how my life would evolve post–high school. I started to adopt what I considered to be sophisticated habits. I took to wearing a beret and walking down Haight Street carrying an antique cane or a single long-stemmed white rose symbolizing peace and spirituality. I started to patronize a café that had just opened in the Lower Haight called Ground Zero. The café hung large abstract paintings on its walls and attracted a clientele of pale college students in thrift-store trench coats clutching beat-up black portfolios. I liked that Dad didn't go there and that no one I knew in San Francisco yet went there. I returned to Ground Zero every week, always ordering Earl Grey tea with milk (another "grown-up" discovery) and reading Tama Janowitz's collection of short stories *Slaves of New York*, which fed my fantasies about the city.

I'd become infatuated with New York en route to Israel. Visiting the city for the first time, I took the subway from our midtown hotel to Astor Place in the East Village. I wandered along St. Marks Place and down Lafayette, eventually finding my way into Keith Haring's Pop Shop. The t-shirt I bought there—Haring's radiant baby in orange on a gray background—became a staple of my wardrobe. Keith Haring would later illustrate the famous *Silence = Death* poster for the AIDS Coalition to Unleash Power (ACT-UP) before dying of AIDS himself in 1990.

Back in San Francisco, with my nose deep in *Slaves of New York*, I dreamed of the life Janowitz depicted: making jewelry, loft living with an artist boyfriend, wearing a neon-green and orange coat, living a quirky creative life informed by the history of Andy Warhol and the Velvet Underground.

In my final year of high school, San Francisco felt provincial to me. Dad was plugged into the vibrant "Queercore" community, playing elder statesman at Klubstitute, Club Chaos, and Uranus, underground scenes he'd later describe in his Pynchonesque novel *The Lizard Club*. But I powerfully longed for my own life, apart from Dad and relieved of my past. I knew I wouldn't find it in San Francisco. I couldn't walk down Haight Street without running into a classmate, ex-coworker, ex-fling, or someone I knew through Dad. I felt an itch to grow and stretch, to walk unfamiliar streets in the great throbbing heart of bohemia, which I then believed to be New York City. Thanks to my "big sister," Dede Donovan, I got there.

My father was pretty hands-off when it came to my school plans. He had a vague idea that I should attend college but was too busy with his own work to focus on the efforts needed to make that happen. Once Dede emerged as someone who would help me, he simply stood aside and let her do it. She wrote to several schools requesting applications. She tirelessly worked on these applications with me, redrafting essay after essay over pots of peppermint tea at For Heaven's Cake. She secured recommendations for me from lawyer friends I'd met at her Christmas brunches. When I was accepted by New York University, I was thrilled. I didn't consider going anywhere else. Dede even secured me a summer job working as a nanny for a pair of her college friends who lived in the city.

Dad was happy for me too, though sad that I'd be moving so far away.

BEFORE I LEFT San Francisco, we took a sauna together. I remember both of us naked except for thin white towels wrapped around my chest and his waist. We chatted a little, but it was too hot to chat more so we decided to play cards instead. Gin rummy was our game.

So there we were, alone on the wood slat bench, naked except for our towels, and I was shuffling the deck. The air was so hot and dry I could barely swallow. My skin felt like it was on fire. I remember the sweat dripping down my back and down my forehead, trickling into my eyes and ears. I had to stop shuffling so I could wipe my face with another thin white towel. Then I cut the deck and let Dad deal each of us a hand. We took turns pulling cards off the open deck, hoping to find a consecutive run of three cards from the same suit or a set of three cards of the same rank.

There was no clock in our sauna. It didn't matter, because there was no place to be. We were neither alone nor burdened by company. There was no pressure to entertain or to find a clever remark or conversational strand. We just played gin rummy, taking turns pulling cards until:

"Three sevens. How 'bout you?"

"Nine, ten, and a queen of hearts. You win."

Over time, the heat of the sauna curled our playing cards so that they reminded me of the little Fortune Teller Miracle Fish cut out of red plastic film that kids would sometimes bring to school. The way it moved in your hand was supposed to reveal your "true heart." A moving head meant "Jealousy." A moving tail, "Independence." If the fish turned over, your heart was "False." If it curled up entirely you were "Passionate."

I remember sitting there and remarking on those curiously curling playing cards, coming to life in our palms, attesting to our love. And I remember our nakedness, which was so natural and easy.

PART V
Departures

And one of the things I'm really happy about is my relationship with you. And your letters. I don't think I ever imagined it would be this wonderful & enjoyable & interesting. I guess when you were growing up I had my hands so full of trying to be with you in the present & keep up w/ your changes that I never had time to imagine what the future might bring. But it's really neat when "the future" turns out better than one expected.

—STEVE ABBOTT, *letter dated December 10, 1990*

15.

WHEN I WAS a little girl, my father and I used to play hide-and-seek among the thick conifers of Golden Gate Park. One day when he was hiding and I was seeking, I couldn't find him. After I called his name, all I could hear was the sound of eucalyptus leaves rustling in the wind. So I sank down onto the nearest park bench, waiting for him to emerge and wrap his arms around me again. But waiting for him, watching all the not-my-dad men walk by, the minutes slowed. I imagined what would happen if I was still sitting on that park bench after the air cooled and the sky darkened to black. Would I join the legions of orphan characters I knew so intimately from books and movies?

For each storybook orphan that rose above tragedy to become king of the elephants (Babar) or to star in the circus and beat up the town bullies (Pippi Longstocking), there were those orphans that were cruelly mistreated before redemption (Little Orphan Annie, Shirley Temple in *The Little Princess*, Jane Eyre) and the orphans who died of neglect before finding redemption in the afterlife ("The Little Match Girl"). I was especially scarred by a 1970s TV version of this Hans Christian Andersen tale, which shows the match girl freezing in the wintry streets while busy Christmas shoppers ignore her offers of "Matches! Matches!" By the light of her last match, she's warmed by a brilliant image of her dead grandmother before ascending to heaven to join her.

I deeply believed (in a ritualized exercise in self-pity) that my father was the only thing standing between me and the fate of the orphans I loved so much. With morbid fascination I studied these stories, thinking that if I familiarized myself with their different shades of tragedy I'd be better equipped to survive should anything happen to him. Every time my father and I temporarily separated—at the market, the street fair, or Golden Gate Park—images of the forsaken orphans would flood in. Who would take care of me now? Would anyone love me like he did?

When I was very small playing hide-and-seek with my dad, I could always get him to appear. If I called out, "Where are you Daddy?" he'd answer, "Here I am!" until the sound of his voice led me to him.

In July of 1988, I moved to New York, living for the first time beyond the sound of his voice.

NEW YORK felt hot: dirty, hot, and sweaty. I was riding in a taxicab from La Guardia Airport over the Brookyn-Queens Expressway. The taxi had no air-conditioning so I kept the windows rolled down. But the wind whipped my hair around my face so I rolled them back up. When the cab finally pulled up in front of a red door in the East 80s, I smoothed down my hair and emerged into the humid evening.

I carried my suitcase to the Weiksners' door, wiped my face, sucked in my breath, and pressed firmly on the bell. Though sticky and tired, I also felt energized, taking in the sights and overripe smells of summer in New York. Then the door opened and I saw a small child with brown bangs and a candy heart necklace.

"San-draaaa! Alysia's here!"

This little girl was my new charge, Sarah Smiley. I gave her my friendliest grin and followed her into the townhouse.

"Hell-*ooo!*" This was the contralto of my new employer, Sandra Weiksner, calling from the back of the house. After lugging my suitcase inside the front door, I walked toward her, stepping over a leather floor mat, which had been tastefully painted to look like an oriental rug with a corner pulled back and overlaid with wind-blown yellow gingko leaves. Trompe l'oeil, Sandra would later explain. "It's French for 'fools the eye.' We had an artist do it."

Sandra sat at her kitchen island with a thick stack of papers, a glass of red wine, and a plate of Boursin cheese and crackers.

Sandra and her husband, George, were friends from Dede's Stanford days back in the sixties. They'd once been sympathetic to the New Left, but now were members of the corporate elite. George worked as an investment banker and Sandra was a part-ner at a prestigious law firm on the bottom tip of the island. She'd been looking for a "mother's helper" to take care of Sarah, her three-year-old niece visiting for the summer while Sandra's sis-ter studied acupuncture in China. Dede had arranged for me to watch Sarah in exchange for room and board.

"It's so nice to meet you. How was your flight? Good? Good. Good. Welcome! Listen, is it okay if Sarah gives you the tour? I've got to finish these notes tonight. You'll meet George later. He's working late. The boys are playing basketball in the neighbor-hood. They're due back for supper. I don't know how they do it in this heat! Isn't it disgusting? So . . . is that okay? If Sarah takes you? Your room's on the top floor." She waved me toward the near-est staircase.

"Yes. Thank you, Mrs. Weiksner."

"Sandra, you can call me Sandra. No need for for-*mal*-ities!" she sang.

As I grabbed my suitcase and followed Sarah up the stairs, I looked back at Sandra. She wore her dark hair short with straight bangs that she kept brushing off her forehead into a middle part.

When she spoke, her eyes were bright and her bracelets jangled up and down her arms with each exclamation. As she settled back into her work, she carefully put each bracelet back in place and took a sip of wine, as if to center herself.

Sarah led me up the stairs to the second floor, an airy, light-filled living room with upholstered wallpaper, Louis XIV chairs, and twelve-foot ceilings. The corners and tabletops were crowded with African sculpture, delicate silver boxes, and painted porcelain fruit the size of babies' fists. The walls were hung with paintings, including a small Braque ("My mother gave it to me when I was sixteen," Sandra later told me), a Sonia Delaunay tapestry ("through a client of George's"), and a Mirò.

I was studying these when the three-year-old grabbed my hand. "C'mon, lets go upstairs!" She pulled me up the carpeted staircase toward the next floor as if she were the grown-up and I the distracted child. I moved slowly, holding on to the thick wood banister with my free hand, trying to absorb my new surroundings. Within the dimensions of the house I felt small—tiny, even. I'd never seen anyplace like the Weiksners'. My only reference for material comfort was Munca and Grumpa's two-bedroom ranch house. Their all-white living room, with its tasteful modern art, black piano, and sliding glass doors facing the deck, had been the height of elegance for me, and the site of many pretend balls as a girl.

After showing me around the third floor, including Sandra and George's room and the "library," Sarah led me to the fourth floor and pointed to a series of doors: "Mike's room. Nick's room. My room. Bathroom. Your room!"

"This is such a beautiful house!" I said.

"Can we go downstairs now? I'm hungry."

"Okay, Sarah. Let me just put my bag down."

I settled my suitcase into the corner of my new room, which

was hung with muted watercolors of clowns and acrobats. I peered out the window facing 81st Street and felt an immediate and powerful urge to rush outside, to walk everywhere and see everything. I forced myself to take a deep breath before heading back downstairs.

Later than night, after a light dinner in the walled garden with the rest of the family—George Weiksner and the Weiksners' two robust teenage sons, Mike and Nick—I lay in my little bedroom in a bed next to the window. Jet-lagged, I had a hard time falling asleep. I imagined my father back in San Francisco where, it being three hours earlier, he might be drinking a latte at the Flore, or be perched on the edge of his futon at home talking on the phone, or sitting cross-legged, scribbling in his spiral-ring notebook.

Did he miss me? Was he thinking about me? I wanted to tell him everything.

At eleven at night, the city was still thick with activity. As I lay in bed, I tried to isolate and identify each sound I could hear through the window. There was the distant pulse of traffic and car horns on Lexington Avenue, a large truck wheezing and rumbling down 81st Street, a group of kids talking and laughing, a radio playing from a distant apartment window. Thinking about all the life happening outside, in every direction, my whole body buzzed. In my head, I started repeating a single phrase over and over, and each time I said it I felt a little more excited: "I'm in Manhattan. I'm in Manhattan. I'm in Manhattan. I'm *in Manhattan.*"

BACK IN SAN FRANCISCO, my father was sitting on his futon, hard at work editing *The Zombie Pit*, a collection of stories by Sam D'Allesandro. Since he was again trying to quit smoking, he was also sucking on a Hershey's Kiss, which he'd unwrapped from its foil after pulling it from a bag he kept in the drawer of his end table. Dad was still not drinking or doing drugs, but quitting smoking seemed harder. His nervous energy was constant, expressing itself through the shaking of his right foot as it dangled over his left leg, and the way he'd fidget with the tinfoil wrapper in his lap. Early the next morning, he'd calm this energy by sitting zazen meditation.

After six years of going to the Hartford Street Zen Center, Dad had evolved into a devout Buddhist. The previous summer we had spent ten days in Kyoto, Japan, an experience that inspired his book *Skinny Trip to a Far Place*, and he sat zazen every morning. He saw his practice as the only reliable way of letting go of unproductive thought patterns and habits. Facing the wall, he'd crouch down, folding his legs around a stiff round pillow on the tatami floor, silently sitting with several other members of the community as incense swirled in the air and the gong rang.

He now had another dimension to his practice: every Friday afternoon Dad walked upstairs from the basement meditation room and into a small room with a rubber tree plant, a hospital bed, and two chairs. There he'd sit for several hours with J. D. Kobezak, a twenty-three-year-old with AIDS.

In 1988, AIDS continued to ravage the gay community. At the end of 1985, there were 15,527 reported cases of AIDS in the US; three years later, that number had swelled to 82,764. But while newspapers ran articles about quarreling AIDS researchers and pundits and bureaucrats argued over policy (with some advocating tattooing AIDS patients), little attention was paid to people actually living with the disease, especially those suffering through its late stages. Men who were still closeted in their hometowns were forced out of the closet once they became sick and bedridden. Often forsaken by their families, these men had to rely on friends and lovers to care for them in their final months. Others fell through the social net and, unable to care for themselves, ended up homeless and on the street.

One day, Issan Dorsey, the abbot of Hartford Street, found a homeless kid with AIDS sleeping under a table in a local laundromat. Issan understood what it meant to live on the street. Decades before, he had performed as Tommy Dee, The Boy Who Looks Like the Girl Next Door!—a cross-dressing opening act for comedian Lenny Bruce. After some years working the North Beach nightclub circuit, he started shooting drugs and eventually would wake up in the gutter. It was through a chance encounter with Allen Ginsberg and LSD that he found his way to Buddhism and a devoted practice that led to his opening and then running Hartford Street, the city's first gay Zendo.

Issan took the homeless kid back to Hartford Street and set up a bed for him upstairs. Within a year, thanks to the generosity of one of the Zendo members, Issan bought the Victorian house next door so he could convert the space into an eight-bed AIDS hospice, the first of its kind in the country. The hospice was named Maitri House (*maitri* means "compassionate friendship" in Sanskrit).

Maitri House was one of a dozen AIDS organizations that formed in San Francisco in response to the epidemic. Much as in the late 1970s, when Anita Bryant and John Briggs had posed a common threat with their anti-gay political campaigns, the gay community was energized by the AIDS crisis. Lesbians, some of whom still felt more kinship with the women's movement than with the gay movement, organized blood drives and marched alongside gay men in angry ACT-UP demonstrations demanding cheaper and faster access to AIDS drugs. Filling the void left by a brutally indifferent federal government, a slew of organizations formed to provide counseling, health care, home visits, and education for anyone affected by AIDS, including the Gay Men's Health Crisis in New York and the San Francisco AIDS Foundation.

This powerful response was due, in part, to the tightly woven sexual communities that had been forming for decades. In *Stage-*

struck, the writer and historian Sarah Schulman argues that the bathhouses, bars, and other meeting places that were blamed for the AIDS epidemic were also the very structures that allowed for efficient organizing and dissemination of knowledge once the epidemic began.

To support the transition of the Hartford Street space from a Zendo into a twenty-four-hour AIDS hospice, Issan asked members of the community to volunteer their time and talents. My father, who'd overseen benefits for Cloud House and *Poetry Flash*, helped organize a fund-raiser for Maitri, and every Friday afternoon he sat with J. D., the kid from the laundromat. Sometimes Dad pushed J. D. in his wheelchair around the neighborhood or out to the Gay Pride parade or the Folsom Street Fair. In a letter to a friend, he described these Fridays as the "happiest time of my week." His experience, as detailed in the epilogue to *View Askew*, was common to many gay men who suddenly found themselves caring for sick friends and lovers:

AIDS is neither a curse nor a blessing: it just is. I see its inexorable progression in a 24-year-old friend whom I've been sitting with every Friday for the last nine months. I got to know J. D. in a healing workshop. He came up to me one night and gave me a hug because, he said, he just felt I needed one.

J. D. is such a beautiful person I found it hard to believe at first that he was sick. But last fall he became bedridden. I wasn't sure if I could cope with helping care for him – I'm not trained as a nurse – but it was just something that needed doing so I did it. I felt awkward at first but he encouraged me and gave me confidence.

Words can't tell what I've learned from J. D. – about myself, about life. Sitting with him every Friday and watching his courage and dignity in the face of this disease has been one of the most intimate, inspiring experiences of my life. Often we've sat for hours together and said nothing, yet said more than most people ever do. His hands flutter like butterflies. He sometimes suffers delusions. But don't we all?

IN NEW YORK CITY, I was the model of an Upper East Side mother's helper. Each day at noon I picked up Sarah from a neighborhood day camp, fed her lunch, and entertained her until dinner and then bed at seven. Some afternoons we took the subway to the Bronx Zoo or walked to the playground in Central Park or wandered the cool marble halls of the Metropolitan Museum of Art. I kept Sarah happy with street vendor pretzels and shaved ice that turned our mouths bright blue. In my free mornings, I walked the avenues studying the windows of the high-fashion shops and watching doormen in their anachronistic brass-buttoned uniforms hailing cabs or helping neighborhood ladies with their packages.

Back at the Weiksners', with the boys at soccer camp, Sandra and George at work, and Marcia, the housekeeper, doing laundry and making beds, I roamed the open rooms examining all the art, playing with Foxy, the family's Abyssinian cat, and writing letters home.

When summer came to a close I moved into my freshman dorm, a new construction downtown with the uninspired name Third Avenue North. Our first night, my new roommates and I looked out our kitchen window and watched the prostitutes who did business on 12th Street.

Though my nanny job had ended, I remained close with the Weiksners. Three nights a week I'd catch the express train to their house for a hot meal and, through Sandra, found work proofreading at her law firm downtown.

I was ten to twenty years younger than all of my coworkers,

who nicknamed me "Seventeen-something," a riff on the then popular TV show *thirtysomething*, but it was an ideal college job. I worked weekends and as often as not was able to while away the hours clipping grocery coupons from the Sunday *Times* and studying my art history and psychology textbooks for school.

While I enjoyed most of the classes I was taking—how thrilling to take art history and then study Giotto paintings at the Metropolitan Museum of Art!—I felt disconnected at NYU. Classes were held in large auditoriums located in one of a cluster of nondescript buildings surrounding Washington Square Park. Once class let out, students were simply absorbed into the anonymous city crowds. There was no actual campus that focused social life. A handful of dorms were located in and around Washington Square, but my own was the farthest-flung, at least a twenty-minute walk from class.

I didn't feel a natural kinship with my roommates either. There was Jane, an actress from upstate New York, and three dancers, all named Rachel, who came to be known by their last names: Goodman, Strauss, and Shaw. They were all smart and fun but the worlds they occupied were very much their own. In the evenings, Goodman, Strauss, and Shaw would gossip and stretch at the kitchen table, while Jane, practicing her vocal exercises, tried hard to round her *O*s and aspirate her *H*s: "Whhhhere is the party? Whhhhat is the plan?"

To remedy my abiding loneliness, I phoned my grandparents in Kewanee every Sunday morning at ten and Dad whenever I wanted, using an AT&T phone card my grandfather had given me. To save money on phone bills, Dad preferred to write to me.

RRRINGGG!!!
It's . . . Alysia! When I talk to you on the phone it seems you're not that far away. When I talked to my Dad about

you not writing, he kept using the word, "weaned." "They get weaned away at college" (like you were a kitten or a puppy).

Issan says we're all home-leavers, leaving the person you were supposed to be, to become the person you are. Being away from home, from San Francisco, I think you'll discover (& create) the person you really are more.

Well, I'll end here – and I didn't even talk about my "boring" friends (even though they always ask about you).

Now that I was living on my own, I wanted to "discover and create" myself, the way I'd dreamed back in San Francisco. This was supposed to be my Tama Janowitz life. But I had no idea how to do this. I'd applied to NYU because I wanted to be in Greenwich Village and find my way into its storied bohemia, but I spent most of my time hanging out with a family on the stuffy Upper East Side. In addition to joining their dinners, I accompanied the Weiksners for weekends at their country house in Connecticut, evenings at Carnegie Hall or the Metropolitan Opera House. They even bought me a winter coat, since I had nothing suitable for the New York weather. For Christmas they gave me an antique pocket watch, which hung from a long silver chain.

Though the Weiksners generously invited me into their privileged life, I knew it wasn't truly mine. I could mostly fit in, sometimes borrowing one of Sandra's scarves or a necklace if she thought I didn't look "fancy" enough for an event. Like a good trompe l'oeil, I could effectively mimic the manners and posture that were expected of me. In my years of traveling between the worlds of home, school, friends, and grandparents, I'd mastered the art of adaptation. But I knew, in my heart, I was different: a pale and scrawny impostor. I was never quite certain what was expected of me or how I could return the Weiksners' generosity.

And I was deathly afraid of making a critical misstep, using the wrong fork, somehow acting gauche.

I would have spent more time among the students at NYU, but outside the Weiksner house I felt totally isolated. Although I casually dated a twenty-something actor-proofreader I met at the law firm, I made no close friends that year. I didn't anticipate how cold and disorienting the city could be—that if I didn't yet know myself, no one else could know me either. I felt lost in New York, swallowed whole.

In San Francisco, I also didn't know myself, but I knew my neighborhood, my friends, and my father. There was a version of myself that I saw reflected back in each of these relationships that was both familiar and acceptable to me. Painfully homesick, I couldn't wait to return for Christmas.

ON THE FIRST EVENING of my visit home, I sat with Dad in front of the TV eating dinner. We'd caught up that afternoon, and as I picked at the chicken on my plate, with the TV news boring into me, I felt a strong urge to leave the apartment. Watching television no longer interested me and I was itching to get out before dark so I could explore my old Haight Street haunts. But I knew I should be keeping my dad company, at least until dinner was finished.

"Is it okay if I head out for a walk?" I asked finally.

"Yeah, sure." The TV light flickered on Dad's face and he turned to me. "Don't stay out late though, okay?"

"Okay."

I walked with long powerful strides down Haight toward Golden Gate Park, eagerly looking for anything familiar. Unlike in New York City, with whom I still suffered the self-doubt and nervousness of a new love, I felt bold and sure of myself walking the streets of San Francisco. I intimately knew the city. When I closed my eyes, I could imagine myself like a ghost floating down Haight toward the Fillmore over to Dubose Park to Café Flore and up the hill of 18th and Castro back toward home over Ashbury Heights. I breathed in the street's peculiar perfume—the faint smell of marijuana, eucalyptus leaves, and wet wood. Walking through the light fog, I even enjoyed the familiar cold dampness penetrating my jacket and jeans, taking up residence in my bones, so different from the razor-sharp winds of New York.

Surveying Haight Street, as I did on each of my subsequent visits home, I made note of the many stores remaining from my youth and those replaced by new ones. The old Shop 'n' Save had closed, to be replaced by a used clothing warehouse called Villains. Etc. Etc. had become the brightly lit Beauty Store. Passing different windows, I searched faces at café tables and in the aisles of boutiques, hoping both to recognize and to be recognized.

When I caught sight of the park, I turned and walked along the opposite side of the street toward home. At the corner of Haight and Schraeder, I spotted a familiar form: Jimmy Siegel, the owner of Distractions. Pulling shut a heavy gate, he had his back to me. He'd shaved his moustache but I easily recognized him: his leather jacket, his short blond hair, his cute, boyish face.

"Hi," I yelled over the loud roll of the closing gate. "Do you remember me?"

He was bent down low, fastening a lock. He turned around, looked at me, and stood upright. "Yeah, I do. How are you?"

"I'm good. I moved to New York. NYU! I'm just back for Christmas."

"That's great."

"Hey, whatever happened to Tommy? Does he still work here?"

I had first discovered Distractions in 1984, after being drawn in by its punk rock window display and the New Wave music playing on the shop speakers. The front of the store had a large glass case full of intricately carved wood and metal pipes, sparkling rhinestone-encrusted cigarette holders, Zippo lighters, and Tommy. He was hard to miss.

Already six feet, he was three inches taller in the roller skates he wore around the store, whizzing back and forth behind the counter. Tommy's hair was styled short on the sides and high on top, which made his big ears appear bigger. His hair color changed depending on his mood—one week it would be purple, another week pink or blue. Beneath his pompadour he had sparkling green eyes and a mischievous, thin-lipped grin. When he smiled, he'd give his eyes a playful roll, like Mae West delivering her best lines.

"Oh aren't you a pretty little plum, but still too green to pick!"

Back when I was being ignored by the high school boys and gender was still a puzzle I couldn't solve, Tommy coaxed me out of my shell. He entertained and flirted with me, and Distractions became a regular stop in my after-school circuit.

I eventually learned that Tommy was not paid to work the register at Distractions. He made his living dealing coke in the neighborhood. He used to brag about his star clients from prominent 1970s rock bands—all references lost on me, a Duran Duranie through and through. Tommy was the ex-lover and best friend of Jimmy Siegel, the store owner, and worked the register simply because he liked to hang out, to soak in the Haight scene. Sometimes his two dogs, a poodle named Cuddles and a terrier named Teddy, would join him behind the register.

When one day I shyly revealed to Tommy that my dad was also gay, he asked with a wink, "Is he a top or a bottom?" When I gave him a confused look, he said, "Well, I am a top, *definitely* a top." I just enjoyed watching Tommy: the way his back arched when he laughed his wicked laugh; his pretty, smiling eyes.

"Tommy?" Jimmy asked. "Tommy died. He died of AIDS six months ago."

Jimmy said it apologetically, as though I were too young, female, and straight to be troubled with such news. As Jimmy spoke, he looked into the middle distance, as though Tommy was just one of many men he pictured in his mind's eye.

"I'm sorry," I said. "I really liked Tommy."

"Me too."

Tommy's death marked a change for me. When I was still living with my dad, my preoccupation with the world of my straight friends had mostly protected me from the effects of the AIDS epidemic. But on these first few visits back from college, I noticed how it altered everything. Dad would later tell me our former neighbor Robert was sick. Another night, seeing a classical concert downtown, I recognized the usher as one of the cute guys I used to chat with at the outside table of Café Flore. "Hey!" I called. "How are you? How's everybody?" He just shook his head, not feeling as chatty as he'd once been.

The street I knew growing up was changing. Some transformations between 1987 and 1992 might have been the effects of the economic recession, but much was a result of the AIDS crisis, as members of the city's gay population went into retreat, either dying or caring for those dying, or else living in a perpetual state of shock about the deaths taking place behind so many closed doors.

It was dark when I turned onto Ashbury Street. Upstairs in our apartment, I found Dad beneath the covers on his futon bed. The TV was still on, the volume loud. Dad squeezed the "clicker," turning down the volume, and then turned to me.

"How was your walk?"

"It was fine."

"Did you run into any of your friends?"

"No," I said, thinking of Tommy. "Not really . . . Shop 'n' Save is closed."

"Yup, you have to walk all the way to Cala to get groceries now."

"Well, goodnight, Daddy. I'm going to bed. I'm still feeling jet-lagged."

"Goodnight, sweetie. Oh, by the way. I bought some new Bic razors. The ones in the Pacific Drug bag you can use. Don't use mine."

ON CHRISTMAS EVE, Dad and I went out for sushi and a movie at the Kabuki Center in Japantown, a favorite outing of ours, and at my suggestion we saw *Working Girl*, about a Staten Island secretary who dreams of her own office on Wall Street. The movie opens with a wide shot of the Staten Island Ferry crossing into downtown Manhattan. As the camera panned over Battery Park and Bowling Green I elbowed my father and pointed out the Cleary Gottlieb office building: "That's where I work!"

At home we opened presents under the tree and I gave Dad a surprise that I'd been working on for weeks: a collection of my best writing from that semester, which I'd printed and collaged with magazine clippings into a book I called "For My Father." The book was divided into four sections: criticism, autobiography, poetry, and essay, which included the essay on Sam D'Allesandro. He loved it so much he pulled me to his lap and squeezed me against his chest. When Sunday came, I was sorry to have to leave for New York. Shortly after my return I received this letter:

> I'm really proud of how you're doing Alysia. Even though I
> haven't seen your report card, I have seen your writing and
> I'm really pleased to see your self-confidence more solid
> than when you left. And when I get a job again, I'm sure

mine will be more solid too. Then we can really enjoy each other's company.

Back in New York, though, I felt increasingly unmoored by my college experience. Ironically, I failed to turn in a final paper in my pragmatism class and was now in danger of taking an incomplete. Furthermore, I had a misunderstanding with the Weiksners. Hanging out at their place one evening, I watched as their teenage boys took turns spinning each other in the basement dryer. It was a stupid game and I told them as much, but I didn't stop them. When Marcia discovered the dryer was broken the next morning, she told the Weiksners who in turn got mad at me. "Why did you let them do it?" Sandra asked me. "You're the adult. Weren't you watching?" Only two years older than their oldest son, I didn't feel adult and I didn't realize that was supposed to be my role.

I wanted to be good, but I never seemed to understand how to be good or even what "good" meant. I noticed how my roommates attended to their figures, slowly turning before the full-length bathroom mirror and measuring the space between their thighs in a standing position, down to the millimeter. At dinner, they ate iceberg salads, mixed with carrots and canned beans. They cut out sugar and white flour to reach their ideal body weight. I can do this, I thought.

That spring, I researched the minimum number of calories and servings of food groups I needed to remain fit and organized my meals around these restrictions. My goal was to eat 1,500 calories a day: 400 for each of my three meals and 150 for each of my two snacks, at mid-morning and mid-afternoon. I drank eight glasses of water a day and avoided drinks other than coffee and tea because I didn't want to waste calories. I memorized the calorie content of each basic food. Banana: 125. Apple: 90. Piece of bread: 125. Snack box of raisins: 50. Cup of plain nonfat yogurt: 90.

On top of my careful diet, I started to budget myself to $15 a day, which I withdrew from the ATM each morning.

Organizing my life around these rules and figures calmed me. If at any point I began to feel anxious or uncertain, I could always find a scrap of paper and quickly tally up everything I'd eaten that day. If I was under goal, I was happy with myself and immediately relaxed. If I was over goal, I knew what steps to take—skip my afternoon snack or spend an extra twenty minutes at the NYU gym—and was also happy. The margins and back covers of my school notebooks became crowded with these scribbled lists.

In high school, I'd fantasized about a New York life that would revolve around SoHo openings and literary parties. I now spent most of my time at the Union Square A&P, a lonely old lady at eighteen. The top of my grocery cart stacked with my clipped coupons, I carefully examined the labels of soup cans and cartons of yogurt, comparing grams of fat, protein, and carbohydrates.

Then one Sunday afternoon while I was working at my proofreading job, one of my coworkers approached me in the bathroom.

"Hey Seventeen-something, are you feeling okay?"

"Yeah, fine," I said. "Why?"

"You look pretty thin."

"Thank you!"

"Are you . . . getting your period?" she asked.

"Yeah, why?"

"Just curious."

I didn't learn until much later that anorexic girls stop menstruating. I saw my close attention to diet and budget as a way of taking care of myself, of setting goals and realizing those goals. I knew I was depressed, the pathetic specter of the A&P, but I didn't know why, so I kept these feelings to myself, which only made me feel more estranged. I longed for change. When Sandra Weiksner said she could arrange a summer job for me in the filing department of Cleary Gottlieb in Paris, I jumped at it.

16.

WHENEVER I THINK back to my first summer living in Paris, I remember a certain day on the Boulevard Filles du Calvaire in the 3rd arrondissement. It was a late Sunday afternoon in June. I was sitting next to the open window in my room at the dormitory where I was living, trying to write a letter to Dad. Whenever I felt stuck, unable to think of what to write next, I'd look out the window and watch the people passing on their way to the neighboring laundromat, large canvas bags balanced on their backs.

I once read a poem by Charles Baudelaire called "Windows," which starts:

> Looking from outside into an open window one never sees as much as when one looks through a closed window. There is nothing more profound, more mysterious, more pregnant, more insidious, more dazzling than a window lighted by a single candle. What one can see out in the sunlight is always less interesting than what goes on behind a windowpane. In that black or luminous square life lives, life dreams, life suffers.

Behind this closed window on the Boulevard Filles du Calvaire was an eighteen-year-old girl living outside her home country for the first time, wearing a white t-shirt and cutoff jeans. Her bobbed hair curled in the humidity.

Fille. I was a *fille.* A girl. I always liked the name of that boulevard: Filles du Calvaire. And I always liked the name of my temporary home there: Foyer Pour les Jeunes Travailleuses, Dormitory for Young Worker Girls. It had a nice communist ring to it. So very like the French in their socio-communist ways, I always thought.

Sandra Weiksner had not only arranged my job working at Cleary Gottlieb Paris, she set up my stay at the dormitory, mailing the headmistress copies of my passport and proof of my employment. To be eligible to live at the Foyer, you had to be between the ages of eighteen and twenty-five, legally employed, and not from Paris. Though I'd have loved spending that summer with Dad in San Francisco, the opportunity to live and work in France on the cheap seemed too good to pass up.

Soon after my arrival, I noticed that the rooms were overwhelmingly populated by girls from former French colonies: the Antilles, Tunisia, Morocco, Vietnam, and Senegal. Each seemed to prefer socializing with girls from her own region, so I gravitated to the only European girls there, two French brunettes: a lean girl from Normandy with conservatively cut short hair and a thin, sharp nose, and a shorter, rounder girl from the Loire with long, kinky hair. We took breakfast together in the kitchen each morning before heading to our respective jobs.

There were no other Americans. I shared my room with a girl from French West Africa, but she spent most of her time down the hall with her friends, stirring fragrant peanut sauces on hot plates. I heard them explosively laughing as they spoke in thick African accents about their *mecs*, their guys. She never invited me to join and would only stop into our room to change before her dates.

Left to myself in the evenings after work, I walked from Boulevard Filles du Calvaire into the neighboring Marais district until sundown. Before heading out, I'd make myself a simple dinner. Other nights, when I wanted to treat myself, I'd buy a falafel on the Rue des Rosiers, which I'd slowly eat on the winding walk home, peering through the windows of small boutiques full of beautiful clothing I couldn't afford. The waning light, a gold wash on the walls of the *vieux quartier*, lingered until eight or nine o'clock, as I meandered through little streets with names like Rue des Mauvais-Garçons (Street of the Bad Boys), appropriate given the neighborhood's recent transformation from a Jewish neighborhood into a fashionable gay enclave. As I neared the Boulevard Filles du Calvaire, the area restaurants would start to come alive—the warm evening air filling with murmured conversation and the music of glasses and tables being set for dinner. The streets were thick with these narrow restaurants, along with bars and nightclubs, what the French call *boîtes*, boxes.

I often felt as if I lived in a *boîte*, this little room on the third floor where I would sit by myself reading or writing letters to my father. It was a square space, with uneven slat-wood floors and room enough only for two wardrobes, two beds, and a desk. The bathroom was down the hall and shared with all of the other girls on the floor. Every night, I waited in line, holding a toothbrush and a cup in my hand. Returning to my room, I spied cockroaches creeping along the edges of the walls.

For three weeks that summer, my high school friend Camille, who was staying with her French father, was my companion and guide. She invited me to a traditional French lunch at her grandmother's and introduced me to kir, a cocktail of white wine and sweet cassis. Drinking these with her on the terrace of a Latin Quarter bar, I felt sophisticated and French. But after she returned to her mother's in California, I was on my own again.

Then one weekend, my roommate left for three days without mentioning anything to me. I looked for her out the window and listened for her laugh in the hallway. I checked with the front desk each night to see if they'd received any news of her. When she finally returned, I told her how worried I'd been but she only laughed. "I'm a grown woman, *une femme*," she told me.

I knew then I was not a woman, just a *fille*.

EVERY SUNDAY at four o'clock, I went to the *cabine téléphonique*, a hexagon of folding glass doors in front of the Foyer. I entered and closed the door, shutting out the sound of busy street traffic, and collect-called my grandparents in Kewanee, where it was ten in the morning. Talking to my grandparents in English, if only for five minutes, was like taking a breath of fresh air after being locked in a windowless room.

There was no problem with my French. Three years out of the bilingual school, I was surprised by how easily and completely it returned. With my pale skin and dark hair I could even pass for a local. One evening, riding home from work at rush hour, the car suddenly filled with a rowdy crowd of American tourists and a man standing beside me murmured in my ear, "It's like we're the only French left!" I smiled at him sheepishly, hoping not to reveal my true identity.

Dad couldn't afford collect calls from France any more than he could afford to call me in New York, so when I finished talking to Munca and Grumpa, I returned to my room and sat down and wrote to him about my adventures.

June 14 1989

Dear Daddy,

You're the best letter writer I know. Almost every week I get a letter. I must say, some of your first few made me cry. So much love was expressed in your words, genuine love. I'm bound closer to you than any one else in the world yet you're so far away. It sounds as if you've been lonely lately. It must be hard having me away for so long. At least I can hear the details of your life by letter. Now you can hear mine:

. . . Five days a week, I spend 9 hours at a little law office called Cleary Gottlieb. Inside that little office I run around, drink liters of water, and talk about Jazz with the American in the photocopy room.

After work, at about 7:30, I eat dinner and take a walk into the Marais. Tonight I walked to the Place des Vosges, the oldest square in Paris, also in the Marais. It was very relaxing sitting on a park bench in the Jardin Louis XIII. I watched a young couple nuzzle and coo, a little girl chasing pigeons, and an old woman with a vivid, pensive face.

But on that one afternoon next to the window, a white sheet of paper, a letter unfinished, lay on top of my desk. I was now looking out the window trying to think of how to answer my father's last letter:

22 June 89

Cher Alysia,

I got a horrid sunburn last weekend & now have had a horrid chest cough. Been tired a lot too (but have had trouble sleeping). My latest t-cell count is 71 (down from 360 three months ago.) It's probably time I get on some AIDS treatment – if I can get on some program when I don't have to pay (because things cost a fortune and I don't have insurance) but the medical bureaucracy is such a maze and experts have so many contradicting opinions and I have been too tired and have no time. But I'll see about it soon.

Been working hard on my job, on 2 books (proofing them, etc.) and my essay on homophobia came out and a lot of people liked it. You probably will be more interested in my writing sometime in the future after I'm gone than you are now.

Hearing about your days & your visit to the Place Des Vosges made me feel I was right there with you. You have a writer's knack for noticing all the fresh, precise details. Rewriting this Atlanta novel is fun in that way – remembering what your mom was like – little details of what she did when she was agitated – and others we knew then too. Not much about you in it @ present (you were 1–2 then) I'm sure you'll be pleased to know that. But if I live awhile, there may be an Alysia book coming.

     love,

     Dad

Looking out the window, I felt myself tumbling. This loneliness in Paris, the loneliness of my room where the African girl never sleeps. There's a greater loneliness out there, much worse than this loneliness. There'll be a time when Dad won't answer my letters. When I won't be able to phone him collect or not collect. When he won't complain and comfort and encourage me. This letter that speaks of T-cells speaks of this time.

"My latest t-cell count is 71 (down from 360 three months ago.)"

The white blood cells that fight off infection are called T-cells. As AIDS progresses it kills these cells, attacking the body's ability to protect itself from any illness. I know this now, but at eighteen I only vaguely did. Sitting in my room, I looked at this part of Dad's letter over and over again, like someone who couldn't read. Then this unfathomable idea started to rise in my consciousness. Now a bone-hard realization, I felt it lift from the bottom of my belly, up under my spine—a large bubble of hard, cool air pushing up and through me, threatening to huff and puff until it blew my house down. Collapsed on the floor, I was suddenly sobbing and breathing so hard and so fast that I was no longer the verb's subject but its object. (Not Alysia taking a breath but a breath taking Alysia.) I continued like this for a long time, rocking back and forth, trying to swallow my sobs, until I was too tired to cry anymore, and I just sat in my empty room, dazed and thirsty.

I stood up, returned to my spot by the window, and looked for the passersby and their big canvas bags of laundry. I needed these signs of the everyday to bring me back to the present.

So on this afternoon sitting by the window, I wrote him a letter finally admitting to and explaining my sadness, begging him to "be careful," and signing it "your melancholy daughter." Two weeks later his reply arrived:

26 July 89

Dear Alysia,

Don't be melancholy (unless you enjoy it, hee, hee). I've been feeling very healthy lately. In fact, when I went to oral medicines this week, the nurse said my gums look better than they had in four months and was so excited she took two photos of them. I'm feeling more vigorous and energetic again too.

I don't do drugs (not even smoke pot) and drink only occasionally (an occasional glass of wine if company comes to dinner). I've even been feeling sexy again. And got laid twice in 2 days (almost a miracle – the second time w/ a very nice person I met at the Anarchists Conference.) This did wonders for my mood.

I don't "have" AIDS yet and am supposed to get on drugs that will fight the advance of the virus soon. Realistically I could stay fairly healthy for another five to ten years – or one or two. I just don't know. It's harder to fight off any illness as one gets older. I know people who have died of cancer or heart attacks younger than me. Death simply gives meaning to life (sets the boundaries of life), and one might as well complain about birth as death because birth is where the suffering begins.

So please don't get so upset you hyperventilate my dear. No need for that. But I want to be honest with you about how things are & not "in denial" ignoring reality and pretending things are always perfect if they're not.

My hope is that by doing this that we'll love and appreciate each other more the next few years & not waste the time we have to communicate or share our growth, hopes and aspirations.

Wish you'd call collect so I could talk to you but I guess I can wait till you return to the US.

> Much love,
> Your loving Dad

By the time Dad had written me this letter, he'd already spent many days and months considering his end. He later told me that when he first learned he was HIV-positive, he panicked. Pacing through the apartment, he kept asking himself, "What about Alysia? What about Alysia?" He focused on his breath and, counting his exhalations, told himself, "It's okay to feel scared." Then he remembered Issan, the abbot at his Zendo. When Issan had tested positive for HIV, he said, "It's not AIDS that's fatal: if you have AIDS you're alive." Dad studied the graceful way Issan accepted his infection and decided to follow his path.

At one of Issan's dharma talks he famously pronounced, "AIDS is the teacher." The talk inspired members of the Hartford Street Zen Center to volunteer. Dad still sat with J. D. Kobezak every Friday at the Maitri Hospice, but now that he was HIV-positive he looked to that experience as a guide. In the epilogue to *View Askew* he wrote:

Because I'm antibody positive, I know I may be in J. D.'s position myself some day – still alive but fading with little control of body or mind. We all die differently just as we all live differently. I don't know what it will be like for me but I'm no longer afraid.

My father may have been "no longer afraid," but I was. He could write about staying healthy for "five to ten years" or for "one to two," but I couldn't think about numbers. The implications of Dad's letter were too painful for me to keep in my head for any length of time. Sitting in my room in Paris, I folded his letter back inside its envelope and closed it in a drawer.

Thousands of miles from Dad, my own life continued. The next morning I woke up and took the Métro to the Champs-Elysées, walked to the offices of Cleary Gottlieb, and spent the day filing legal briefs for bespectacled young lawyers, chatting up my French officemates and drinking liter bottles of water. That weekend I went on a picnic with the French girls to the Bois du Boulogne and walked with them through the woods, all of us getting drenched in a sudden summer rain.

I RECENTLY DISCOVERED that this letter Dad sent to me in Paris isn't the first in which he mentions being HIV-positive. On March 23, nearly three months before I left for Europe, he wrote, "Got results from my blood test. My t-cell count is 363. That's below average – which is 450–1500. So I'm getting physical & evaluation @ UC AIDS Clinic. Maybe they can put me on some experimental drugs before I get sick." But I have no memory of reading this letter, or even reacting to it, while in New York.

Which is why I focus on that day at the window. It was the first time I remember thinking of Dad with AIDS.

I never understood why it was so hard to recall Dad as HIV-positive before Paris. Then, carefully sifting through Dad's journals, I found a copy of a letter he wrote to Dede Donovan that same summer of 1989:

> Alysia knows I have some health problems but I haven't
> wanted to alarm her about their seriousness. But one reason
> I've wanted her to learn to fend for herself more is that it's
> not unlikely that she'll be without her remaining parent
> in 2–3 years, if not before. I haven't told her grandparents
> about this either.

Dad was indeed careful not to alarm me about the seriousness of his health. In the letters he wrote to me while I was at university, news on the progress of his infection was always couched between news of the banal—updates on plans for his fall tour promoting his novel, *Holy Terror*, and his book of essays, *View Askew*, troubles with the chatty roommate sleeping in my old room ("He has talk-arreah!"), and his many unrequited crushes: "What I mostly am, my dear, is celibate. It seems too much bother to get these boys in bed. But I <u>do</u> love them."

Unconsciously I took my father's lead. If Dad didn't want to give me reason to worry about the status of his health, I didn't look for it. Why should I cooperate with the possibility of this loss, with the dissolution of my world? Besides, there was still so much life to live.

IN FRANCE later that summer, I learned to ride a bicycle for the first time. The headmistress at the Foyer had organized a weekend trip to the countryside, driving the rowdy Filles du Calvaire in a rented bus to a dormitory on the Brittany coast. The trip cost us each thirty francs, then the equivalent of six dollars. On the five-hour drive from Paris, the girls in the back of the bus sang along to French pop songs playing loudly on a cheap transistor radio.

When we arrived at the dormitory in Brittany it was already dark, but I noticed next to the front door, under a bare bulb buzzing with moths, seven pink single-speed bicycles leaning against the wall outside our rooms. Over dinner the next night, the Norman girl with the sharp nose suggested that we go for a ride before bed. I sheepishly confessed that I didn't know how to ride a bike, a fact I'd somehow managed to hide from my friends for most of my life.

"Then you'll learn," she said in French, her thin lips curling into a smile. "I'll teach you."

She took me out that evening on an abandoned road near the rooming house. As we started along the wooded path, the dorm shrinking behind us, I wanted to tell her that I'd changed my mind, that I'd rather go to the beach, watch TV, do anything else. But though my French was good I didn't feel competent enough, or intimate enough with this new friend, to jettison our plan without seeming rude. Instead, ten minutes later, this twenty-two-year-old girl wearing pearl earrings and a conservative navy sweater with tiny white buttons, this girl whom I'd known only two months, dug her neat canvas sneakers into the dirt and patiently held my bicycle steady as I tried again and again to pedal forward without falling over. This girl, whose name I can't even remember, worked so hard to keep me aloft on that rusted pink bike that her cheeks flushed and a thin moustache of perspiration appeared above her mouth, which was drawn tight with concentration. I felt heavy and stupid on the bike and was grateful that no one was around to see us. I was thinking of how to rescue us both from what was clearly a futile pursuit when suddenly I was moving forward on my own. I felt like I was flying.

The sun was low on the horizon as I pedaled back and forth down that patch of dusty dirt road, gaining speed as I gained confidence. I bicycled into a nearby clearing, passing fields of grass in which I could see small farmhouses and rolled bales of hay painted golden pink by the evening sun. It was just like the Monet paintings I'd studied in my freshman year and I had to laugh at this almost prepackaged postcard moment. The fresh evening wind blew into my face and I couldn't stop smiling. Pedaling in large swooping circles, I accepted the wind as a reward for my perseverance. Behind me, the Norman girl was laughing and clapping.

I later wrote Dad about that day. I wrote him about the Norman girl (my heroine! my Joan of Arc!), who'd later take me to meet her family in Rouen, including her welcoming father, still grateful to those Americans who stormed the beaches of Normandy in World War II. I wrote about how I'd never felt as good as I had in that moment, riding a bicycle in the countryside of Brittany, the westernmost province in the western arm of France, which stretches into the Atlantic as if trying to reach the distant United States.

17.

RETURNED TO NEW YORK in the fall of 1989. I continued traveling to the Weiksners' Upper East Side townhouse every week, clinging to it as a familiar base. One cold Monday evening that October, I was typing a paper in their upstairs office (formerly my bedroom) when their fourteen-year-old-son Nicky burst into my room. He'd been in their library watching game three of the World Series on TV. It was a match between the Oakland A's and the San Francisco Giants, the so-called BART game, named after the subway that connected the two cities.

"Alysi*aaa*!" he called as he thundered up the stairs. "There's been an earthquake in San Francisco! The Golden Gate Bridge *collapsed*!"

I immediately telephoned my father, who informed me that it was the Bay Bridge, not the Golden Gate, and that only a portion of the upper freeway had collapsed, crushing two vehicles beneath. In our dining room the mantelshelf had cracked and fallen, destroying two blue marble goblets handmade by a friend.

As a San Francisco native, the fear of "the big one" had always been a part of my identity; it pained me to not be there. Although the quake's epicenter was in the hills of Loma Prieta Santa Cruz, eighty miles north of the city, to miss the Bay Area's worst earthquake since 1906 fractured my foundation, my sense of self. I felt as if a part of me, the San Francisco me, was somehow slipping away.

Though he didn't say so, Dad's journals reveal that the Loma Prieta earthquake made him feel disconnected also, but differently:

> I was on Haight Street bus and didn't feel it. Saw a couple broken windows & a toppled chimney & folks outside talking excitedly but I went to Flore for coffee & then sat zazen. Only afterwards did I begin to understand the magnitude of the event: walking home in total darkness & seeing my bookcase toppled, 2 windows broken. Didn't want to be alone & walked around the city looking for open bars. In a way I felt friendless during this time.

Two days after our phone call, I received an overnight package from Dad. He'd sent me crisp copies of the *San Francisco Chronicle* and *Examiner*, with their extensive reporting on the quake. Paging through the coverage in my hometown papers, instead of in the *New York Times*, the news felt more real. The earthquake killed sixty-three people throughout northern California and left more than 12,000 homeless. Along with the newspapers, my father mailed me a t-shirt. On the front, printed in red serif type, was "October 17, 1989. 5:04pm." Above the type was a black-and-white photo, the same image featured on every front page, showing the Bay Bridge, its upper roadway collapsed.

Thumbing through these papers and then pulling my new earthquake t-shirt over my head, I felt overwhelmed with love for Dad. Somehow he knew just what I needed at that moment. I ached with a longing to return home, to our apartment, to him. I wanted to fly home for the holidays but he'd already dipped into his savings to pay for the East Coast tour promoting *Holy Terror* and *View Askew* and didn't have the money. So while he was peeling and mashing ten pounds of potatoes for the Hartford Street Zen Center Thanksgiving, I was snacking on shrimp cocktail in the Weiksners' country home, feeling as fake as the painted papier-mâché fruits that decorated the dinner table.

I knew I was lonely and unhappy in New York. After a three-month respite from calorie counting in Paris, the margins of my school notebooks were again filling up with my detailed meal accounting. Then one night I hatched a plan. I could transfer to one of the highly rated University of California colleges, which could return me to California's warm bosom. The next day I phoned UC Santa Cruz and UC Berkeley, both close to the city, and asked them to mail me applications.

I made an appointment with an NYU counselor to explore what I'd need for a transfer. The counselor had me sit in a chair opposite hers in the dark office cubby where she worked. Adjusting her wire glasses, she asked me exactly why I wanted to leave NYU. I considered telling her about the earthquake, about Dad and his falling T-cell count, but I hadn't even told the Weiksners about Dad and just thinking about all of this made my head heavy and thick.

"I want to be closer to home," I sighed.

I returned to Third Avenue North that afternoon with a stack of NYU transfer forms, which I kept on the corner of my desk beneath the glossy UC applications that started arriving by mail. They pictured grassy campus quads under clear blue skies, a planet away from my bitter New York winter. But as the year progressed, I found myself caught in a powerful gust of readings, deadlines, and midterm exams. The UC applications and NYU forms were soon buried under a pile of clothes and books.

In San Francisco, my father was keeping himself busy. He organized an event with poets Judy Grahn and Allen Ginsberg at the University of San Francisco, attended by more than 600 people.

And he was invited to speak at the San Francisco Out/Write conference, which brought together 1,800 lesbians and gay men for three days of readings, panels, and talks. His panel was "Outrageous Queer Journalism."

The writer Edmund White attended the Out/Write conference the following year, 1991, where my father also organized a number of panels. In his *New York Times* op-ed about gay literature, "Out of the Closet and Onto the Bookshelf," White noted the irony that at the very moment that gay literature was flourishing, so many gay writers were threatened with extinction:

> Every other writer at the Out/Write conference appeared to be ill. People who were HIV positive (like me) exchanged T-cell counts as though they were the latest Wall Street figures. Many who were robust a year ago were now dramatically thin or blind or covered with lesions. During the last session of the last day of the conference a member of the audience seized the microphone, ostensibly to denounce [keynote speaker] Edward Albee once again. But in an instant the pale, emotional man had segued into a cry from the heart: "I wanted everything to be perfect since obviously I won't be at the conference next year."

Although Dad didn't share with me details of either conference, he did mail me articles he was writing on the impact of the AIDS crisis on the gay community for the *Sentinel*, the *Advocate*, and a new column of his own in the *Bay Guardian*. Young guys came up to him in bars and clubs saying how much they liked his writing, which delighted Dad greatly. But his journals reveal that finances were an ongoing concern. He'd cut down his involvement with *Poetry Flash*, which he'd stopped editing but where he was still a regular contributor, because he wanted to focus on better-paying assignments. Yet the money he was paid for editing Sam's anthology and for the articles and columns he wrote for the *Sentinel* and various weeklies was meager at best.

He was well liked at the University of San Francisco, where he was now teaching two expository writing classes three times a week, but a senior administrator there said that unless he got a master's degree he wouldn't be able to return in the spring. My father had been pursuing a master's in English at Emory University when he met my mom in the late sixties, but dropped out before graduation. To secure his job, he was now pursuing a graduate writing degree at San Francisco State.

For the last year, my father had been supporting himself with freelance legal summarizing which he did from home, but his boss had disbanded the company for "personal reasons." The AIDS Emergency Fund paid Dad's rent that March.

He applied and interviewed for several jobs, including one at *Mother Jones*. But halfway through that interview he was asked to name his greatest character defect. "Moodiness," he answered. "I'm not going to write that down," said his interviewer, "or you'll immediately be disqualified." She then advised my dad to pick up some books on interviewing techniques. In his journal he wrote, "She must have liked me to give me this advice." He didn't get the job.

Despite these setbacks, Dad continued to send me money, as he had started to do as soon as I left for New York. "I will be sending you $2,000 of your social security checks over the next four months," he wrote to me when I started school. "Will make it tough on me financially but its yours & I want you to have every opportunity over this next year. It you don't need it for school, you could put in into savings & use it to pay for travel expenses or whatever."

In fact I did need it for school. When Dede helped me apply

to NYU, she assumed it would be priced like the University of California system. Instead NYU, which billed itself "a Private University in the Public Service," was among the most expensive colleges in the country. What my grandparents couldn't cover I made up with student loans, financial aid, and my father's Social Security checks. Another incentive for transferring into a University of California college was that it would be much less expensive. In letters, Dad checked on my progress: "Hope you've gotten your applications in for UC Berkeley & UC Santa Cruz too. I hear the latter is best for undergrad, but if you went to Berkeley you could stay here again. It would be nice to see more of you, kiddo." But for some reason I failed to complete these applications, let alone mail them in. While I missed Dad and the city, I was also ambivalent about returning home—I suspect, because I was afraid.

In French class that spring I made friends with a Jersey girl named Lauren. The spitting image of Raphael's Virgin Mary, she loved opera, small dogs, and everything French. She'd even named her shih tzu Bisou ("kiss"). Whenever Lauren became excited, which was often, her face flushed crimson and her voice trilled like a young girl's. One day as we were heading to a favorite café after class, she told me she'd applied to NYU's junior year abroad program in Paris.

"I just spent last summer in Paris," I told her. "I worked at a law firm near the Champs Elys—"

"Oh. My. God," she interrupted, gripping my arm. "You should *totally* apply! We could be there *together*!"

When we finished our cappuccinos, she walked me to the Maison Française, NYU's "French House," where I picked up an application.

Remembering my summer as a Parisienne, the beauty of rural Brittany, and the kindness of the Norman girl, I completed my application that evening. When I received the letter in April telling me I'd been accepted into the NYU in France program I telephoned my dad, ecstatic. He was thrilled because I was thrilled. But of course, instead of moving closer to him, I was making plans to move farther away.

18.

I FELT A DEEP CHILL walking along Avenue Mozart. On a Sunday night, all the area shops were closed. Only a few *boulangeries*, with their pristine tarts and pastries glistening under glass, still welcomed the neighbor picking up her last-minute dessert or baguette for dinner. Other than the yellow glow emitted by these bakeries, the neighborhood was a resolute gray, all the windows shuttered. There were few if any pedestrians, and the ones I did see were hushed, buttoned up in their secret journeys. Everything here felt sealed, like flower buds before the bloom, all the beauty hidden.

We are a neighborhood, the 16th arrondissement told me, not a playground. Our streets are walked only by our neighbors.

I was a neighbor. I lived at 23 Rue de la Source. My Métro stop was Métro Jasmin, which I jokingly referred to as Métro Jasmine, as though it were a hippie refuge and not the heart of bourgeois Paris. The intersection of Avenue Mozart and Rue de Passy, near the NYU in France building, was teeming with young BCBGs (*bon chic, bon genre*), French preppies who wore pearls, headbands, and cashmere sweaters. They kissed each other twice on each cheek, instead of the customary one kiss, and were notoriously *coincé*, uptight.

But I was not *coincée*; I didn't belong to this neighborhood, I simply lived here, in the Lazars' *chambre de bonne*, the maid's room. Through the glass front door I could see the lace curtains of the concierge's window part, her coal-black eyes suspiciously following me, whenever I came in and out of the building.

Every year the Lazars took in students from the NYU program. In exchange for lodging in their sixth-floor walk-up attic, the students were to iron the Lazars' laundry for two hours a day and be an English-speaking "presence" for their twelve-year-old son between his return from school and their return from work.

Like many French families, the Lazars owned a washer but, with no dryer, line-dried all of their clothing. To remove the resulting stiffness I ironed every article, from their dishtowels to their underwear. Edouard, their doughy redheaded teenager with a lazy gait, preferred to watch TV and eat *les brownies* than to speak English with me, so I let him. At seven o'clock, when the Lazars returned from work, I walked up the back stairs to my little garret, where I'd eat alone and read back issues of *Madame Figaro*, kindly given to me by Madame Lazar.

"I have this private joke between me, myself and I," I wrote to Dad early that fall. "A lot of my friends are looking into health clubs. For $300 they want access to saunas & Stairmasters and I have to laugh because I get all of this for free at the Lazars'! I steam my face as I iron, and walk 6 flights of stairs at least 2 times a day going to my room."

As far as maid's rooms go, mine was, in fact, quite comfortable. I had a wardrobe to hang my clothes, a small refrigerator, sink, counter, and hotplate where I stirred instant Knorr soups, which Monsieur Lazar brought me from his job at Nestle. I slept in a full-size bed layered in blankets, where I read books for school and watched the French evening news on a small black-and-white TV. Looking out my window I could see the tiled roofs of the 16th, where pigeons gathered in pockets of gray and black.

I was happy to be back in Paris. My fluency in French and the Métro, and the occasional visits with Camille (who was studying that year in Madrid), gave me a sense of possibility. "In Paris where life is already more liveable, I am a free agent," I wrote to my dad. "I have my own space and that is important."

But by January 1991, a deep malaise had set in. The Weiksners generously flew me to New York for Christmas, but I had to return to France by January 2 to resume my work for the Lazars. School was closed for winter break and the friends I made in the fall were all home for the month. Théophile, a slim blond Frenchman whom I'd met at a Cleary Gottlieb holiday party and had recently started dating, was stationed outside Paris, on military service. The previous August, Saddam Hussein had invaded Kuwait, and George Bush was counting down the days before American troops were to invade Iraq. NYU faculty advised us to avoid groups of loud Americans, not to sing American songs, and not even to walk home the same route twice, thinking that if we did we might be attacked by local Muslims. All the garbage bins in the Métro stations were removed for fear of bombs. The only thing that made the winter of 1990 bearable for me were my father's letters.

Each day I arrived at the NYU Center, the first place I stopped was my mailbox. It was in this thin wooden slot, sandwiched between other mailboxes, that I found the source of my sustaining hope and joy. Arriving two, sometimes three times a week, Dad's letters made me notorious in the program. No other student received so much mail, especially from a parent.

My father's letters always arrived in business envelopes, long and rectangular, deliciously heavy. I delighted in the mountain range of As that crowded the front of the envelope: Steve *Abbott*, 545 *Ashbury*, *Alysia Abbott*. As I tore open the envelopes, the pages of ruled paper, edges frayed from being ripped out of my dad's spiral notebook, unfurled like Christmas wrapping in my lap. The gift inside this wrapping was the density of my father's script, filling each narrow college rule: words, sentences, paragraphs, and pages—all for me!

These words were written, I knew, to the rhythm of my father's twitching foot. Deep in thought, he always wrote with his right leg crossed over his left, his notebook balanced on his right knee, his dangling right foot twitching from side to side as though it alone motored his overactive intellect.

Even now, when I remember my father writing, I unconsciously throw my right leg over my left and mimic his twitching. It feels remarkably natural, this twitch. That right foot can get going with instinctual ease, but when I try to reverse the legs and twitch my left foot I can't do it. There's something in that right foot, something I like to imagine I inherited from him.

With my yearly trips to Kewanee, Dad and I had been writing to each other for years. But something changed that year in France. With both of us living on our own, thousands of miles apart, we relied on letters to be close. And in these letters we were no longer looking to the other as the cause, or solution, of our respective problems, but instead as a loving witness, a devoted and concerned audience.

Where Dad had described our needs mixing "like fire and oil" when I was a teenager living at home, in letters we felt free to confide crushes, test new ideas, and wrestle with frustrations and fears.

I no longer criticized his boyfriends (or the boys he wished could be more than friends). If I didn't have anything nice to say about another misbegotten crush (Alex, Jeremy, Myles, Olivier), I could easily keep those feelings to myself. I was no longer disappointed by Dad's preoccupation with work, because I no longer looked to him as the source of my company and care. The ups and downs of his romantic adventures, his professional trials and economic woes, no longer crowded my living space.

Because we sometimes had to wait two weeks for a response, each carefully composed letter became an act of faith, like a coin thrown into a well, along with a fervent secret wish. After writing, I hoped most to hear that echo, that confirmation that my wish would be heard and answered. Since I didn't want to wait for Dad's reply before writing to him again, I decided early on to write whenever I wanted. We wrote each other almost every day, our letters like diary entries, especially Dad's:

> Yesterday I was thinking you're the only person I love. Others I'm only fond of from time to time. Sometimes I feel loved but oftentimes I feel that no one loves me, no one I ever want is attracted to me & that I've lost the capacity to love. I have to keep constant vigilance with myself so as <u>not</u> to fall in love w/ Alex. What he wants & needs is just my friendship.

It's Dad's emotional availability that most strikes me. Making my way through the pages of his letters, I feel as if I'm settling into a bathtub full of warm water. Weightless and floating, at peace, I am caressed by the near-constant expression of my father's trust and attention. In this watery world I am that version of self that I knew before any other: daughter. And in this role I am loved as only a child can be loved: wholly and without condition. With my father I felt no pressure to behave in any particular way. I could be trite, boring, selfish, petulant. I never felt there was anything I could do or say that would jeopardize his affection. This is the father I always wanted. This is the father that I miss the most.

There are the many articles and essays he clipped for me from the local paper, about Paris's Moreau museum or the latest research on why girls suffer low self-esteem. He writes one letter on the back of Sylvia Plath's poem "Daddy." "Certainly a different take on Daddy than you have – or is it?" he jokes before going into an analysis of why it works. "Plath's genius in this poem is to invest very <u>simple</u> language (nursery rhyme & fairytale) with intense power & anger."

There are his own impromptu poems:

> *The arms of the bookstore are full*
> *of postcards & tee-shirts.*
> *The coffee has triumphed.*
> *I got several letters today & read*
> *Yours (of Dec. 4) first.*

And there is the vividness of his San Francisco, which was also my San Francisco—his seeing a film noir series at the Roxie, picking up a biography of Baudelaire at the Adobe bookstore, or sipping on a mocha at the Macondo.

Am sitting in Tassajara Café. Very cute guy sitting @ next table w/his friend or boyfriend, unfortunately. I assumed he was gay right off, before hearing them talk even – something about his delicate manner. Straight guys tend to be more aggressive, less refined, in their non-verbal behavior. Baseless stereotype? <u>You</u> be the judge.

And then there is that version of me. I never liked my self as much as the self I saw reflected in my father's eyes. He continued to delight in my letters, even with my incessant worrying, my silly self-pity: "Lauren spends money like it was nothing. Her mother was just here and bought her all these clothes. Everything Lauren wears looks so new!!!"

Again and again he asks me questions. He entertains, instructs, and inspires, always working to build me up, up, up.

I always enjoy reading your letters, even when you're blue. When Henry Miller lived in Paris he always ate off friends. And Appollinaire was so poor he imagined the favorite meals of his childhood when he was hungry. Lynn Tillman says she was the poorest person she knew in NYC, even though she once worked for Malcolm Forbes. Money isn't everything. I certainly value my friends & having time to write more.

When I despaired over my confusion about what to do with my life, fearing that I'd already failed, Dad offered advice on ways to clarify my goals and then detailed how he met his own:

I know you're sensitive to all the expectations that your grandparents, the Weiksners, me, etc. have for you. And that's an irritating bother to say the least.

But how about this: make a list of what kind of life you want (don't worry "can I do it, get it" whatever – just honestly list what you want regardless of whether it seems unrealistic or not). Then: prioritize. What do you think you really want most? What goals seem more realistic or doable to you? What steps would be needed to realize them? Is taking those steps something you enjoy?

For me, for instance, I wanted to be a writer – a famous writer. (Now I don't care so much about the "famous" part). The steps involved a) reading a lot to see what other writers are doing or have done b) writing & improving my writing and c) getting my writing out in the world – which meant taking risks & overcoming fear of judgment or ridicule at times.

But this didn't happen for me @ age 20 – it didn't really get started till I was 32 & afterwards.

When I wrote him about Lauren's growing friendship with another classmate in the program, and how their friendship made me jealous, he advised me to transcend these feelings, teaching

me the precepts he'd learned in his Zen practice, yet never pushing me down a Buddhist path.

> Through meditation or reflection or whatever, find out how
> to go to that place in yourself that can observe without
> judging. If you feel jealous, or depressed, or guilty – just try
> to pay attention to how your body feels. Where does the
> physical feeling start? Does a tightness go up or down your
> stomach for instance. If you notice that you're being critical
> of yourself – then try to observe yourself doing this without
> judging it as good or bad.
>
> This observer self is the deepest part of you – deeper
> than your fearful self, guilty self, emotional self, or intellec-
> tual self. By observing what's happening to your body when
> you go into these head states, you can learn little tricks to
> alter your body & mood. Like if you catch it early, try coun-
> tering the negative physical feeling or emotion by doing
> something nurturing for yourself (exercise or pleasant bath,
> calling a friend, going to a movie, or whatever).
>
> Anyway, this is something I started doing at a time in my
> life when I was wracked by jealousy, loneliness, self-doubt,
> excessive self-criticism. And overall it worked.

Until this chapter, I've relied on my father's journals and published work to understand the nature of his creative passions,
addictions, and relationships, but rereading these letters I feel
him right here with me, like a beloved whispering in my ear—the
way he ends with "Think of you <u>always</u>!" or draws on the back of
an envelope in big block letters: "Believe In Yourself! Love Life!
NEVER GIVE UP!"

My father worked so hard to nurture me in these exchanges
because he knew his time was limited—which is why the hand-

written letters feel like such a gift now. Each is a unique artifact, pressed with the imprint of his pen on the paper. Each one has a different sign-off, with postscripts scribbled in the margins, the occasional cartoon to illustrate a point.

These missives are all the more poignant for me now because I know that he was suffering from a fatal disease. He was the one facing his mortality and living in a community steeped in death. The week before I left for France, Issan Dorsey, Hartford Street's abbot and Dad's beloved spiritual teacher, died of AIDS.

Despite the loss of his friends and countless acquaintances, Dad spent page after page attending to me in far-off Paris, especially when I worried over the idea of a life without him.

I asked Theo whether he thought it a good idea if you stay with me when you come to Paris. "I don't know," he answered, "you have 6 flights of stairs and your dad's not that young anymore." I started thinking about not having you around to give me your words of wisdom and unconditional love . . . I ended up going into the bathroom and weeping until I regained control. I didn't feel like crying in front of Theo. That's not to say we're not close. In fact, I become more in love with him each day. I just don't feel like going into the details of your *maladie*. And of course, your sexual preference.

When I wrote this letter in April 1991, Dad had just had a tube put into his chest so he could give himself infusions of ganciclovir, prescribed for the CMV retinitis stripping him of his vision. "I feel like both Frankenstein and Frankenstein's monster," he joked. But he was sad too. He wrote how he would never swim again, would never take a sauna again. But I, an oblivious twenty-year-old, didn't respond to these reports or even consider the effect of these losses on his morale. Instead it was he who did the heavy lifting, the hard work of calming and distracting me from that terrible inevitable.

As for my health, you needn't weep until I die. I mean I know you'll die sometime soon too, everyone will, but I needn't focus on that. You needn't either. What you tell Theo about my health is up to you. I think the more honest you can be (esp. with those close to you) the happier one can be. Secretiveness = loneliness. You could tell him I have health problems w/o going into details – like I have retinitis & lung trouble or something. The girl in Femme Nikita doesn't tell her boyfriend anything about her past, esp. that she's an assassin – but he finds out anyway. And still loves her.

It was easy for me to minimize the decline of Dad's health because his letters were still so full of humor:

Odd, the more trouble my health is in, the better my spirits. I can hardly read or see to recognize anyone on the street so I make jokes about it, say it's like being on an acid trip. What else can one do?

In another letter:

I'm getting fat since I stopped smoking. I did weigh an average of 145 lbs. now it's a bit over 150. I can hardly squeeze into any of my jeans. But I'm going to keep all these smaller jeans cuz I may end up w/ wasting syndrome sometime & they'll be baggy on me. (a little joke, hee hee).

I didn't respond to these reports beyond the occasional "Please be healthy" because I was reluctant to invest in them any more power than they already had. I also hoped that if I ignored this subplot in our story, it might recede and I could freely enjoy my Paris adventures unhindered. For the most part, this strategy worked. That is, until my father came to visit me in the summer of 1991.

19.

WHEN MY FATHER came to visit me in Paris that June, I was already living the life of *une femme*, a woman, or what I then considered the life of a woman. I'd completed my junior year and now, at twenty, I was in my first serious relationship, living with a twenty-four-year-old Frenchman in his apartment in a mostly Muslim section of the 18th arrondissement. Théophile was the youngest in a good Catholic family of six but considered himself *branché*, "plugged in." When we started dating, he told me he liked the Smiths, adding, "I wear black on the outside because black is how I feel on the inside."

Over my six months dating and two months living with Théophile, or Theo, as I called him, I transformed myself into a model French girlfriend. I cultivated my own version of the BCBG style—less *coincé*, more retro. I wore my hair in a neat bob, with flirty dresses and lipstick, and a polka-dot scarf knotted around my neck just so. And every night I prepared us a three-course dinner: appetizer, main course, followed by a dessert or cheese plate. I enjoyed finding recipes in the small paperback cookbook given to me by Theo's elegant, perfumed mother.

It wasn't so difficult to prepare a decent trout almondine or chicken dijonnais with crème fraîche, I discovered, as long as you had fresh ingredients. I loved shopping at the outdoor markets, planning our meals for the week, and making sure the bowl on the front table was always full of fresh fruit.

Living with Theo, I cultivated a fantasy of my adult self: independent, sophisticated, mature. We played the Sundays and the La's on our stereo, their dreamy pop harmonies filling the apartment, providing the soundtrack to our still new love. I felt that everything was as it should be.

One June afternoon, sitting in our living room, I wasn't planning a meal but sifting through a stack of Paris hotel guides, while Theo sat in the sun-dappled kitchen drinking his morning *café* and reading *Libération*. Applying myself to this task with the same rigor I'd applied to my research papers earlier in the year, I copied numbers out of *Paris Pas Cher* into a small notebook, phoned each hotel, noting their rooms' availability and cost, and then marked a neat check next to those that had a refrigerator guests could use. Dad needed a refrigerator for his medication.

I'd been urging Dad to visit all year. "What I'd really like for Christmas is you," I wrote to him. But he kept insisting he hadn't the health or money to travel. Finally he booked tickets for May with his friend Alex, but had to cancel this trip because of a complication related to his CMV retinitis. Determined to visit, he rescheduled the trip for June against the advice of his doctor and friends.

MY FATHER was a rich man in Paris. In San Francisco we'd skimped and saved. No piece of furniture was bought new; everything was found at garage sales or marked down, as were our clothes. But in Paris my father was loose with his francs, buying any blouse or dress that caught my fancy. "I like to see you in nice clothes," he told me as I posed and turned in the shop mirrors. We went out every night and he barely looked at the check before spreading his francs like Monopoly money across the tabletop.

What my father didn't spend that week he put in an envelope

and handed to me before taking a cab to catch his flight home to San Francisco. There was this feeling that we're in Paris—this world is not our world. This is not real money. Why worry?

But on our first afternoon together in Paris, when we met for a coffee in Montmartre, I didn't yet know the flush side of my father. I explained to Dad how it was cheaper to take a coffee standing at the bar than to sit at a table. I was still tight with money, still used to being a student. But he wanted to sit. His legs were tired. He was easily tired that trip. So we sat on the terrace outside. The sun was shining, so every other seat was taken. The cobblestone streets were stacked with parked *motos*, the Vespas that young Parisians drove everywhere. The angry wasp buzz of their engines echoed through the neighborhood's narrow alleys and hills. We sat at Café des Abbesses across from a blinking merry-go-round. The trees were in bloom. The summer air warmed me and I felt good.

Our plan was to walk up to Sacré-Coeur, but Dad didn't know if he was up for the hill and the many flights of stairs. "It's not far from here," I said, splitting a cube of sugar for my espresso. He sat tapping the saucer of his *café crème* with his narrow, cigarette-stained fingers.

"That's okay," he said, looking at the table.

I suggested we go to the Musée d'Orsay, my favorite Paris museum, the next day. That semester I'd studied nineteenth-century history along with the French realist writers Flaubert and Balzac. I enjoyed seeing the art of that period against the literary and historical context I knew so well.

"That's okay," he said again.

He'd already seen the Musée d'Orsay. Just as he'd already seen Notre-Dame and the Musée Picasso and Place des Vosges and everywhere else I suggested we visit.

"I've seen them all," he said, then after a pause added, "I'm here to see you."

He spoke his words calmly as he sipped his *café crème*. And for a moment I felt uncomfortable, just as many times in my life my father's love left me feeling uncomfortable—how at thirteen I had snarled "What are you smiling at?" when I caught him grinning at me with big eyes across the dinner table, and he had answered, "I'm just amazed that I've raised this beautiful young woman."

His love always surprised me. It could be jarring, because it would spring from nowhere and certainly seemed to bear no relationship to my actions. It was as though my father loved me for just sitting there in front of him, before his eyes, and returning his gaze, listening to him, and speaking. This was how he looked at me that day at the café. It was too easy.

It had been a year since my last visit with Dad and I was careful to notice any changes in his appearance. He still wore his round tortoiseshell glasses. He still wore his hair cut short and dyed brown, which made him look younger than his forty-seven years. He still had his smudgy moustache and goatee, which he kept trimmed with scissors from the kitchen drawer. He even still had weight to his face and body. But after we left the café, he stopped every other block to catch his breath. And he talked. He talked a lot, mostly about the past. I remember passing through the turnstile of the Métro back to my apartment and my father's mouth just going.

"I didn't really have my first relationship until I was in grad school myself. Sometimes it takes a while to get your self-esteem up for it. But I always had lots of interests—reading, art, travel, getting involved in politics—where I could get my satisfaction, so when I *did* get interested in someone, like your mom, there was something to be interested in ... Why's this not working?"

"Dad, you're putting in the wrong ticket. You have to use a new one. Try again."

"A main thing your mom and I had in common, at first, was

the antiwar movement. *There, that's better.* We were in a social-
ist group that sold militant newspapers. Your mom was the top
salesperson!"

I nodded. Smiled. And, looking around, felt embarrassed. The
French have a habit of openly staring at anyone who stands out,
and Dad was standing out. I wanted to explain his behavior but
barely understood it myself. It was as if his life were passing before
his eyes and he wanted to describe everything he saw, now,
before dementia stripped him of his memories. But I didn't have
a tape recorder, and I was still not attuned to this idea—*his end.*

Aside from his fatigue, and the cooler of medical supplies we
lugged from the airport to the hotel, and his rambling voice, I was
struck by a certain gentleness in his face. It still startles me in a
photo we took the next afternoon with Théophile at the Jardin des
Plantes. Dad is standing in a window, awash in sun, wearing an
R. Crumb t-shirt and a blue denim shirt, unbuttoned and rolled at
the sleeves. As he looks at me through the camera's eye, his head
is tilted slightly back, as though he's both surprised and delighted
that I am capturing him on film. Then there's that sweetness. It
was as if all his rough edges had been filed down—all the negativ-
ity, the irritability and know-it-all-ness that bothered me when I
was a teenager. It was as if AIDS had reduced Dad to his essential
core, which was gentle and good.

When I look at this photo now, I have a powerful desire to
swoop in and protect that sweetness. I want to wrap him in a blanket and feed him hot tea. I want to apologize too, for all the trouble
I caused: for my disrespect and the petty meanness I sometimes
resorted to, wanting to hurt him because I was hurting. I want to
make him happy.

But I wasn't capable of these feelings then. I still wanted him
to make *me* feel better, to keep *me* warm and safe. I believed he
owed me that security. And his coming to Paris the way he did,

lugging that cooler of medical supplies, planning to tell me what he planned to tell me, felt like betrayal.

AFTER OUR VISIT to the Jardin des Plantes, Dad, Theo, and I went out for an early dinner at a Greek restaurant. It was still warm and sunny when we sat down on the terrace. We drank sweet white wine from a carafe, listened to the music pouring out of a nearby window, and watched the neighborhood Greek restaurateurs accosting potential customers as they passed in the street. Dialogue between Theo and Dad was stilted but friendly. They shared an interest in history and Baudelaire, but the level of Dad's French and Theo's English prevented anything but superficial conversation. When Theo excused himself to use the bathroom, I turned to Dad and asked him what he thought of my first real boyfriend. Dad stared into the middle distance before answering, "Bourgeois. You're both much more bourgeois than I was in my twenties. But I'm okay with that."

My face crumpled in disapointment before he added with a chuckle, "No, no. Theo seems very nice. But don't you think it'd be hard to marry someone from another culture?"

Wait, what? At twenty I hardly knew what I was going to do for the rest of the summer, let alone with my French boyfriend. But before I could answer, Theo returned and we changed topics. Later, after dinner, we walked my father to the closest taxi stand, and as we crossed the busy Boulevard Saint-Germain, my father turned to me, looked into my eyes, and said, "I only wish I could see you as a harried mother."

THEO WAS AT WORK when Dad and I took the train to the grounds of Château Fontainbleau. We were sitting outside, near the spot where Emperor Napoleon bid farewell to his guard before going into exile in 1814, when my father finally revealed his news: "Last November I was diagnosed with pneumocystosis."

"I know, Dad. You wrote me about it. It's like a really bad cold. Sounded awful. I'm sorry."

"Pneumocystosis is a form of pneumonia. PCP pneumonia. Where before I had ARC—AIDS-related condition—this diagnosis means I now have full-blown AIDS."

I looked around the magnificent grounds of Fontainebleau, which stretched out across the horizon. The perfect order of the landscape was marred only by a huddle of tourists ambling by, taking pictures and shading their eyes from the severe noon sun. I looked back at Dad, who was staring intently at me with gentle green eyes. His hands were busy, moving in the air, explaining. Though I knew he was talking to me, I felt as if I were far away. I imagined myself joining that clumsy crowd hurrying back to their bus. I could see myself boarding the bus and then watching the father and daughter talking on the bench as the bus pulled away.

"Pneumocystosis means full-blown AIDS," he repeated. He might only have a year to live. Or six months. "You have to make arrangements to graduate early and move home," he said, "now that I have full-blown AIDS."

Such a strange expression, I thought to myself: "full-blown AIDS." Why "full-blown"? I imagined being blown away, as in, "Wow, that really blew me away." Or I thought of an orchid in the summer, its petals expanded to their full blossom, exploding with gaudy color, sticky nectar, and scent. I pictured something blown apart, like a dandelion, fully blown until nothing is left but the naked stem.

Before that trip to Paris, my father's illness was just a series of letters—HIV, ARC, AIDS—and the letters he wrote me describing the ailments that attended these acronyms. *CMV-blah-blah-itis. Pneumo-blah-blah.* No matter how much detail he provided about his condition, these were still abstract concepts scribbled onto a page. I returned the letters to their envelopes just as I put away the feelings these letters provoked. I wrote off Dad's ailments as just more complaining.

We were both famous complainers, after all. When we lived together in San Francisco, I bought him a card for his fortieth birthday depicting the front cover of a fictitious magazine, *Bad Mood Monthly,* with headlines like "143 Ways to Say 'I Don't Like It,'" "How to Make Your Loved Ones Feel Like Hell," and "Whining & Dining." We kept that card stuck on our fridge with a magnet for years. It was a playful reminder of our cranky natures. Calling Dad from my NYU dorm, I entertained him with tales of my miserable trip to the A&P and the walk home in the spitting rain, my arms straining from the weight of the grocery bags. He always laughed in the right places. Complaining was our inside joke.

Not until he visited me that summer in Paris did I see how these ailments he detailed were not only real, but as his daughter they were my concerns as well. Each was like a heavy stone being laid on a road toward his inevitable death.

THE CONVERSATION that had started at Fontainebleau continued later that night outside an overpriced brasserie in Montmartre. As Dad and I meandered after dinner, he started to list what he'd leave me: an old PC that barely worked, his computer table, his shelves of dusty, dog-eared books, and of course any profits from his writing.

"I've named Kevin Killian my literary executer. He'll make sure you get anything the books could make. I've drawn up papers."

"Okay." I blinked at the apartment buildings and the people swarming around us. Swallowing hard, I avoided Dad's eyes. A tightness gripped my chest.

"More importantly, how soon can you graduate?" he asked. "Do you have money saved to leave at a moment's notice if you need to?"

Shut up, I kept thinking. "I don't know," I answered quietly, teeth clenched, "I have to see."

My twenty-year-old self was imploding. Wills, executor, computer table, graduate early? For months he'd told me not to worry or cry over his sickness. All that exists is right now, he told me. And then he comes to Paris, *my* Paris, where on a recent weekend I'd effortlessly cooked up rhubarb from the garden of Theo's country house. With just a little water and sugar it was so delicious and so sweet. I'd looked forward to Dad's visit for months. I wanted to share these discoveries with him, to introduce him to Theo and our life here. And he then comes to tell me that this life is over. That I must return home, that the time to worry is now. Because he has full-blown AIDS.

Dad was unremitting. Dodging tourists on their way to Sacré-Coeur, he chased me around the narrow cobblestone streets, trying to hammer out this crazy plan of his. I felt a great weight pressing down on me, pulling on my shoulders and chest, like the lead apron dentists make you wear before taking your X-ray. I wanted so much to lie down, to unburden myself of this conversation and float away into the Paris sky. But my father pressed on, his energy renewed by determination.

"You have to look into this," he said, stopping me so he could look me squarely in the eye. "I think you should plan to move home by Christmas. Do you think you could move home by Christmas?"

"Okay!" There was no question; of course I'd move home. If

not me, who? But my head kept spinning, unwilling or unable to absorb what all of this meant.

Before the introduction of protease inhibitors in the mid-nineties, AIDS was considered a death sentence. And that death was a hard death, promising either physical degradation (purple lesions, wasting syndrome,) mental degradation, or both. But for all the fear AIDS provoked, the nature of the disease was inherently confusing, especially as it was diagnosed in stages. You could test positive for the HIV virus without having symptoms. You could be sick with AIDS-related condition (ARC) without "having" AIDS. Only when you were diagnosed with certain specific illnesses—pneumocystosis, for example—did you have "full-blown AIDS." Only then was death near.

Before Dad came to Paris, I'd sought refuge in my ignorance about these stages, in the dense thicket of medical jargon that separated living with HIV from dying of AIDS. Dad was my accidental conspirator—downplaying his HIV status before he showed any symptoms, insisting he didn't have AIDS when he was only suffering from AIDS-related condition, and only telling me he had full-blown AIDS when he felt it necessary for me to make plans to return home.

He wanted me to enjoy my college experience as fully and for as long as I could. But the problem with this otherwise sensible strategy was that when it came time for him to tell me he was truly sick and dying, I was unprepared for the reality.

I tried to recount my night to Theo. He already knew Dad was sick with an AIDS-related condition, but like me had a hard time grasping the distinction my father detailed. I raged at his "stupidity" before devolving into a puddle of tears in the bathroom.

When I finally told Munca that Dad had AIDS, I wanted to throw up. I was sitting on the floor of our kitchen, leaning against the closed door in a parody of privacy. Munca seemed to respond to my news as though she were expecting the call.

"Yes, okay," she answered calmly. "What do you need from us?"

Choking back sobs, I couldn't answer at first. I felt dumb and foolish.

"I don't know," I said finally. "Nothing, I guess."

Theo lacked the intuition to understand why I had a meltdown in the freezer section of our local grocery store later that afternoon, exploding into tears because of a conflict over frozen moussaka. And he didn't know why I started crying the next day when, late to meet my father, I didn't have time to buy fresh fruit at the open market.

"But I need to eat a piece of fresh fruit every day," I yelled.

"What is *wrong* with you, Alysia?"

"I always have fresh fruit. *Don't you understand? This* is what I want. I don't want this *other* life!"

July 2nd, 1991

Dear Alysia –

Just got home and unpacked. It's 11:20 pm SF time. I guess Paris time is 8:20 am July 3rd.

Somehow I'm sad right now – back in the same old rut of medical appointments & visits to the same old tired cafés here. Paris felt so much nicer to be in, but I suppose the longer one would live there, the more one would just get into ruts there – take all the beautiful architecture for granted like you said.

If I tried to imagine a "perfect daughter" I couldn't imagine any one better than you. I could tell you and Theo really put effort into making my stay enjoyable – not only getting that nice hotel but also the places we ate, fixing food for me yourself, lugging around w/ me to the party at the Pompidou Center & the Jardin des Plantes. And I want you to know how much I appreciate your love.

I'm sorry too that the state of my health is, understandably, a sadness for you. I think some of your irritation & grouchiness were probably because you feel bad & you get angry that this is my situation – our situation. But it would probably be better to know you're angry because I have AIDS & that doctors haven't found a cure for it yet than to shift your anger to all sorts of other things – not having time to get fruit or whatever.

Sometimes I get really angry too. I got especially angry when I had to cancel my earlier planned trip to Europe – but as it turned out, I probably had more time to visit with you than I would have otherwise. Or I get angry that I can't see like I'd like to. So I get angry & feel the emotions & then I realize – since there's nothing I can really do to change things – I might as well accept life as it is. Hanging onto anger only wears one out – & it's hard on those around you. And I realize there's still a great deal in life to enjoy & be thankful for. In fact AIDS has become my spiritual teacher teaching me what's important & what's not & to let go of unproductive mental habits that aren't really necessary.

I really like that I can now imagine you more vividly in your environment – in Theo's kitchen cooking, or sitting reading, or walking down the street or in the Metro.

Will head off to the post office now.

much love,
your Dad

20.

AFTER DAD LEFT France, I was restless. I no longer wanted to wait in Theo's empty apartment for him to return from work. Neither did I want to live off his meager wages for the remainder of the summer. I could have returned to New York, but there was nothing requiring me there before September and I didn't want to leave Theo; we were still in love. So I went job hunting, diligently submitting resumés, signing up with employment agencies, working job boards and all of Theo's contacts. But jobs in Paris were scarce, especially for young Americans on student visas. No one answered my applications and my follow-up calls were ignored.

By the time I walked into La Criée I was three weeks into my search. I sat in a booth across from Véronique, the skinny brunette manager of this seafood chain in Neuilly-sur-Seine, a wealthy suburb north of Paris famous for its mayor, the future French president, Nicolas Sarkozy. The lunch hour had just finished and she was interviewing me. "La Criée hires new waitresses every summer," she explained, barely meeting my eyes. "With the terrace open, it's our busiest time of year." She said all of this in French with me eagerly nodding along, hoping to elicit a smile that never came. "We're looking for someone with restaurant experience. Are you experienced?"

Everything about Véronique was stern, from the severe high ponytail that stretched her face taut, to her thin-lipped grimace, to her immaculately applied makeup and manicured nails. Véronique was the first person to answer one of my applications (and perhaps the last), so I boldly lied, telling her that I'd worked in a restaurant before (I hadn't) and that I was planning to stay in Paris through September (I was leaving at the end of August).

After asking me some questions about my studies, she looked me up and down and, after pursing her lips, gave me the job on the spot, along with my uniform—a pleated navy blue skirt, matching blue and white striped shirt, and a small folding corkscrew I was to keep hooked over my skirt's elastic waistband.

On my first day, I was trained by Maggie, an eighteen-year-old daughter of Moroccan immigrants. She'd left home at sixteen, quit school because it bored her, and had been living on her own ever since. Though two years younger than me, she was hard as nails and it was clear that she resented having to train me, this privileged, know-nothing American. She tsk'ed at my every question, rolled her eyes at my every mistake. And I made many mistakes.

La Criée, "the Shucker" in French, was known for its raw bar. This meant that each appetizer and entrée required a unique fork and side. Oysters on the half shell, for example, required a tiny oyster fork be placed outside the salad fork, and were accompanied by a little dish of vinegar and minced shallot (*mignonette*). Lobsters required a separate set of flatware, including a lobster pick and a nutcracker. In addition to keeping track of these various tools and sides, there was the challenge of carrying everything. La Criée's terrace was located a floor below the main restaurant. You picked up your order in the kitchen—say, a mixed raw seafood platter (*fruits de mer*) presented on a bed of ice chips—then you had to snake through the indoor tables past the front door and a large line of people waiting for a table, then gingerly descend a set of concrete steps to your customers on the terrace below. The steps were steep. My first day on the job I saw another girl drop a platter of cocktails on her way downstairs and burst into tears. I later learned that the cost of the drinks and glasses was taken from her paycheck.

Véronique was the only French native on staff. The waitresses could have formed a model UN, with girls from Spain, Poland, Austria, Germany, Tunisia, and Thailand, Maggie the French-Moroccan, and me, the American. After a few days on the job, I figured out why. Management worked us like dogs. Only girls working under the table would put up with this shit.

Everyone worked the five-hour lunch and dinner shifts four days a week. The girls each had one day a week on which they worked only lunch, but on this day you worked seven hours, polishing the brass bar, mopping the floor, pulling up and hosing the upstairs rubbernet flooring, and replenishing the wine and spirits from the dank wine cave. As exhausting as this work could be, it was a cakewalk compared to the dinner shift.

La Criée had no busboys. Each waitress had to set her own tables, pour water, take orders, serve, and clear between courses and at the end of dinner, all in humid 90-degree temperatures. It was the hardest job I ever worked. From lifting and balancing trays of food and drinks back and forth in the restaurant, up and down the concrete stairs, my uniform was soaked with sweat by ten o'clock every night.

The bartendress, a kinky-haired Tunisian, stirred up tall glasses of cold water and Torani crème de menthe syrup for each of the waitresses to swallow as we passed her station between the kitchen and the terrace below. She handed us the drinks when we whizzed by, as if we were marathon runners in our final lap.

I was especially grateful for this gesture, because the bartendress was otherwise not my fan. The *idiote Américaine*, as she called me, didn't even know how to properly uncork a wine bottle. And since 99.5 percent of my tables ordered a bottle of wine with dinner (this being France), my inability to open bottles became a real liability. I tried to smile my way through these trials. While my customers amiably chatted amongst themselves, I turned my back and struggled with the corkscrew. Screwing it in sideways, twisting it back out, and then screwing it in again, I probably broke one out of every five corks my first week. Each time I ran over to the bartendress so she could fix my mess, she sucked in her teeth and then cursed under her breath, *"Quelle conne."* What a dumbass.

All restaurant staff except management were fed simple pasta before La Criée opened, and, by the time it closed, we were all starving. Sometimes we'd clear an empty table and, standing together over the garbage bin in the kitchen, greedily slurp down whatever raw seafood the customers had left. There was still more work to do. Once we locked the restaurant doors and cleared and wiped all the tables, we had to empty the garbage. But the cheap bags, heavy with spent lobster and oyster shells, empty wine bottles and rock-hard baguettes, would easily tear, oozing a rancid summer-baked slime on our bare legs. Avoiding this mess required two or three girls to hoist and carry each bag from the downstairs to the Dumpster. When we finished with the garbage, we stacked the tables and chairs and hosed down the terrace. We performed these tasks as efficiently as possible. No one wanted to miss the 1 a.m. train, the last Métro back to Paris.

On top of everything, we didn't even pocket our tips. (Insult, meet injury.) In France service is *compris*, which means that the 15 percent Americans typically leave on top of the final bill is simply included in the final bill. La Criée pooled and distributed tips to the staff on a points system. If you were a new girl, like me, you got three points. More experienced girls made four or five points. Management like Véronique had eight points. If a table was especially happy with your service they might leave you change on top of the bill—this you could keep.

After two weeks, I wondered if the labor and anxiety of this job was worth the slim paycheck. Working four nights a week, I barely saw Theo. We clutched each other tightly during the few hours we shared in bed before he was off at 7:30 a.m. for his job. I missed him especially those days I cleaned the restaurant after lunch. The bartendress, busy steaming her glassware, would play a pop radio station—Oui-FM—and every sentimental song reminded me of Theo and the tenderness I was missing.

My stomach rumbled with dread every day I headed off for La Criée. To calm my nerves on the long Métro ride from Theo's place in central Paris to Neuilly-sur-Seine, I read a book my father had bought me before returning to San Francisco: *L'Écume des Jours* by Boris Vian. In addition to Vian's book, he gave me Georges Bataille's *Story of the Eye* (fittingly, since Dad was starting to go blind). My father loved Bataille and Vian and it delighted him that I could read them in French, since he could only read their books in translation.

In Vian's story, first published in 1947, the protagonist's girl-friend suffers from a rare and fatal disease which causes a water lily to grow inside her chest cavity. Her breath grows thinner and thinner each day and the protagonist has to keep her room as warm as a hothouse and filled with flowers to prolong his beloved's life. Reading *L'Écume des Jours* made me feel closer to my father. As I progressed through the book, I thought of him sick in bed. What was growing inside his chest cavity? And I thought of our year ahead in San Francisco. What could I do to prolong his life?

My father was, in fact, not sick in his room but spending two weeks at the Jack Kerouac School of Disembodied Poetics at Naropa University in Boulder, Colorado. He'd been invited to teach a summer class called "Writing Against Death." It was a great week for him. He reunited with several old friends, includ-ing Allen Ginsberg who, on learning Dad was sick, personally prepared for him a macrobiotic dinner. He wrote me about the week on his plane ride home:

> One of the things I like especially about having been in the poetry scene is all the really marvelous, interesting people I've met. I hope your life puts you in touch with as many wonderful people . . .
>
> My workshop and reading went very well. I read "Elegy," then a poem about someone with AIDS, then some prose <u>by</u> someone with AIDS. There were about 75 people in the class & things really began to get emotional, especially when I had students write about death & read their work. Afterwards, several people said they liked my class better than any, that I was a really good teacher, that I was very brave. (I guess because I let myself emote & tear up a few times – which gave others permission to do the same.)

Unfortunately, Dad had not taught me the same. Like being a waitress, my emotions were something I knew little about.

AFTER FOUR WEEKS at La Criée, I'd dropped ten pounds and built muscles I didn't know I had. I'd also managed to find my rhythm at work, had memorized the place settings and organized my tasks. I even earned the grudging respect of my cowork-ers, including Maggie, who started driving me to the taxi stand at Place de Clichy on the back of her scooter whenever I missed the last Métro. My points were bumped up from three to five, so I was earning more per paycheck. By the end of each night, my personal tip glass was filled with franc coins. Only the German, Hilde, received as many. She earned her tips because of her sheer competence as a waitress. I think I impressed with an American brand of table service, a smiling, friendly patter that can be rare in French restaurants.

Then one night at the peak of the dinner shift, another scorcher, a table ran out on me. I'd happily bid "adieu" to the well-dressed young couple, convinced they'd left extra money on my table. When I discovered they'd in fact stiffed me, I figured I could chase them down in the street. I ran after them in my blue and white La Criée uniform. I forgot to put down my corkscrew and it made sharp imprints in my squeezed palm.

"*Attendez!*" I yelled. Wait! "*S'il vous PLAÎT, atten-DEZ!!!*"

When I finally caught up with them and grabbed the man's shoulder, he turned and I realized I'd chased down the wrong couple.

"*Je suis desolée*"—I'm sorry—I wheezed. "*Bonne soirée.*" Good-night.

I returned to the restaurant depressed. I explained to everyone what had happened, hoping for their sympathy. Véronique reminded me that the cost of the bill would be docked from my pay. This was policy. All I received from the waitresses was disdain. "*Quelle conne,*" I heard behind my back. "*Quelle conne.*"

The next afternoon, as I mopped the floor after the lunch shift, Oui-FM played REM's "Losing My Religion." I fell fast and hard into the comfort of this song with a homesickness that hollowed my insides. The song's mandolin riff coupled with Michael Stipe's plaintive lyrics—he didn't know if he could "do it"—tunneled a brief escape out of that gloomy dungeon of a job, as if the sound of something from my old life could be a portal back to that life. By the time the song finished, I knew I had to leave La Criée. I had only a couple of weeks left in Paris and I didn't see the point in suffering through them.

The next day, I confronted Véronique. It was the end of lunch and she was sitting in an upstairs booth, delicately forking a plate of smoked salmon, which was forbidden to the waitstaff. Reading the paper, she ignored everyone rushing around clearing tables and sweeping the floor.

"Il faut qu'on parle." We have to speak, I said, easing into the booth across from her.

I watched her eyes narrow and her lips pull into a tight smirk and in that moment, I made a split-second decision to play the one card I knew would allow me to extricate myself from the job with the least confrontation.

"Mon papa, il est malade. Il va mourir." My father, he's sick. He's going to die.

In any other circumstance, "my father is dying" would be an incredible lie to get out of a job. And because I was using this news to facilitate my departure, it felt like a lie. The sudden burst of tears that followed also felt like a performance. But it wasn't. I really was sad. So, so sad. It was as though, in that instant, I finally realized just how sad I really was.

Looking around, she quietly stood and pulled me into the back office next to the bar. Wiping my eyes, I said, *"Je suis desolée. Il faut que je parte."* I must go. I started to weep again.

What was odd about this moment is that it was the first time I'd let myself cry about my father in front of anyone. With Theo, I hid myself behind the bathroom door. On the phone with my grandparents, I tried to swallow my tears. With my dad I only felt angry; I couldn't cry at all. The depth of feeling aroused by my father's illness frightened me. I imagined it as a large and powerful black hole that would suck up everything in its path. So I worked hard to conceal the depth of my grief. I don't know if I didn't trust my friends and family to receive my sadness or if I didn't trust myself to properly reveal it. All I know is that these emotions felt dangerous to me.

But here in this office with this skinny French woman with the severe ponytail and icy demeanor, this woman whom I didn't like at all, I freely wept. With a clear purpose to my grief—get out of this godforsaken job—I finally felt at liberty to grieve, to feel the full weight of what my father had dropped on me before boarding the plane back to the United States. He was dying. He was dying. He was dying. And there was no way around it.

"Je suis desolée," she said, clasping my hands in hers. She felt terribly sorry for me, for my *"pauvre papa,"* my poor daddy. It was as if she suddenly saw me for the young girl I was. She let me go that day—that day!—and said if I wanted to return after my father was better I could, that there would always be a job for me. I thanked her, saying how much I appreciated this job (I didn't), saying how I'd call and write (with no intention of doing either). As I waited for the Métro back to Theo's, I felt incredibly light and clearheaded. I knew what to do: I had to wind up my summer, finish my semester in New York, and return to San Francisco.

21.

"HE GAVE HER A JOB. She gave him a . . . *raisin* to live!"
Brad and I were laughing so hard that we were blowing crumbs all over the table at Bruno's, our daily café stop near the NYU campus. We had another twenty minutes before our first class, and we were finishing up our third cup of coffee. (Bottomless coffees, along with ricotta-filled *sfogliatelles*, being Bruno's great draw.) Brad had just offered the tagline for a movie we'd concocted, *The Sun-Maid*, inspired by a small raisin box I had in my backpack. We'd cast Sean Connery as the steel-eyed owner of the grape vineyard and Winona Ryder as the bonnet-wearing sun-maid he employs and who eventually melts his heart.

Brad and I had met during my second semester in Paris, when he transferred from NYU in Germany. He looked like a blond Hugh Grant down to the "butt cut," as he called the floppy parted hairstyle that Grant later wore in *Four Weddings and a Funeral*. The son of a Midwestern lawyer and the middle of three children, Brad had had a very different upbringing from mine. But we had an easy rapport and were fast friends. I felt with him the same sort of affectionate ease and playfulness I felt with Dad. Theo was initially jealous of all the time we spent together. He didn't know, as I wouldn't for years, that Brad was gay.

With Brad's help, the New York I returned to in the fall of 1991 felt like a different city from the one I'd left the previous spring. Where New York had been confusing and cold, the city now felt electric, as if anything was possible.

My first order of business on returning to the city was to find a place to live. After sifting through the *Village Voice* classifieds, I found a share on Lafayette Street, just south of Cooper Union. The building smelled strongly of bleach and pesticide, but it was cheap. For a mere $125 a month I slept in the "main space" on a futon hidden behind a freestanding trifold screen. Next to me behind the screen was a tall, round fish tank, whose inhabitants were obscured by a thick film of dirt and algae that went ignored, week after week. I didn't mind becasue I was rarely home.

Brad was my constant. Weeknights we met for dinner at NYU's Weinstein cafeteria, where Brad had a meal plan. Since I didn't, we set up complicated ruses to get me in. One day we were looking for a "friend" named Jennifer. Another day I tearfully claimed to the guard that my wallet had just been stolen. We'd then fill up at the salad bar and buffet stations, the mediocre food more appetizing because it was free. I'm sure the guard was wise to our tricks or likely didn't care, but we were energized by the cleverness of our plots. We called ourselves the Meal Plan Bonnie and Clyde.

But just at the moment I'd feel most buzzed, returning from a night roaming the East Village bars with Brad and our friends, I'd open my mailbox and find a letter from Dad:

September 15, 1991

Dear Alysia –

I just wrote a short letter to Theo. My eyes are so bad I can't read the paper anymore or even write a letter unless I put a blank paper over the lines above. With my eye problems lines of print or writing collapse into each other – so

I can read the top line but then the following lines blend together or some lines are big, some lines tiny.

I could probably read better if I put a patch over my right eye like a pirate. Got your letter today & even using a magnifying glass & putting a paper above each line I was reading I still could hardly read it. It would help me if you typed (& double-spaced) your letters. Otherwise I'll always have to have someone else read them to me.

"Pigeons in the grass, alas!" to quote Gertrude Stein.

I miss you but I don't want to be a drag on you. I feel this is the time you should have for school, etc. – NOT having to get tied down caring for me. I guess I worry about being helpless & dependent on anyone. See! I can worry too. Actually, I don't worry too much though cuz all that exists is the present moment & right now I'm fine. I hope you are too. And that you can accept that you are.

> Love,
> Dad

My father didn't want to be a "drag" on me but, inevitably, because of letters like these, that's the role he played. I'd like to say that I was a thoughtful, good daughter, attuned to his needs and to my commitment to take care of him. But I was young and callow, still hungry for whatever fruits New York could offer. Brad had found an internship working for a national TV show and I was determined to land one as well. When not studying, I spent my afternoons paging through job binders at student services. The state of Dad's health, as reported in these letters, felt like an intrusion in the life I was trying to build. Unfortunately, I felt close enough with him that I told him so.

9/21/91

Dear Dad,

I received your letter yesterday. Sometimes reading a letter from you can be depressing. You complain so much about your bad health and ill luck!

I'm not asking you to censor these aspects of your life. But if you accentuate less the negative I would enjoy your letters more.

My life is often frustrating too. To get internships I have to send off my resumé. I've written my resumé but I haven't found a good block of time when I can type it. This stresses me out because then I think I'll lose the internships.

. . . I really enjoyed our conversation the other night. That we can laugh about what to do with your ashes is a big step for me. I have a lot more trouble accepting your condition than you do. I suppose that parents take on a mystic quality in the eyes of the child. To a young duckling the father duck is omniscient and like god, never dies. I'm used to having you in my life. You know me well.

Sometimes I feel you provide a security and support that could never be matched. I'm starting to learn that isn't true. My relationship with Theo attests to the fact that my life is growing, opening up in new directions.

Gotta go.

love, Alysia

By October I found an internship at Columbia Records. I spent three afternoons a week in their Blackrock building, addressing envelopes to radio stations across the country and stuffing them with CDs and press materials for all the bands the label was pushing. In my free time I poked my head into offices, saying hello to whomever was inside regardless of their rank. What did I have to lose? And each week I came home with free CDs given to me by my new record exec friends, which I gleefully shared with Brad.

Through a girl in my French class I also found a weekend job hostessing at a midtown French restaurant called La Brasserie, which piped the hits of Jacques Brel and Edith Piaf on a continuous loop. After my adventures in France I easily got the job, which entailed greeting people at the door and strategically situating them in the restaurant so that it always looked full.

Walking from my apartment in the East Village to Brad's in the West Village, I felt young and free and fierce. I'd worked and lived in Paris, with a blue-eyed Parisian who still wrote me letters proclaiming his love in fresh ink. Rigorously applying myself to my studies, I was getting all As, making the dean's list. The fall air was thin and crisp, sharpening my senses. I moved in long strides across the avenues. I moved so fast, I felt as if I was flying.

As the year progressed, Dad continued to write me accounts of his declining health but, thoughtfully, he now headlined these sections in case I wanted to skip them. Of course I couldn't, and the effect was no less painful:

Complaints (I'm labeling so you can skip):

1) Headaches, diarrhea past 2 days (bad enough to keep me home) medical safaris eating half my time, feeling wiped out, Kaiser never sending me the right stuff so I have to stay home all day for next 2 days.

2) Loneliness – my roommate's been gone a lot & I've been spending most of my time alone. I used to go to certain clubs & cafes to socialize but my lack of energy, health problems has just about cancelled all this. Also I used to enjoy going to sauna at the Kabuki w/friends, which I can no longer do. So I find myself more & more iso-

lated which is itself depressing, alienating, & not good
for immune system. I've always been a bit of a loner but
AIDS seems to make me more so.

3) Career. Can't get through to this woman in NYC who
I want to be my agent. She's always gone, on phone, etc.
Not a good sign. In a way I even feel abandoned by New
Narrative group of writers, which I founded and first
published and reviewed. They don't include me in read-
ings any more.

I wonder if it's partly my illness. I recall my reluctance
to visit Sam D'Allesandro when he was sick. AIDS makes
people nervous, uncomfortable & they want to avoid being
around it. Maybe they think I want to remain alone – or am
too sick to do anything.

Okay – enough complaining!

In another letter, Dad directly addressed my future as his care-
giver:

I'm enclosing some newspaper clippings for your (hopeful)
enjoyment. Also a flyer on homecare (not to depress you
but so you'll see there's help in this area). I think a key thing
in homecare is to take care of yourself so you don't burn
out. Namely (whenever that time might come) I'd try to
set it up so my friends could have a schedule of helping out
so that you'd have free time to get away & do other things.
Also, Kaiser has nurses that would come in a few days each
week. So it's not like you'd have to do it all, all the time.

Dad believed he was being considerate with these notes, easing me into what I could expect in the year ahead. Instead, I felt

besieged. Couldn't he see? I was just getting everything into place in New York: the apartment, the internship, the job, the friends! I convinced myself that if I had enough engines revving at once, I could drown out the siren call of Dad back in San Francisco. There'd be too much to leave. Dad would understand and let me stay.

So instead of preparing for my early graduation and eventual return, as I'd resolved to do in Paris, I sought out even more work and activity. Brad and I waitered dinner parties for the Weiksners uptown, earning extra cash. Though I was planning Theo's visit that Christmas, I sought out attention from cute guys, flirting with a busboy at La Brasserie who was into rave music and a waiter at Dojo's who gave me free slices of carrot cake whenever I came in.

In phone calls with Dad early that fall, we had joked about what I'd do with his remains after he died. We imagined the havoc my kids would wreak if they accidentally knocked over his urn ("Billy, stop playing in grandpa's ashes!"). But as the inevitable approached, I started to push against the boundaries of our agreement: "Maybe I should just finish the school year, Dad. It's only a few more months."

"I want you to come home," he answered.

"But I've only been in this internship for a month and a half," I said. "And I'm meeting so many people! I could get a job at Columbia Records!" But my father never wavered. He continued to write letters, presenting himself as the loving but ailing father. And he never let me forget my promise.

11/20/91

Dear Alysia –

Went to see the doctor yesterday. He doesn't know what my skin rash is. He said it looked like scabies but you don't

get that on your neck and forehead. So he gave me an anti-
biotic, which made me a bit feverish last night. Meanwhile,
the itching drives me crazy.

Ten more days and my roommate will be gone. I can
hardly wait. Anyone would drive me nuts if they stayed in
the apartment all day everyday . . . Considering the trouble
I have living with one roommate, how will I manage living
in a hospice w/10 or so others. No privacy at all!

Time for me to do my infusion now. Then Danny
Devito's "Other People's Money." A light escapist film
appeals to me right now.

Now after the movie – I'm having a cup of peppermint
tea in a cafe at Fillmore & Haight. Lots of beautiful shots
of NYC. From skyscraper offices & wealthy apartments
it sure looks fine. If you're living in a nice apartment and
enjoying your job & friends, I can see why you want to stay.
3 and 1/2 years ago you didn't want to leave home & I more
or less pushed you out of the nest. Now you don't want to
come back.

Well, NYC will still be there in a year and I may not be.
So if you stayed there & missed being with me, you might
even feel worse and more guilty . . .

One night, as Brad was walking me back to my apartment, I
told him I had only a few months left in the city.

"What? That's crazy. You can't leave now."

"I have to," I said. "It's my dad." My face flushed. I felt dizzy and
sick with emotion, like I was confessing to some crime, as if by
articulating my dad's illness I would somehow make it more true.
"He's going . . . blind."

I can't remember if I used the word AIDS. Brad thinks I did. We
didn't talk about it again. Not my return. Not Dad's health. Brad

and I resumed our New York escapades, as if nothing was going to change. And I quietly prepared my leave.

THAT DECEMBER, I turned twenty-one. On the night of my birthday, the Weiksners took me out with Brad and another friend to the Gotham Bar and Grill, a sleek Union Square restaurant famous for its dramatically towering entrées. Spotlit from above, each plate looked like a death-defying circus act. Sandra and George sat at their own table in a distant, but still visible, corner of the restaurant, leaving my friends and me to our own conversation. At night's end, the Weiksners picked up our tab. They even sent over a birthday bottle of fine champagne.

Then it came time to open my presents. I got a travel alarm clock, a comment on my perpetual tardiness. Brad gave me a mug from Bruno's and a cassette of Nirvana's *Nevermind*, which had come out that fall. In Paris, Brad and I had bonded over the Pixies. We loved everything about the power-punk band—lyrics inspired by surrealist filmmaker Luis Buñuel, badass bassist Kim Deal, and especially the controlled chaos of the music. We joyfully slam-danced watching them perform in Paris and that fall in New York. Banging my body into strangers with all my force, I felt both light as a feather and hard as a brick.

Like the Pixies, Nirvana made beauty out of mess, juxtaposing feedback and screeching guitar with the vulnerability of Kurt Cobain's broken voice and lyrics that yearned for a "Leonard Cohen afterworld." *Nevermind* provided a framework for my mixed-up feelings about leaving New York. As I packed up my apartment to move home, I listened to the tape over and over, clinging to Cobain's poetic rage as if it were my own.

The night before my flight home I forgot to set my new alarm clock, and the next morning woke up late. I rushed out the door and found a cab to LaGuardia. When I arrived at the terminal, it was thick with families and harried singletons wearing Walk-mans, all lugging suitcases full of Christmas presents. I waited in the check-in line with my bags for the better part of an hour. When I reached the ticket agent, I gave her my ticket and ID card.

She looked at the ticket and frowned.

"Your plane is leaving from *Kennedy*. In about"—she looked at her watch—"forty minutes. You might be able to make it if you leave right now." She pushed the ticket back toward me over the counter. Already overtired and distraught, I broke down in hic-cupping sobs.

"Kennedy?"

I tried to wipe away my tears but they kept coming, washing down my face and drawing curious stares from my airport-weary neighbors.

"It's going to be okay," said the ticket agent. "It's going to be *okay!*"

"You don't understand. I have . . . I have to go home to see my dad! I've got to . . . I'm going to . . . *I can't make it to Kennedy in thirty minutes!*"

She started furiously tapping on her keyboard.

"Okay. I found you a spot on a flight for San Francisco with a layover in Denver. But it's boarding now. Grab your bags. You've got to run."

Taking my hand in hers, she passed me off to another attendant who rushed me through security and instructed me to run to my gate, which I did as fast I could. Sticky and out of breath, my heart beating in my throat, I squeezed myself between two annoyed strangers and, closing my eyes, sank into an exhausted fog. I was heading home.

PART VI
Return

Serene stands the little captain,
He is not hurried, his voice is neither high nor low,
His eyes give more light to us than our battle-lanterns.
                    —WALT WHITMAN, *"Song of Myself"*

22.

I DON'T KNOW what happened with Theo and me. I'd been looking forward to his visit to San Francisco that Christmas, but from the moment he landed nothing felt right. 545 Ashbury appeared grimy and tiny through Theo's eyes. And I was defensive when he made fun of the cheap caviar Dad served on Christmas Eve and the sparkling wine Dad mistakenly called champagne. Theo's gifts to me—a small bottle of Chanel perfume and a pair of pistachio green, fur-trimmed gloves—now seemed frivolous and silly, belonging to another life, another person. We fought over this and stupid things and Theo said I had a *mauvaise caractère*. I felt justified in my annoyance. How could he not see the pain I was going through? How could he not know what I needed? But in truth, I didn't know what I needed. I just knew that there was no room for Theo within the confused emotions of my return. We didn't break up before he boarded the plane to Paris, but I knew it was over. His letters continued to arrive for months. They piled up on the spool table unopened, worthless promissory notes of a dream unfulfilled.

After Theo left, I tried to throw myself into a job search, but the country was mired in an economic recession. Waiting for responses to my applications, I had nothing to do but linger next to Dad's bed watching him count out pills in the palm of his hand, and accompany him on depressing visits to the doctor. With my friends still at college and few activities to distract me, I fell into deep pits of despair.

Then I got busy. I started weekly GRE classes to improve my chances at getting into graduate school and chased down every job opening I could find. By March, I found a full-time $300-a-week job selling videotapes of the news to local Fortune 500 companies, and an internship at *Movie Magazine*, a radio program broadcast from the nearby college station, KUSF.

By spring, I swaggered past the storefronts of the Lower Haight and inner Mission. I wore big silver hoop earrings, white V-neck t-shirts, Dad's black suit vest (just the right vintage), and form-fitting jeans. The tattooed, grunge-tinged scene that permeated cafés like the Horseshoe and Café Macondo now felt like my scene despite the fact that I had no tattoos, nor odd piercings. My generation was reveling then in the gritty and the authentic, and nothing felt more genuine than my life with Dad.

Entering the Horseshoe café one afternoon, I was ready to forget for a moment why I was in San Francisco and not in New York. I noticed the blue-eyed boy behind the counter. I flashed him large dark eyes then looked down, smiling demurely. After finding a seat in a dingy corner with a mug of Earl Grey tea, I watched the boy pass my table. Dinosaur Jr.'s "Freak Scene" played fuzzy loud through an overhead speaker. Watching the counter boy clear tables, I pushed my hair behind my ears. I pulled a navy corduroy newsboy cap down over my head, feeling slim, young, pretty—twenty-one.

The counter boy asked if he could sit. He sucked hard on a lit cigarette. We exchanged names and chatted. He'd moved from New Jersey and was going to break into San Francisco's music scene. He just needed to get the band together. I noticed Scott wore a skull ring but, with his café apron, diminutive stature, and thrift-store fedora, he looked cute and boyish. When I announced I had to go, I asked Scott if it was too forward for me to want his number.

Soon Scott and I were dating. Though our romance lasted only six months—he'd drop me as his band started getting bigger and things with me too serious—lying on Scott's unmade bed in his Mission apartment, sheets smelling of cigarettes, the floor cluttered with empty beer bottles, notebooks, and CDs, I tried to erase myself, obliterate all evidence of my life past and present. But even after a passionate night with Scott, I'd burst into tears holding his thick arms tightly while he sat rocking me, saying nothing.

Whenever I returned to 545 Ashbury, I was hit by heavy and oppressive warmth. Sweat trickled down my back. There was no forgetting in this air. At home I was again, always, my father's daughter. I was also a nurse, helping him count pills from the many vials that covered his end table. And a maid, wiping the floor around the toilet and picking up the stiff, crumpled tissues that gathered around his bed. Every week I bought gallon after gallon of juice to replenish the fluids he lost during his night sweats. He woke up looking like he'd been doused with a bucket of water.

Some weekends, Dad would accompany me to the Café Flore in the Castro. I had to slow my pace so he could keep up, but we still loved sitting at our favorite corner table on the outdoor terrace, drinking up lattes and the beautiful boys that surrounded us. But as his illness progressed, his eyes worsened and he couldn't make the trip anymore. "It breaks my heart," I wrote in my journal. "What's the point of going to a café if you can't see anyone?"

That's when the boys started coming to our house. These were the young men I got to know through Dad and his letters. The Alexes, the Larry-Bobs, the Oliviers, and the Dans now showed up every few weeks to help or to distract. Dan delivered Marx Brothers movies to lift Dad's mood. Alex and Larry-Bob brought over Philip K. Dick books, and issues of the *Bay Area Reporter*, which they'd read aloud, since Dad could no longer read to himself. Olivier helped with groceries a couple of times and, once, washed our windows.

Other days, Dad lay in bed watching television. He now had a violent cough. Sometimes his cough was so loud and sustained that it overwhelmed the sound of the TV, distracting me from my GRE prep tests, and reinserting his illness into the "healthy" world I was trying so hard to grow.

Use the following words in a sentence: **aberrant, faculties, assiduous**:

> *For many, my father's was an **aberrant** lifestyle.*
> *Each day my father loses more and more of his **faculties**.*
> *In an attempt to distract herself from her very real sadness, she was **assiduous** in all that she did.*

(I barely wrote in my journal during this time but did keep these lists of GRE sentences.)

Sometimes Dad's coughing was just too much. "Shut *up*!" I once yelled from my desk. Even though his coughing had subsided, I believed he hadn't heard me through the French doors separating our bedrooms. But then he brought up the incident later, shaming me. "I cough so much sometimes I think I'm going to throw up," he said. "I can't help it." I felt terrible.

I was overwhelmed by the task of caring for my dad, but I also loved him and wanted to comfort him. At least once a week he asked me to run the vacuum, not to clean but because he liked the sound of the muffled motor. He told me it reminded him of being a little boy at home in Lincoln, Nebraska. The sound of his mother vacuuming always made him feel safe and loved. As he huddled beneath bedcovers, the Hoover droned loudly, upright and immobile next to his bed, while I lay on the sofa beside him staring at the ceiling.

In the mornings, we sat together at the large spool table. I made him a bowl of cold cereal, then gave him a quick kiss on the forehead before pulling on my fingerless bicycle gloves, strapping on my helmet, and lifting my mountain bike over my head, down the stairs, and out the door. In the fresh morning air, I soared down Haight Street, past the hills of Divisadero and Laguna, down to South of Market and my job at Video Monitoring Services. I zipped between cars, breaking rules, running lights.

Faster. Faster. *Faster.*

VIDEO MONITORING SERVICES became my only reliable escape during my first several months at home. I loved playing the eager little salesgirl, dialing all the numbers on my morning call sheet, catering to clients like Gap, Levi's, and Nike. Immersing myself in their PR campaigns and selling them news video and transcripts, I could finally compartmentalize my feelings about Dad.

VMS had three departments: monitoring, production, and sales. Because we were the sales department, needing to access whatever magic might convince clients to spend a hundred dollars for two minutes of tape, we were given free rein to design our environment. We played music on a boom box and wore whatever we wanted. When things felt too stressful—managing a Chevron oil spill, say—we took turns lying down on the carpeted floor with a lavender-scented silk beanbag draped over our eyes. We called it the "cosmic eye pillow."

In the early nineties, Video Monitoring Services was a journey point for waves of alternative-minded liberal arts grads and aspiring creatives who came to San Francisco in search of a media job but who couldn't live off bookshop wages. Through VMS I'd meet future roommates, editors, and boyfriends, but I first became close with Jon, a super-mellow cycling enthusiast who turned me onto toe-clips and fingerless gloves, and Karin Demarest, who'd hired me to replace her when she was made general manager.

When I sat down to be interviewed by Karin, with her warm smile and large blue eyes, I decided to do something I'd not done in previous interviews: I told the truth. I told her that my dad was sick with AIDS and I'd graduated early and moved home to care for him. This openness would characterize my relationship with Karin who, along with Jon, took on the role of older sibling and mentor. When I first started at VMS, my fingers resting on Karin's old Rolodex and petrified to make my first call, she gave me a note, previously kept over her desk and which I taped over mine:

"Be brave. If you're not, pretend to be. Nobody knows the difference."

In truth, we were all pretending, all of us kids playing grown-up. We made sales presentations touting the importance of "proactive" versus "reactive" PR. We used computer monitors so big they took up our entire desks. We faxed "rush" orders to other offices and shipped huge stacks of VHS tapes all over the country so those PR folks could show their bosses they'd done a good job. Selling the news every day, we learned that much of what was broadcast wasn't news at all but one big public relations effort. Unwittingly, we even looked forward to disasters. Every oil spill, airline crash, and product recall meant we'd make our monthly goal. We watched so much TV that the absurdity of the enterprise overtook the tragedy.

It was easier for me to manage the crises of my clients than the crisis I was facing at home, so I threw myself into work and the world of Karin and Jon. At the end of each day, I bicycled with them to the Rosemont Estates, the name given to the apartment complex where they lived with half a dozen of their friends on Rosemont Street, a San Francisco version of *Melrose Place*. In their shared backyard, the site of future ecstasy-fueled costume parties,

I met Karin and Jon's neighbors reclining in a bubbling hot tub beneath a big hand-painted sign that read "George Clinton not Bill Clinton."

I watched as Karin and Jon kicked off their shoes and rolled a joint or popped a beer, inviting me to do the same. But, much as I wanted to, I rarely could. I always had to get back to the Haight, to Dad.

Returning home from work one evening that summer, Dad's mere presence on the bed, in the same position in front of the television where I'd left him eight hours earlier, forced a pained sigh from my lips. Where Dad used to vociferously disdain TV as "the idiot box," this role now fell to me. "Does it *always* have to be on?" I pleaded. Because my father couldn't read anymore, television provided him both company and cultural text. Without books to critique, he applied his intellect to old reruns of *Burns and Allen, Perry Mason,* and *Bewitched.*

"Don't you see," he pointed out to me, "*Bewitched* is all about the conflict between anarchical spirituality, Samantha, and the repressive patriarchal quest for order, Darrin."

"Never noticed that, Dad."

In other circumstances I'd have loved to engage Dad on the cultural subtext of sixties TV, but I couldn't see past the inherent sadness of our situation. After seven months of living at home, I'd long since exchanged my *Harold and Maude*–inspired fantasies of the fearlessness of the fatally ill—Stealing cars! Outrunning police! They had nothing left to lose and the world was theirs for the taking!—for the tiresome reality of nurse visits and pill vials and Open Hand meals delivered night after night by another kind-faced stranger. (Project Open Hand, started by San Francisco retiree Ruth Brinker, then provided hot meals to over 2,300 AIDS patients around the city, free of charge.)

"How was *your* day?" he asked, as I moved awkwardly through the dining room with my bike.

"Fine," I mumbled, resting my bike against the spool table. Unbuckling my helmet, I asked, "How was yours?"

"Well," he chuckled, " I was heating up the Open Hand meal for lunch, and, well . . . I fell asleep and it burned."

"So you didn't eat?"

"No."

Hearing my father's pitiful "no," I felt myself propelled from the room, eager to jump back onto my bike and head to Rosemont Street or to Scott's or to anywhere. I wrestled with my conscience then, and I wrestle with it still. Had I not left him alone, maybe he wouldn't have burned his Open Hand meal and he would have eaten. Maybe he wouldn't have tried to change the dining room lightbulb on his own: wouldn't have dropped the glass shade, wouldn't have cut his finger.

SOME DAYS Karin and I made VMS sales calls in San Jose or Palo Alto, and on these days I took the bus instead of my bike. Returning home in my mint green Ann Taylor suit, I weaved my way through the smelly throngs that were always parked on the corner of Haight and Ashbury, skinny white kids with dreadlocks, tattoos, and piercings. They asked me for change as I passed my corner, and I surveyed the gang of them. Amongst their bedrolls and beat-up paper bags, they made stacks of peanut butter sandwiches and played bad guitar. A teenage girl with a nose ring clutched a big-eyed puppy. A young guy with a sunburned face took a swig from a paper-sheathed bottle.

Haight Ashbury had been a mecca for runaways and freedom-loving drifters since the late 1960s, but now the hippies were joined by the "gutter punks" who, unlike their middle-class sixties counterparts, had often run away from abusive homes. They didn't sing songs of love and peace; they favored heroin, meth, and crack over

LSD and pot. The increasing numbers of these kids—camped out on corners and on front stoops, begging for change, shooting up in the bushes, or drinking themselves into oblivion—became for me an ugly reminder of all the changes to my neighborhood, of all the beauty and magic that I'd already lost and was now painfully losing. By the late fall of 1992, the energy of Haight Street was as angry as I'd ever seen it, seeming to reflect back my own freefloating anger, which only made it worse.

My neighbors, including many former hippies, were angry too. I watched them patrol the area in the evenings, wearing neoncolored t-shirts and carrying signs that read: "RAD: Residents Against Druggies." The countersigns popped up within a week: "DAMN: Druggies Against Mad Neighbors." Many felt drugs were an integral part of the local culture, but with the harder drugs came crime.

The homeless kids were sometimes robbed or attacked in the park where they slept. That November there was a shooting off Haight Street, a drug deal gone wrong. Another night an alarm went off in Coffee Tea & Spice, where I'd bought my gummy bears as a girl. When the police arrived they found the front window smashed in. Amongst the shards of glass, a scruffy kid was stuffing his face with candy. Several shop owners hired security guards to walk a section of Haight Street, but that only deepened the neighborhood's collective malaise.

The public restroom in the Panhandle became a shooting gallery. The playground where I used to play was littered with empty bottles and hypodermic needles. In the doorway of my apartment building there was a near-constant stench of urine. I couldn't walk to the grocery store for Dad's biweekly juice runs without having to weave through the kids or risk walking into car traffic to get around them. I was hit up for change every single time I passed. It was exhausting and depressing.

"Yuppie," was hissed at my back, or—and this one *really* got me going—"How 'bout a smile at least?"

"I don't think I can do this much longer," I announced to my dad one evening after work, perched on the edge of his bed.

Quietly he listened to me, propped up by a surplus of pillows and lumpy throw cushions. And he smiled. The light from his eyes shined at me serenely, even though his vessel was failing while mine was still young and sturdy.

"Of course you can. You can do anything you set your mind to."

Peacefully, he looked at me. The television blared, yet only I seemed to hear the penetrating noise. It washed over him like a lulling wave.

Looking away from him, rocking back and forth, I continued with my plan. "I need a limit. A year. I moved here last Christmas, and after this Christmas I want to move out, maybe even move back to New York."

He said nothing.

"I don't think I can do this," I repeated. "I'm not *ready* for this."

Then he answered me, his words a slap: "I wasn't ready to care for you when your mother died. But I did."

I had no reply for that.

WHEN I WAS A GIRL my father never questioned me when I wanted to stay home from school sick. He never felt my forehead or stared suspiciously into my eyes, trying to catch my lie. He answered, "Fine," whenever I said I wasn't feeling well, and sent me back to my wooden loft bed. Lying under the covers, I would listen to my father in the kitchen mixing cherry Jell-O, pausing between beats to take a drag on his Carlton Regular. I could hear him slicing the bananas that would float in the Jell-O mold's shallow waters. This was step one in our sick-day ritual. While the

Jell-O was cooling in the fridge, he went out to buy me comic books—*Mad* magazine and *Betty and Veronica*—to read in bed. And for lunch he served me Campbell's Chunky Chicken Noodle Soup with extra pepper, a favorite of both of ours.

Now that he was sick, I could have phoned the offices at Open Hand and said, "Thanks, but we don't need you anymore. I'm dedicating myself to my father." I could have abandoned my nine-to-five job; I could have ignored all the slim-hipped young men that caught my eye; I could have let go of the radio internship that didn't even pay, the GRE prep course. Few of these lasted anyway. Each romance flamed out. The grad school applications were never mailed.

But I feared that if I halted my trajectory—the vision of myself as a body in motion—my burgeoning adult self would be completely absorbed by Dad and his needs. And increasingly, his needs frightened me. It wasn't just that it was unbearably sad to watch my dad lose weight and get weaker. That was bad enough. But I felt so alone in it, so angry that this had become my life. The only way I could keep going was to cultivate a vibrant self of my own, separate from "daughter"—just as my father needed to be someone other than "Daddy" back when he was caring for me after my mom died.

Growing up, I fantasized about having a bigger family. Now especially I longed for someone to help with the quotidian work of caring for Dad. But on another, equally powerful level, I also relished the intimacy of our one-on-one relationship.

The meals Dad prepared for the two of us when I was a kid seemed tailor-made for our single-parent, single-child family. He'd buy a single chicken leg for us to share, bake it until the skin was crispy golden yellow and the juice and butter pooled together on the tinfoil lining our pan, then he'd cut the leg in two, keeping the thigh for himself and giving the perfect-sized drumstick to me. For dessert, we'd split a package of Hostess cupcakes, which were sold in packs of two. I developed elaborate methods of eating mine to prolong the experience, holding the cupcake upside down in my cupped palm, eating the spongy cake first, then the white center, finishing with the chocolate frosting and, finally, the hardened white sugar squiggle.

Having just enough for two and no more for the possibility of a lover, mother, brother, or sister only heightened the romance of our relationship.

Still, I was not a nurse. That October it became clear that I couldn't give Dad the care he needed without quitting my job. He couldn't make his own meals anymore and could barely get from his bed to the bathroom and back. Because of his many years' involvement with the Hartford Street Zen Center and Maitri Hospice, the administration said they'd have a bed for him when he was ready. He was ready now.

ON A COLD weekday morning, my father was lying on the futon mattress while I busied myself at the dining room table, stacking *San Francisco Chronicles*, sorting mail. I'd taken the day off work. My high school friend Camille, back home from UC Santa Cruz, was to pick us up in her mother's car at noon. Through the heavy curtain separating my father's room from the dining room, I could hear him clear his throat.

"I don't see how we can possibly be ready by noon," he called.

"Noon? That's four hours from now," I answered. "We have plenty of time."

"I sometimes don't get up until afternoon. It seems rushed to me. I get exhausted just walking to the bathroom."

"I'll do the packing. I'll do the lifting. You won't have to worry about anything." I continued sorting mail. "Just sit there. I'm here for you. You understand that, right? That's why I was born."

"They call it 'attendant care,' when all they do is intrude on my life. They poke and prod and say, 'Now here, have this medicine . . . have that.'"

"Is that the way they are at the hospice?"

"That's the way they are at the hospital," he said.

"You're going to the hospice, not the hospital. You don't know what they're going to be like. Do you even know where you are going, Dad?"

No answer.

THREE HOURS LATER. "Do you want an egg salad sandwich before we drive to the hospice?" I asked.

"Half of one," Dad said.

"There's half a chicken sandwich in the fridge, isn't there?"

"It's a chicken sandwich and I don't want a chicken sandwich," he answered.

"It's pretty hard to make only half a sandwich," I said, with my hand on the refrigerator door. "Are you sure you don't want a whole sandwich and save the other half for later if you can't finish it?"

"All I want is half an egg sandwich," he answered, leaning up from his pillow. "I already said that. Do I have to draw a picture?"

"Do you even appreciate that I took the day off?" I asked him.

"I'm sorry. I guess I'm kind of grumpy today."

Though Dad was little, wee in his now shrunken frame, he was still the captain—silently, cleverly in control. He was the rock then. And I was free-floating and wild. He knew well the power of the powerless, the steel of the rubber spine. He could refuse to eat my meals. And though the hospice provided TVs for all of their residents, he refused to leave home without his own. "I'll raise such a fuss they won't take me!" he argued. I pulled a muscle carrying it upstairs to his new room.

Of course, it's now obvious why he was so angry that day. People don't move into hospice to live but to die. And that half an egg sandwich I ended up making him—that sandwich was the last meal he ate in our Haight-Ashbury apartment, our one true home.

23.

O N A W E E K D A Y evening, the air was cooling quickly as the fog moved down the hills of 18th Street into the Castro Valley. I unlatched the low, wrought-iron gate at the Maitri Hospice and walked through the small garden and into the door of the three-story Victorian building. In the front room, frail, old-looking men watched television, accompanied by plainclothes nurses and volunteers. I motioned to the attendant nurse in the kitchen and said, "I'm here to see my father, Steve Abbott."

As I hurried up the stairs, two steps at a time, I could see the blue light of the TV flickering on the floor outside his room. The door was open.

"Hi," I announced, walking in.

He turned to me and grinned widely. For a moment he looked like a giddy little boy. But then, he always was a little boy. His attention made me uncomfortable. He was too sweet, too good.

"Hi, Daddy."

Dad's room was sparsely decorated. A small tin Buddha he'd bought on his trip to Kyoto sat on the bedside table; against it leaned a picture of Issan, the blue-robed abbot of the Zen Center who'd died of AIDS the previous year. Next to the Buddha stood a framed picture of me beside a vintage brown and beige Rolls-Royce convertible on a Paris street. My grandparents took this photo when they visited me during my junior year abroad. At the foot of Dad's bed was the television I'd lugged from home the day he moved into the hospice. It was almost always on. And next to his bed stood a large rubber tree plant.

I'd arrived just before dinner. Maitri had nutritionists on staff who prepared vegetarian meals for all its residents: black bean burritos, winter squash stews, and organic vegetable and rice pilafs. Dad had grown to hate these wholesome meals, as he reminded me each visit. He craved the sort of potato chip–crusted casseroles and mayonnaise-drenched tuna fish his mother used to fix for him. It became my job to rescue him. During one Saturday visit, he told me he wanted a chicken salad sandwich, so I found one easily at the corner deli. Another afternoon he asked if I could get him an ice-cream cone. I raced over to Castro Street and bought two cones—rocky road for him, mint chocolate chip for me. It was an unseasonably warm afternoon and the ice cream was melting down the outside of my clenched hands. I considered running but feared if I did the scoops would tumble off the cones and into the street. So I walked back as quickly as I could, looking like one of those ridiculous "fast walkers." The whole way I licked the chocolate and mint ice cream as they melted down my left and right fists respectively.

Tonight, I'd stopped by the local sushi restaurant and bought us both miso soup and what we called "safe" sushi—sushi without raw fish, which can be fatal for someone with full-blown AIDS. Dad sipped his miso soup loudly.

When I was younger, I used to glare at my dad whenever he ate soup or cereal in my presence. The sounds of his eating, the sluicing and guttural gulping as he downed his cereal milk, always grated on my nerves. But as I watched him now, sitting next to me in bed, loudly sipping his miso, I reveled in these sounds. I didn't want them to stop.

Aside from Dad's eating and the scraping of our plastic spoons on the bottoms of the Styrofoam soup bowls, we sat together in silence. Dad told me that he liked visiting with me above anyone else because other people, he explained, "need to be entertained."

"And I don't always have energy to be cheered up," he added.

I took his hand in mine.

I FELT BETTER with Dad out of the house, knowing he was well fed and looked after. For the first time since returning to San Francisco, I felt like I could breathe. The house was quiet too. But it was a disturbing quiet.

One night, some weeks after my father moved out, I decided to sleep in his futon for a change. But I went to bed after taking a bath, with my hair still wet. Shivering, clutching a single blanket, I imagined what it must have been like for him, so sick and weak those many months in our drafty Victorian apartment. Picturing him, I felt chilled to the bone. I couldn't get warm. No matter how much I rubbed my hands and legs together, no matter how much I twisted myself in the blanket, I couldn't shake the cold. Suddenly I felt as if I was the one who was sick, as if I *was* my father, and I started to panic.

I moved to my loft bed, but I couldn't relax there either. From my window I saw a terrible fight between some kids and a drug dealer across the street. Even after I closed my eyes and turned my back, I couldn't shut out the scene. They were so angry and loud, it felt as if they were in the bedroom with me.

I climbed down my ladder and called Karin. She was with a friend, but when I explained to her what was going on, she immediately drove over. She followed me up the ladder to my loft bed. Spooning me tightly, she stroked my hair until I finally fell asleep.

I made myself busier and busier. I pitched movie reviews at *Movie Magazine* and worked late hours at Video Monitoring

Services. Since Scott the musician didn't want to date me any-more, I sought out the company of young men I met at VMS or KUSF—anything to distract me from the quiet of the house, the big quiet ahead.

I visited the hospice several nights a week. But one night late that November, I found my dad perturbed. He was so worked up, I could hardly understand him.

"They're taking them," he told me.

"Who's taking what?"

"The nurses. They're taking my t-shirts."

"The nurses? I'm sure they're not *taking* your t-shirts," I said.

I couldn't imagine why anyone would want Dad's shirts. Though his political Queer Nation and Boys with Arms Akimbo t-shirts held sentimental value, they were worn thin, marked with odd yellow stains, the edges frayed. I wondered whether his para-noia was a product of his sickness or whether he was still upset about the freedom he lost by moving out of our apartment.

"Well, they're disappearing. I used to have seven and now I only have four."

"Maybe . . . maybe they're getting lost."

"I used to have seven and now only *four*!"

"Okay, Dad. I'll get you more shirts."

I vowed to get him t-shirts that no one could lose or steal, and planned to do so while visiting my grandparents that Thanksgiv-ing. Every trip to Kewanee required a stop at Breedlove's, the local sports shop that supplied the logo-embossed t-shirts for the town's school teams: the Kewanee Boilermakers, the Wethers-field Geese. Our family loved Breedlove's because the shirts were inexpensive and came in every color of the rainbow.

On that first day of my visit, my uncle David drove me down-town to the store. Flipping through stacks of t-shirts, I picked out the brightest hues I could find: kelly green, royal blue, fire engine red, and emergency orange. All size medium. I thought Dad would look so sweet in these shirts, the bright, saturated cotton offsetting his increasingly pale, almost transparent skin. I asked for my father's name, "Steve," to be printed in small capital letters on the shirt's upper left side, just above the heart.

When I picked them up that Saturday morning, I beamed with satisfaction. No one could lose these t-shirts, because these shirts were exploding with color. No one could steal these shirts, because who would want to wear a t-shirt printed with the name "Steve," except someone named Steve? There would be no question as to whom they belonged.

Later that Saturday afternoon, my uncle and I were walking with Munca through the icy streets near her house. As we passed Windmont Park, I decided to break off from them.

As I walked into the park, it started to rain. Instead of heading back to my grandparents', I walked farther in, following the paved perimeter of the lake I'd circled countless times as a child and teenager. The water reflected the gray sky above, and Windmont Park was emptier than I'd ever seen it. After I walked around the lake, letting myself get drenched, I stopped at the big maple tree next to the tennis courts where Munca used to play. The biggest leaves looked like open palms. I watched as they collected rain until the water became too heavy to bear and the leaves collapsed, sending the water to the ground with a splash.

As I walked around Windmont on this gray winter day I tried to say it, practicing aloud, because I could: "My father is dead." Circling the lake again and again, I repeated these words, because I knew it might soon be time. I knew I had to get used to these vowels and consonants in my mouth. "My faa . . . Myfatherisdead. My father *is* dead. *My* father is dead. My father is *dead*." By saying these words without any catching in my throat, by making the phrase sound natural and real, I felt guilty, as if I were betraying something. Everything seemed to conspire with me. The gray and white landscape said, embrace death. As I looked out at the distant bleached horizon, my sadness felt very, very right. In this wet park, alone, I felt more myself, more at home, than I had felt all weekend.

I returned to San Francisco on Sunday night. I was supposed to visit Dad at the hospice Monday, since I'd been away for Thanksgiving. I had planned to give him his t-shirts then. But the next day at work I phoned him.

"Dad, I can't make it over tonight. I have to work on my radio piece."

"Oh?"

"I can't make it until Wednesday. I'm so sorry."

"That's okay," he said. "I know how busy you are."

TUESDAY AFTERNOON the hospice rang me at work. The desks in the sales office overlooked the large garden of a home for the elderly. I was watching an old Chinese woman with a back so stooped she looked like an apostrophe watering a lush hydrangea bush, when the Maitri nurse informed me in flat, even tones that my father's lungs had collapsed.

Without any cues from the nurse, I didn't know how to take the news. "We've put your father on morphine," she continued matter-of-factly. She did not sound alarmed. She did not say, "You should come to the hospice right away." She did not say, "You may never see him alive again." It just seemed to be something she needed to tell me, like "Your father cut his finger so we gave him a Band-Aid."

"Okay," I murmured before hanging up.

Right before the hospice phoned, I had received a call from an important client needing footage of the 1989 earthquake. It was a rush job. Remembering this, I moved to the filing cabinets in the corner. I was combing through printouts of monitoring sheets looking for the "V" our transcribers used to signify video footage. Mesmerized by the shuffling pages, I kept forgetting what I was looking for. I kept needing to start over from the top of the massive stack, always looking for "V-earthquake. V-earthquake."

I pictured the earthquake t-shirt my father had sent me back in college. Shuffling, shuffling. That picture on the front of the t-shirt: the Bay Bridge, its upper roadway collapsed. As I knelt on the office floor, the industrial carpet chafed my bare knees and I forgot again what I was doing and then remembered: "V-earthquake. V-earthquake."

Karin came in. "Who was that on the phone?"

"That was a nurse from the hospice. My dad's lungs collapsed. They put him on morphine." I parroted what the nurse told me in her same flat tones and looked to Karin for a response.

She blinked as she registered the news, and I returned to the stack of monitoring sheets on my lap and on the floor.

"What are you doing?"

"I have to find this footage for J. Walter Thompson. It's a rush job." It wasn't yet five o'clock and I thought I could finish up before the day was over. "They need footage of the '89 earthquake."

"They can wait," Karin said.

She asked if I needed her to drive me to the hospice. I answered yes, still not knowing why I should go over there. Still not understanding the significance of any of it.

On arriving, we walked upstairs to my dad's room. I could feel the warmth as I approached, the ripe smell of his static body rooted in damp bedsheets. I went over to him.

"Daddy?"

He was sitting up in bed looking straight ahead. I moved very close to his face. But because of the morphine, he looked right through me as though he were looking at the large plant behind where I stood.

"Dad!" I repeated a little louder. And then I shrank back.

With Karin next to me I suddenly felt very uncomfortable, embarrassed. She had to know that this was not our relationship. This was not my father.

"This is not my father," I told her.

And we left. Walking downstairs, I stopped and turned to Karin and, looking her squarely in the eye, repeated, "That was not my father." I wanted to distance myself from the memory of whoever that was in my dad's clothes, in my dad's bed.

"That was not your father," she answered.

The next day, I went back to work. I don't know why. It was someplace to go. I wanted to be around people. I just went to work and sat at my desk looking out the window facing the garden.

Then I got a call from the nurse at the hospice. "This is it," I remember her saying. Although she couldn't possibly have said these words, her meaning was clear.

This time Jon drove me over. We arrived just after five. The room was already full of people. I don't remember speaking with them at all—just being aware of their physical presence. Dad's ex-roommate Sam was standing, reading, against the wall. His pink face looked more pink than usual, but his blond hair was neatly combed to the side. Bruce Boone was seated in a nearby chair, looking long-legged and distant in his small round glasses. Big-eyed Dan Fine sat against the wall and I think waved to me. Though everyone was close, no one seemed to interact. We were each in our own realities, experiencing our own versions of my father's death.

The only force uniting us was the rhythmic wheeze of the breathing machine hooked up to my dad, a loud inhalation then a quick exhalation. It operated through a mask sealed tightly over his mouth and nose. I remember the room as uncomfortably warm. It smelled faintly sour, like Dad's night sweats. His hair, which used to stand up in animated tufts, was matted down so that the shape of his skull was visible. His skin looked waxy, not like skin at all. His slight frame, looking shrunken next to the large machine, was propelled by the push and pull of the air through his lungs. In and out. Up and down. This is why we were assembled. *In and out. Up and down.* This sound and this movement reminded us that he was still alive.

Jon and I were in the room perhaps half an hour when I said I was hungry. We walked two blocks away, and I ordered a burrito but couldn't eat all of it because my stomach hurt.

And then we returned. Everyone was still in the same positions against the wall. Attendants walked in and out of the room as though to check on my dad, but his state was unchanged. On a small table next to his bed I noticed a pile of letters and a boom box. I had this notion that my father, unable to see or talk, could perhaps still hear. Though he couldn't reach me, I wasn't convinced that he couldn't be reached.

I put on an audiocassette of his pianist brother, my other uncle David, playing a Mozart concerto, a cassette he'd sent my dad by mail. I began reading him letters from friends that had been arriving at the apartment. I spoke to my father as I went through each of these motions. "Now we're going to play a cassette from Uncle David. Now I'm going to read you a letter from . . . Diamanda Galas! Isn't that nice of her to write?" I narrated these actions much as I used to speak to my toys and stuffed animals as a girl.

When I tired of this, I pulled a chair up close to the left side of his bed. And, finally, I forgot everyone else in the room. I took my father's left hand in mine, and stared. I could only look at his hands, because the rest of him was unrecognizable. I knew those cigarette-stained fingertips, and pressed them to my lips. There was hair on his wrist, which seemed to have crept down from his arm. Little blue veins formed a road map leading to each of his fingers and thumb. These hands were as soft as silk. I thought they might melt in the heat of my palm.

The hands still looked strong to me. I remembered them gently, lovingly, holding me on his lap. I remembered pulling on these hands when I was tired on walks home from Golden Gate Park. I remembered them tying double knots on my shoelaces when I was late for school, or steering the mesh-wrapped steering wheel of our Volkswagen bug. I remembered the hands opening cans of Campbell's soup, stirring the dinner as the TV news blared in the background, and putting down the pot to take a drag on his cigarette.

I was studying his fingers when the mechanized rhythm of the breathing, which had been steady—and calming in its steadiness—suddenly paused. Everyone in the room stirred, the tension building as we waited for the next heaving inhalation.

It never arrived. There was no sound at all.

Then at once everyone's voices rose up in a single chant:

"We love you, Steve. We love you, Steve. We love you . . ."

I collapsed over my dead father's hands and wept. Exhausted and relieved.

MY FATHER DIED on December 2, 1992, two months after moving into hospice, four days before my twenty-second birthday, and three weeks before Christmas, the date I'd told him I wanted to move out.

The day after he died, I emptied his bank account at the neighborhood ATM. Nine hundred and eighty dollars. As I withdrew the money, in three separate batches, I looked around, nervous that I would get in trouble if someone saw me, as though I were stealing my dad's money. I then walked over to the nearby

Haight Street shoe shop, peeled off one hundred and fifty dollars from the wad in my pocket, and bought myself a pair of lace-up steel-toed boots.

I wore those boots every day. I loved the feeling of the thick leather hugging my shins and calves. I loved the heaviness of my feet as I trekked down Haight Street in long sure strides. I felt supported by these boots. Though military footwear was ubiquitous in early nineties San Francisco, I felt they particularly suited me. They grounded me in the street, in the city, in that moment in time.

I loved the weight of my steel-toed boots just as I enjoyed the weight of my father's leather motorcycle jacket, which I now also wore everywhere, because at night, when I took them off, I felt perilously light. I felt as if I might fly away. Without my dad around, I didn't quite know who I was. I didn't know what to do now that I didn't have him to look after or worry over. I never even gave him his t-shirts, which, never washed or worn, sat in my dresser for months until I finally donated them to the local Goodwill. I felt unmoored, like there was very little keeping me together. There was little that made sense anymore.

The only thing that did make sense was my grief. So I got drunk on it, literally. I took up drinking single malt scotch, neat. I liked the way it softened my brittle edges. I liked the way people looked at me when I ordered it in bars and I looked back, without blinking. Every night I lit candles throughout the apartment. I shut off the lights and played over and over the saddest music in my collection: Mozart's *Requiem*, *Carmina Burana*, and REM's *Automatic for the People*.

"Remember me!" commands the ghost of Hamlet's father, and like that dutiful Dane, I remembered. I leaned delicate photographs and framed portraits of my dad all around our one-bedroom apartment, which now seemed impossibly large. Sitting with Karin and Jon, I read aloud Dad's letters, his lively, humorous voice filling the room. I bicycled through the narrow paths into Golden Gate Park past Hippie Hill, where we used to play hide-and-seek, and over to Lloyd Lake, where we posed for the cover of his book *Stretching the Agape Bra*. I fingered the many IDs in his wallet, which pictured him with his lopsided leather cap, a hat I openly disliked but which he persisted in wearing. I caressed his round tortoiseshell glasses with the scratched lenses, things once so important but now valuable only to me.

In the time immediately following my father's death, I reveled in my onlyness and clung to my grief like a birthright. Perhaps my father's family, all living in Nebraska, would have come out in those final months of his life had I urged them. Perhaps, too, my father's friends could have helped me sort the twenty-year accumulation of things in our apartment which I sifted through in the months following his death. But if anyone had been available, if anyone had entered the delicate two-step of our final year, I'd have had to share the noble light of caregiving. And if I was going to have to suffer through my dad's death, damned if I was going to share that noble light with anyone.

It didn't occur to me until after Dad died that the lack of a long-term boyfriend in his life was due, at least in part, to my overarching presence in our apartment as a teenager. I scowled. I was rude. I neglected to deliver phone messages and objected when my father kicked me out of his bedroom/our living room. Except for my close attachment to Dad's first two boyfriends, the men that passed through our life were mostly useless to me. They could never replace my mom. All they could do was take my father from me, divide his precious love in two.

THERE WERE TWO memorial services for my father: one organized by his family in Nebraska and one in San Francisco attended by my father's adopted family, his community of poets, students, intellectuals, and freaks. Within this second audience, as my father's only attending relation, I held a singular position. I chose a large photo to display at the Buddhist ceremony in the basement of the Hartford Street Zen Center—a commanding black-and-white portrait of my father taken by Robert Giard that had hung in our apartment. I found an excerpt from one of Dad's essays—the epilogue to *View Askew*—which I photocopied and distributed at the service. I picked a poem to read at the service's close.

The funeral was held on December 11, 1992. I wore jeans, a black t-shirt, and my father's leather jacket. I was small in that jacket, my frame shrunken from the stress of those final months. But the leather on my shoulders, so thick and stiff that it squeaked whenever I moved, made me feel safe and close to Dad, as though I were wearing his skin.

The resident monk, poet Phil Whalen, tall and bald and big in a long blue robe, performed the ceremony, chanting sutras and lighting incense. Smoke snaked through the air. The ceilings were low. The room seemed small. And in my father's leather jacket, I felt warm. At first I stood along with everyone else in the cramped basement space, where my father and the other Zendo members sat zazen every week. Perspiration trickled down my neck and back. After Whalen completed the service, I took the stage.

I looked into the mass of bodies all standing at attention, awaiting my delivery. I recognized Kush and David Moe, both grizzled with age. Joyce Jenkins in her big glasses. Kevin Killian, Dodie Bellamy, Bruce Boone, and Bob Glück clustered together. I spotted Father Al Huerta in one corner, Karin and Jon in another, and Yayne with her dad, Mengeshe, who saw me and smiled. There were faces I remembered from the Café Flore and others from Haight Street, including many I hadn't seen in years.

I held my father's book, *Stretching the Agape Bra*, in my hands.

On the cover we're posed together: an unsmiling gothic father and his unsmiling ten-year-old daughter. He wears a pin-striped suit and two-tone spectator shoes and holds a long-stemmed white lily. I stand behind him in a high-neck white dress, with one arm to my side and one behind my back. He'd taken me out of my fifth-grade class so that I could pose with him that day in Golden Gate Park. We are standing in front of a grand marble-columned portico, the ruins of a Nob Hill mansion destroyed by the 1906 earthquake which was turned into a monument to that disaster called *Portals of the Past*.

I turned to the book's last poem, "Elegy." In the poem, my father imagines what it's like to die. He imagines first losing his sense of sight, then sound, touch, taste, and, finally, smell. He liked to imagine his past lives in ancient history, and sees his spirit floating up after escaping the stake in the sixteenth century. Taking my father's words in my mouth, I mimicked the rhythms I'd learned from accompanying him to scores of readings, the only child in the room. Commanding this audience to listen to me, I felt powerful. My voice never wavered, even when reading the lines he wrote about me:

"Babar's mother was killed by a mean hunter and that makes Alysia sad even now."

My father stares out from behind me in his black-and-white incarnation. In the photo, he is handsome, his face still almost plump in 1989. He wears his black button-down shirt and his Jesus bolo tie. He's not smiling, but staring serenely at the camera's lens with wet, light eyes, watching in a sort of knowing, affectionate way. I continue reading, sensing him there, saying to me:

"You. Yes, you. Who else could read this but you?"

ELEGY

The first timepieces were encased in delicate silver skulls
Memento mori. *You may smile to hear this*
since much of what we say is gallows humor. We would die
      laughing
but time encases us both as we are young & healthy.
It was not always so. I recall floating up
from one wrinkled corpse with total delight. It was maybe
the 16th century & I fled into exile to escape the stake.
First goes sight, then hearing, touch, taste, and finally smell:
so say the Tibetan monks who wrote their Book of the Dead.
Whether fire, loneliness or love hurts more than death I don't
know but I'm reminded of driving 14 hours to Key West
& lying beside you only to hallucinate your beautiful face
a grinning skull. I lost the poem that told of this.
When I lost my first lover, murdered by an AWOL Marine,
I drove round all night howling helplessly
yet no one could hear me. The windows were up. Before my wife
died, she dreamt of our fish tank breaking & all the fish
flopping into the street. No one would help her save them.
She was a psychologist & fell in love with a psychotic patient,
a kid who wanted to kill everyone in a small town. He was
fantastic in bed. Altho he hated queers he imagined me
coming toward him like Jesus with a garland of roses on my
      head.
I knew this boded ill fortune.

                              The dead
communicate to us in strange ways, or is it only because it is so

ordinary we think it is strange. I don a dark suit & wear a white
    veil,
pretend I'm a monastery prefect reading the Cloud of
    Unknowing.
The top of my head floats effortlessly into past or future perfect.
An ancestor of Virginia Woolf, one James Pattle, was put in a
    cask of spirits
when he died & thus shipped back to his wife. She went crazy.
    It's difficult
to conceive what the black death meant to 14th century Europe.
    That Hebrew
tribes & Roman Legions massacred whole cities is generally
    forgotten
but then so too Auschwitz. Life is bleak enough
under the best of conditions. I wonder if a book of poems has
    ever
been written about murderers. If not, I'd like to write one.
Caligula, Justinian—one could do volumes on the late Roman
    Emperors alone.
But what is more terrible than the death of one child?
The last poem would be about Dan White, the Twinkie killer,
& his love for green Ireland, its terrible beauty.

When I learned my wife's skull was crushed by a truck, my
    head
swam like an hourglass into a tv set. All the channels went
    crazy.
Crickets sounded like Halloween noisemakers & I remember
    explaining the event
to our 2 year old daughter with the aid of her Babar book.
Babar's mother was shot by a mean hunter & that makes
    Alysia sad even now.

*We distance ourselves for protection, wear scarves when it's
 cold.*
*What seems most outlandish in our autobiography is what
 really happened.*
It is only circumstances that make death a terrible event.
She dreamt of our fish tank breaking & all the fish . . .
*You should not have to burn your hand every day to feel the
 mystery of fire.*

EPILOGUE

AFTER MY FATHER died, nearly twenty years ago, the lights in fairyland went dark. I left San Francisco for New York in the hope of rekindling the adult life I had to snuff out when Dad got sick, but the world I rejoined there was mostly young and straight. I could count on one finger the number of friends who'd even met my dad. At first this was liberating. I could reinvent myself. I could be someone other than "daughter." But I also felt this persistent sense of dislocation. With few people to share memories of my father, I had no outlet for my grief. I started to feel as if the life we'd shared existed only in my head and in the pages of Dad's out-of-print books, his journals, and the letters I ritualistically reread on his birthday and on the anniversary of his death. This disconnect intensified after the introduction of protease inhibitors in the mid-nineties changed AIDS from a death sentence into a manageable disease. Those who hadn't lived through the epidemic would come to know almost nothing of it, as a cultural amnesia set in. The heavy warlike losses of the AIDS years were relegated to queer studies classrooms, taught as gay history and not American history.

All along, my memories of those years have followed me, along with my father's papers, from an apartment on the Lower East Side to a Brooklyn loft and finally to the house in Cambridge, Massachusetts, that I now share with my husband and two young children. All along they spoke to me, and I to them, and in the course of that conversation this book emerged, more by fits than starts. Finally, now, nearly twenty years after I first sat down in that closet full of notebooks, the book is written.

But something happened along the way. Researching Dad's life, I've made contact with his old colleagues and friends and others we knew—people like Joyce Jenkins of *Poetry Flash*; and Jimmy Siegel, who owns Distractions; and Sean, the smiling Southerner who worked at Coffee Tea & Spice. Speaking with them, I got to hear three powerful words, three words I didn't know I so badly needed to hear: "I remember you."

With these words, the lights switch on. The music plays. The carousel starts up again and those glittery and colorful horses move up and down and around, delighting my every sense. For a moment, I get to be a child again. I feel wholly me.

Working late one night, with my kids and husband peacefully sleeping upstairs, I decided, for the first time, to research the B.A.R. obituary database. The B.A.R., or *Bay Area Reporter*, where Dad sometimes covered books and arts, was an important barometer of the AIDS epidemic, the papers dramatically thickening as the number of dead increased. Those obituaries are now online, thanks to the GLBT Historical Society, part of a database searchable by name or year.

Sitting in the dark alone, I easily found the obituaries of friends like Robert ("a devout Wagnerian"), Tommy ("Teddy and Cuddles were by his bedside"), Jono ("An incredible kisser, a perfect listener"), and Sam ("Goodbye, my mystery"). Then I searched out names from Dad's journals, men I didn't know but who were among his friends. Then I just started browsing, randomly clicking on names, reading stories and staring at picture after picture of the dead. All of these Peter Pans, young men frozen in their eighties haircuts and sweaters, never to realize the potential of that first book of poetry, that well-received play or generous heart ("His friends *were* his life"). And soon I was sobbing, sobbing until my eyes were puffy like a boxer's. I felt battered with grief. How strange, I thought, when the crying finally subsided. I'm not gay. I'm not a member of this generation of men that lost so many friends that whole phone books had to be tossed. This grief, I now realize, has always been with me. I'd just never located it.

This place where Dad and I lived together, our fairyland, wasn't make-believe but a real place with real people, and I was there. And though I haven't lived in San Francisco since 1994, and though the life I live is very different from the life we shared, one Dad might even consider bourgeois, I am very much a product of his world. Though I am straight and haven't had a living gay parent for almost twenty years, I still feel a part of this queer community. This queer history is my queer history. This queer history is our queer history.

LIST OF SOURCES

Part I: Fairytales

Bronski, Michael. *A Queer History of the United States.* Boston: Beacon Press, 2011.

Shannon, Margaret. "College Politics and the New Left." *Atlanta Journal and Constitution Magazine*, October 27, 1968.

"Former Kewaneean Killed in Accident." *Kewanee Star Courier*, August 29, 1973.

"Two Killed in Highway 11 Wreck." *Sweetwater Valley News*, August 30, 1973.

Part II: Motherless

Hatfield, Larry D. "Love and Haight." *San Francisco Examiner*, August 17, 1997.

James, Scott. "A Near-Forgotten Casualty of AIDS: The Haight's Gay Identity." *New York Times*, November 24, 2010.

Pennington, Greg L. "Mirrors of Our Community: A History of the Gay Pride Parades in San Francisco." *San Francisco Bay Area Gay and Lesbian Historical Society Newsletter* 1, no. 4 (June 1986).

Shilts, Randy. *The Mayor of Castro Street: The Life and Times of Harvey Milk.* New York: St. Martin's Press, 1982.

Sides, Josh. *Erotic City: Sexual Revolutions and the Making of Modern San Francisco.* New York: Oxford University Press, 2009.

Left/Write. Edited transcripts of 1981 Left/Write Conference. Edited by Steve Abbott. 1982.

Note: Quotes from poets at Cloud House party are taken from transcripts of the Left/Write conference panel with these same Cloud House members in 1981.

Part III: Borrowed Mothers

Abbott, Steve. "10 Years of Poetry Flash." *Poetry Flash*, April 1983.

Clendinen, Dudley. "Anita Bryant, Singer and Crusader." *Saint Petersburg Times*, November 28, 1999.

Fetner, Tina. *How the Religious Right Shaped Lesbian and Gay Activism*. Minneapolis: University of Minnesota Press, 2008.

Gold, Herbert. "A Walk on San Francisco's Gay Side." *New York Times*, November 6, 1977.

Left/Write. Edited transcripts of 1981 Left/Write Conference. Edited by Steve Abbott. 1982.

Mathews, Tom. "The Battle over Gay Rights." *Newsweek*, June 6, 1977.

Shilts, Randy. *The Mayor of Castro Street: The Life and Times of Harvey Milk*. New York: St. Martin's Press, 1982.

Part IV: The Quake

Abbott, Steve. "Gossip and Scandal: Poetry Newsletters & Reviews." *Poetry Flash*, February 1983.

———. "10 Years of Poetry Flash." *Poetry Flash*, April 1983.

Adler, Jerry. "The AIDS Conflict." *Newsweek*, September 23, 1985.

Alter, Jonathan. "Sins of Omission." *Newsweek*, September 23, 1985.

Clark, Matt. "AIDS." *Newsweek*, August 12, 1985.

Fetner, Tina. *How the Religious Right Shaped Lesbian and Gay Activism*. Minneapolis: University of Minnesota Press, 2008.

Harris, Kaplan. "Causes, Movements, Poets." Unpublished manuscript.

———. "New Narrative and the Making of Language Poetry." *American Literature* 81, no. 4 (December 2009): 805–32.

Lindsey, Robert. "20 Years after the Summer of Love, Haight-Ashbury Looks Back." *New York Times*, July 7, 1987.

Roy, Camille, Mary Burger, Gail Scott, and Bob Glück, eds. *Biting the Error: Writers on Narrative.* Toronto: Coach House Press, 2004.

Seligman, Jean. "The AIDS Epidemic, The Search for a Cure." *Newsweek*, April 18, 1983.

Snyder, Ruth. "'Gay Bashing'—AIDS Fear Cited as Attacks on Male Homosexuals Grow." *Los Angeles Times*, April 10, 1986.

Tremblay-McGaw, Robin. "New Narrative: A Queer Economy of Insufficiencies & Excess." Unpublished manuscript.

We Were Here. Documentary film. Directed by David Weissman and Bill Weber. Red Flag Releasing, 2011.

Part V: Departures

Bronski, Michael. *A Queer History of the United States.* Boston: Beacon Press, 2011.

D'Allesandro, Sam. *The Zombie Pit.* Foreword by Steve Abbott. San Francisco: Crossing Press, 1989.

Leerhsen, Charles. "Hard Times Ahead." *Newsweek*, August 12, 1985.

Schneider, David. *Street Zen: The Life and Work of Issan Dorsey.* Cambridge, MA: DaCapo Press, 2000.

Schulman, Sarah. *Stagestruck: Theater, AIDS, and the Marketing of Gay America.* Durham, NC: Duke University Press, 1998.

White, Edmund. "Out of the Closet, Onto the Bookshelf." *New York Times*, June 16, 1991. Reprinted in White, Edmund. *The Burning Library: Essays.* Edited by David Bergman. New York: Knopf, 1994.

We Were Here. Documentary film. Directed by David Weissman and Bill Weber. Red Flag Releasing, 2011.

Part VI: Return

Irvine, Martha. "Teenage Runaways Find an Alcoholic Haze in Haight Ashbury." Associated Press, September 15, 1996.

Marine, Craig. "Streets of Their Dreams Surrounded by Madness." *San Francisco Examiner*, February 20, 1994.

Walker, Thaal. "The Haight Getting Dangerous, Residents and Cops Say." *San Francisco Chronicle*, May 10, 1993.

Works by Steve Abbott

Transmuting Gold. San Francisco: Androgyne Books, 1978.

Wrecked Hearts. San Francisco: Dancing Rock Press, 1978.

Stretching the Agape Bra. San Francisco: Androgyne Books, 1981.

The Lives of the Poets. San Francisco: Black Star Series, 1987.

Skinny Trip to a Far Place. San Francisco: e.g. Press, 1988.

Holy Terror. San Francisco: Crossing Press, 1989.

View Askew: Postmodern Investigation. San Francisco: Androgyne Books, 1989.

Lizard Club. San Francisco: Autonomedia, 1993.

Lost Causes. Unpublished.

ACKNOWLEDGMENTS

Libraries are endangered treasures. I relied enormously in my research on the informed and dedicated staff of the San Francisco Public Library's History Center, especially Susan Goldstein and Tim Wilson, and the GLBT Historical Society. The staff at NYU's Bobst Library and the Woodberry Poetry Room helped me locate important letters and books. I spent the majority of my writing hours at Harvard's Widener and Lamont Libraries and at the magical Collins Branch Library, where staff serve patrons butter cookies and hot tea every Thursday afternoon.

To write you need space and quiet. I'm grateful to the Ragdale Foundation for granting me three weeks on the prairie; the dear friends who put me up on my research trips to San Francisco, especially Roger, Mishiara, and little Elodie; and Maggie and Joe, who offered me their beautiful home in my final stages of editing.

I must thank the many friends, family members, and colleagues of mine, and my father's, who shared their stories and patiently answered my repeated questions, including Elaine Abbott, Niki Berkowitz, David Binder, Bruce Boone, Anne-Marie Burger, John Dale, Karin Demarest, Dede Donovan, Dan Fine, Camille Floquet, Jon Fox, French American International School, Nina Friedman at the Cradle, Farris Garcia, Bob Glück, William B. Hampton, Kaplan Harris, Joyce Jenkins, Kevin Killian, Lara Klemens, Gerard Koskovich, Ginny Lloyd, Sean Monahan, John

Norton, Andrea Richardson, Larry-Bob Roberts, Jim Siegel, Ron Silliman, Janet Smith, Robin Tremblay-McGaw, Ken Weichel, Sandra Weiksner, and Yayne Wondafarow.

I want to thank the readers who helped at various stages of writing this book, especially Martha Bebinger, Noel Black, Michael Bronski, Nazila Farhi, Andrea Meyer, Vanessa Mobley, Honor Moore, Rose Moss, Miranda Purves, Beena Sarwar, the New School gang (including LL, Lisa, and Nancy), Kate Tuttle, AQ, and detail-oriented Kris Wilton. The brilliant Alexander Chee also gave me needed perspective and extensive notes at a critical juncture.

I am grateful for the existence of Brad, the better half of "Hambutt Productions." His pun-laced humor has kept me buoyed these last few years, and then some. I'm also lucky to know little p. Her faith in this project has been steady for almost two decades.

Thank you to my wonderful copy editor, Allegra Huston, and to the talented staff at W. W. Norton, especially Elizabeth Riley, Anna Mageras, and my editor, Amy Cherry. Amy guided me through the writing of *Fairyland* with generosity, intelligence, and grace. I feel so fortunate to have met you, Amy.

Though I've been writing this book in my head for nearly twenty years, I didn't focus on the project until I became a Nieman Affiliate. I want to thank the Nieman Foundation for creating an atmosphere that fostered intellectual curiosity and growth. Without this space, I'd have never have met David Patterson, the editor-turned-agent who helped me find a good home for *Fairyland*. Thank you, David, for your gentlemanly manners and sympathetic ear.

And then there's Jeff. Though often busy supporting our brood with his own varied projects, he took time to read my grotty drafts and provided me with crucial advice when I needed it most. It's been a long journey to the publication of *Fairyland*. I couldn't imagine sharing this achievement with anyone else.

CREDITS